MICROECONOMIC CONTRIBUTIONS TO STRATEGIC MANAGEMENT

Advanced Series in Management   Volume 16

Series Editors: A. BENSOUSSAN   and   P. A. NAERT

University of Paris-Dauphine
and INRIA
Paris, France

INSEAD
Fontainebleau, France

Previous Volumes in the series:

VOLUME 1:	*Competitive Economics: Equilibrium and Arbitration* K. H. Kim and F. W. Roush
VOLUME 2:	*New Trends in Data Analysis and Applications* J. Janssen, J.-F. Marcotorchino and J.-M. Proth (eds.)
VOLUME 3:	*Mathematical Theory of Production Planning* A. Bensoussan, M. Crouhy and J.-M. Proth
VOLUME 4:	*Intra-Industry Trade: Empirical and Methodological Aspects* P. K. M. Tharakan (ed.)
VOLUME 5:	*EEC Accounting Harmonisation: Implementation and Impact of the Fourth Directive* S. J. Gray and A. G. Coenenberg (eds.)
VOLUME 6:	*Replacement Costs for Managerial Purposes* J. Klaassen and P. Verburg (eds.)
VOLUME 7:	*Designing Efficient Organizations: Modelling and Experimentation* R. M. Burton and B. Obel
VOLUME 8:	*Data Analysis in Real Life Environment: Ins and Outs of Solving Problems* J.-F. Marcotorchino, J.-M. Proth and J. Janssen (eds.)
VOLUME 9:	*New Challenges for Management Research* A. H. G. Rinnooy Kan (ed.)
VOLUME 10:	*Strategic vs. Evolutionary Management: A U.S.-Japan Comparison of Strategy and Organization* T. Kagono, I. Nonaka, K. Sakakibara and A. Okumura
VOLUME 11:	*Product Standardization and Competitive Strategy* H. Landis Gabel (ed.)
VOLUME 12:	*Applied Stochastic Models and Control in Management* C. S. Tapiero
VOLUME 13:	*Managing International Manufacturing* K. Ferdows (ed.)
VOLUME 14:	*Policy Implications of Antidumping Measures* P. K. M. Tharakan (ed.)
VOLUME 15:	*Corporate and Industry Strategies for Europe* L.-G. Mattsson and B. Stymne (eds.)

NORTH-HOLLAND
AMSTERDAM · LONDON · NEW YORK · TOKYO

MICROECONOMIC CONTRIBUTIONS TO STRATEGIC MANAGEMENT

Edited by

Jacques THEPOT
University Louis Pasteur
Strasbourg, France

Raymond-Alain THIETART
University Paris IX Dauphine
Paris, France

1991

NORTH-HOLLAND
AMSTERDAM · LONDON · NEW YORK · TOKYO

ELSEVIER SCIENCE PUBLISHERS B.V.
Sara Burgerhartstraat 25
P.O. Box 211, 1000 AE Amsterdam, The Netherlands

Distributors for the United States and Canada:

ELSEVIER SCIENCE PUBLISHING COMPANY, INC.
655 Avenue of the Americas
New York, N.Y. 10010, U.S.A.

HD
30.22
.M53
1991

ISBN: 0 444 89082 3

©1991 Elsevier Science Publishers B.V. All rights reserved.

No part of this publication may be reproduced, stored in a retrieval system or transmitted in any form or by any means, electronic, mechanical, photocopying, recording or otherwise, without the prior written permission of the publisher, Elsevier Science Publishers B.V., Permissions Department, P.O. Box 521, 1000 AM Amsterdam, The Netherlands.

Special regulations for readers in the U.S.A. – This publication has been registered with the Copyright Clearance Center Inc. (CCC), Salem, Massachusetts. Information can be obtained from the CCC about conditions under which photocopies of parts of this publication may be made in the U.S.A. All other copyright questions, including photocopying outside of the U.S.A., should be referred to the copyright owner, Elsevier Science Publishers B.V., unless otherwise specified.

No responsibility is assumed by the publisher for any injury and/or damage to persons or property as a matter of products liability, negligence or otherwise, or from any use or operation of any methods, products, instructions or ideas contained in the material herein.

pp. 219-234: Copyright not transferred.

Printed in The Netherlands

THE EDITORS

Jacques Thépot is professor of management at the University Louis Pasteur-Strasbourg. He was on the faculty of the European Institute of Advanced Studies in Management from 1978 to 1982. He holds a doctorate in applied mathematics (1974) and a doctorate in management from the University Paris IX-Dauphine (1983). His research interests are in the fields of industrial economics and operations management. He has published extensively in scientific journals. His last publications include a book "Optimisation pour l'Economie d'Entreprise" (1991).

Raymond-Alain Thiétart is professor of management at the University of Paris IX-Dauphine and at the Ecole Supérieure des Sciences Economiques et Commerciales. He is a graduate from the Institut National des Sciences Appliquées (Insa, 1967), Ecole Supérieure des Sciences Economiques et Commerciales (Essec,1969) and hold a M.Phil. (1973) and a Ph.D. (1974) from Columbia University. His research interests are in the field of strategic management. His research uses economic and organization theory to clarify how corporations work and how managers make their strategic decisions. He is the author of more than fifty articles and five books. His last book, "Stratégie d'Entreprise" (McGraw-Hill, 1990), has received two awards: the Harvard-l'Expansion best book of the year and the best European management book.

AKNOWLEDGEMENT

Without the help of several individuals and organizations, this book would not have been possible. We would like to acknowledge their respective contributions.

First, we would like to thank the authors and the referees who agreed to participate in this attempt at bridging economics and strategic management.

Second, the French Foundation for Management Development (FNEGE) and its Secretary General, Jean-Claude Cuzzi, deserve special thanks for sponsoring the first workshop on Microeconomics/Strategic Management Interfaces held in Brussels in late 1989 and for providing financial support for the preparation of the present manuscript. FNEGE has a long tradition of supporting interdisciplinary endeavours.

Third, we would like to thank the European Institute of Advanced Studies in Management (EIASM) and its Director, Alain Bultez for hosting and organizing the workshop on Microeconomics/Strategic Management Interfaces. The EIASM has played a significant role in stimulating management research on a European scale by building networks between European researchers and sponsoring conferences throughout Europe. The role of the Institute in creating a European consciousness in management research continues to be crucial.

Fourth, we acknowledge our publisher, Elsevier, and the two editors of the series, Alain Bensoussan and Philippe Naert, who have consistently supported our project.

Last but not least, a hearty thanks goes to Essec, which provided technical assistance, and to Marie-Pierre Dormeval, who coordinated and prepared the entire manuscript. Without Marie-Pierre's good will, humor and professionalism, the book would still be "forthcoming".

TABLE OF CONTENTS

INTRODUCTION: MICROECONOMIC - STRATEGIC MANAGEMENT INTERFACES   1
by Jacques Thépot and Raymond-Alain Thiétart

PART ONE : STRATEGIC ECONOMICS

CHAPTER 1   A DUOPOLY MODEL SUGGESTING A TAXONOMY OF COMPETITIVE SITUATIONS   7
by Gabrielle Demange
DELTA Ecole des Hautes Etudes en Sciences Sociales
and
Jean-Pierre Ponssard
CNRS and Ecole Polytechnique

CHAPTER 2   BRAND LOYALTY AND ADVERTISING: A NOTE   23
by Damien Neven
Université Libre de Bruxelles and Insead
and
Jacques-François Thisse
CORE Université Catholique de Louvain

CHAPTER 3   COST-REDUCING STRATEGIES WITH SPILLOVERS   33
by Raymond De Bondt
Katholieke Universiteit Leuven

CHAPTER 4   BARRIERS TO ENTRY AND STRATEGIC MARKETING INVESTMENTS   51
by Jan Karl Karlsen
Centre for Research in Economics and Business Administration
and
Kjell Grønhaug
Norwegian School of Business Administration

CHAPTER 5   DYNAMIC DIVERSIFICATION AND LEARNING EFFECTS   73
by Jacques Thépot
LARGE, Université Louis Pasteur

CHAPTER 6   MULTIMARKET COMPETITION: ENTRY   93
            STRATEGIES AND ENTRY DETERRENCE
            WHEN THE ENTRANT HAS A HOME
            MARKET
            by Marc van Wegberg and Arjen van Witteloostuijn
            University of Limburg

PART TWO : ORGANIZATIONAL ECONOMICS

CHAPTER 7   THE DYNAMICS OF POWER AND CONTROL: 123
            A CASE STUDY OF BULL
            by Raymond-Alain Thiétart
            Université Paris IX-Dauphine and Essec

CHAPTER 8   VERTICAL INTEGRATION: WHY   143
            TRANSACTION COST AND RESOURCE
            DEPENDENCE EXPLANATIONS CAN'T BE
            EASILY SEPERATED
            by Guido A. Krickx
            University of Pennsylvania-The Wharton School

CHAPTER 9   INTER-FIRM ALLIANCES: THE ROLE OF   169
            TRUST
            by Christian Koenig and Gilles van Wijk
            Essec

CHAPTER 10 STRATEGIC MANAGEMENT AND VERTICAL   185
            DISINTEGRATION: A TRANSACTION COST
            APPROACH
            by Christophe Boone
            State University of Antwerp
            and
            Alain Verbeke
            Free University of Brussels

CHAPTER 11 ORGANIZATIONAL CHOICE AND ENTRY   207
            DETERRENCE
            by George Hendrikse
            Tilburg University

CHAPTER 12 TOP MANAGEMENT INCENTIVES FROM   219
            BONUSES AND FROM LABOUR MARKETS
            by Harry G. Barkema
            Tilburg University

INTRODUCTION

MICROECONOMIC-STRATEGIC MANAGEMENT INTERFACES

J. THEPOT and R.A. THIETART

Microeconomics is an old lady. For more than a century, she has ceaselessly drivelled, telling the same boring story on consumer preferences, production functions and equilibrium conditions. What have such colorless ideas to do with the intricate reality of business life today, especially with the ubiquitous spread of new technology, the increase of international competition and the overall deregulation of financial markets? Since the fall of the Berlin wall in 1989, ideologies are no longer in fashion. This is a consequence of the victory of the marketplace and of technology over dogma.

But microeconomics does not deserve to be relegated to the realm of economic dogma, an exhibit in dusty libraries for the reference of future paleo-economists. We believe that microeconomics and its application to industrial organization provide, more than ever, a conceptual framework which is essential for mastering the complexities of the industrial world and for helping managers sharpen their understanding of their activity.

Traditional strategic management research is organized by topic. These include diversification, acquisition, innovation, cooperation, and revitalization. Traditional microeconomics research is conceptual and theoretical. Strategic management has a problematic and empirical bias. It gives answers to practical questions and it investigates problems as they are asked and formulated by managers. However, it is limited in scope. It does not facilitate accumulation of knowledge and renders theory-building-- the construction of a general framework in which particular themes can be understood as specific applications-- extremely difficult. Microeconomics has a theoretical bias. It gives the broad picture but, too often, it is not overly concerned with the realism of its assumptions. Rarely are its findings backed by empirical evidence. Of course, between these two extremes, scholars have recently started to build bridges. Researchers in strategic management rely on more conceptual and theory-based frameworks and microeconomists make more realistic and empirically-based investigations. The book by Barney and Ouchi (1988) is a case in point. It illustrates the present trend toward synthesizing the two fields. This book seeks to add another span to the theoretical bridge between strategic management and microeconomics.

In the present book, four major micro-economic contributions are used to study strategic management problems: transactions cost economics, agency cost theory, industrial organization and game theory. They offer a conceptual framework for explaining how strategic decisions are made and how organizations work.

Transactions cost economics (Coase, 1937; Williamson, 1975) addresses a fundamental question: "how should economic activities be organized? Should one rely on the market or on an organizational hierarchy?". In this theoretical framework, the unit of analysis is not limited to the corporation. It is extended to the entire economic activity. Transactions costs are a general concept which can be used to explain all kinds of hierarchies. It is a paradigmatic shift in the way we look at corporations. It transcends traditional organizational borders. It attempts to provide answers to such questions as: why are firms organized the way they are, why are some activities kept inside or outside traditional boundary lines. Organizations are not presented as sets of individuals and groups. Instead, they are described as a nexus of contracts. The focus of analysis is on contracts between individuals, between individuals and groups, between groups and groups, both within and outside of the "organization". A great deal of attention has already been given to this theory in the strategic management literature and it will undoubtedly continue to be a focus of research for years to come.

A complementary body of literature is agency cost theory (Jensen and Meckling, 1976). This theory looks at governance stuctures and more specifically at the relationships between shareholders and managers (i.e. the relationships between power and control). It addresses the following question: how can a firm owner (principal) delegate power to his/her managers (agents) and, at the same time, design a control system to keep their decisions in line with his or her own interests? Although, most of the literature has focused on these two actors (owner and manager), the theory can potentially be extended to other relationships involving the delegation of power and control.

Game theory is useful for grasping the dynamic interplay between competitors. The making of strategy is a dynamic phenomenon. It is a succession of moves and countermoves which can only be understood in a dynamic format. Strategy consists of anticipation, action and reaction. The traditional strategic management paradigm does not take into account the time dimension which is implicit in game theory. Even though game theory is limited in term of the actors involved, it gives us a better understanding of what firms should do when making a decision. Industrial organization "à la Porter" (Porter, 1980), based on the SCP paradigm (Bain, 1956; Caves, 1980; Mason, 1939), focuses on the nature and the structure of competition to determine which strategies lead to higher performance. Industrial organization theory (Tirole, 1988) deals with the neoclassical conception of the firm. It represents market interactions and other interdependencies between firms as "stylized facts". Even though empirical validation is not the focus of this approach, it succeeds in explaining many aspects of strategic management.

Introduction - Microeconomic/Strategic Management Interfaces

The book covers many of the issues raised here. It is divided into two major parts. The first part, strategic economics, deals with economic contributions to strategy. The second part, organizational economics, covers the management dimension of the firm and deals with the question of how to manage and organize economic activities.

In the first part, "Strategic Economics", six contributions have been grouped together. The first Chapter "Duopoly Model Suggesting a Taxonomy of Competitive Situations" by Demange and Ponssard is devoted to a general analysis of the relationship between oligopolistic market structure and firms' strategies in a game theory framework. Customers'loyalty, a specific element of consumer behavior, is analyzed in Chapter 2 "Brand Loyalty and Advertising: a Note" by Neven and Thisse. These authors analyze the effect of advertising on market equilibrium, under the assumption that advertising affects the distribution of consumers' loyalty. De Bondt (Chapter 3, "Cost Reducing Strategies with Spillovers"), develops a game-theoretic model of the effects of technology spillovers on R&D investments which generate externalities between oligopolists. Diversification strategies and learning effects, in a dynamic two-product monopoly, are studied in Chapter 5 ("Dynamic Diversification and Learning Effects"). Using an optimal control formulation, Thépot clarifies the dynamics which are inherent to the well known BCG approach. Entry strategies and preemptive investments designed to influence market structure are successively analyzed in Chapter 4 ("Barriers to Entry and Strategic Marketing Investments") by Karlsen and Grønhaug and in Chapter 6 ("Multimarket Competition: Entry Strategies and Entry Deterrence when Entrant has a Home Market") by Van Wegberg and Van Witteloostuijn. The second set of contributions are grouped under the rubric of "Organizational Economics" in part two of the book. This part contains research seeking to explain organizational issues such as make or buy decisions, cooperative arrangements between firms, management control systems, decentralization levels and incentive structures. In the first chapter of this second part (Chapter 7, "The Dynamics of Power and Control: a Case Study of Bull"), Thiétart explores the evolution of power and control over a fifty years of a firm's life. Based on agency cost theory and transactions cost economics, he shows how control evolves as a response to changes in the power structure of a firm. In the following chapter (Chapter 8, "Vertical Integration: Why Transaction Cost and Resource Dependence Can't be Easily Seperated), Krickx relates two disparate bodies of the literature: transaction cost economics and resource dependence theory. He shows how they can be used as complementary theories to explain vertical integration. He identifies several linkages between them. The two theories stress uncertainty and they rely on two very similar concepts: resource dependence and asset specificity. In Chapter 9 "Inter Firm Alliances: the Role of Trust", Koenig and Van Wijk study the role of trust in strategic alliances. Trust, which is defined as a set of mutual obligations, is used as an informal mode of control by the cooperating partners. The authors argue that the emergence of an alliance and its stability depend on this important factor. In Chapter 10 "Strategic Management and Vertical Desintegration: a Transaction Cost Approach", Boone and Verbeke propose a new conceptual framework to explain the recent tendency of industries toward "vertical disintegration". The authors enrich the transactions cost paradigm with contributions from the organization and strategic management literatures in order to compare the costs and benefits of vertical integration with those of other governance structures. Hendrikse, in Chapter 11 "Organizational Choice and Entry Deterrence", studies the impact of organizational structure on entry deterrence. He shows that a centralized organizational form charges higher prices and locates products closer together than a decentralized structure. Finally, in the last chapter (Chapter 12, "Top Management Incentives from Bonuses and from Labour Markets") Barkema looks at the relationship between motivation bonus-based incentives, internal labor market pressures and monitoring from the market for corporate control. Based on an agency theory framework, the author shows that bonus-based incentives and internal labor market pressures influence motivation when and only when monitoring does effectively exist.

Within the diversity apparent in the various chapters of this book, one also finds convergence: the constant effort to relate and apply economic theories to organization and management concepts. We are convinced that this effort will be fruitful and hope that the present contribution will stimulate other investigations along the same lines.

References

Bain, J.S., 1956, Barriers to New Competition, (Cambridge, Mass., Harvard University Press).

Barney, J.B., and W.G. Ouchi, 1988, Organizational Economics, (San Francisco, Jossey Bass).

Caves, R.E., 1980, Industrial Organization, Corporate Strategy and Structure: a Survey, Journal of Economic Literature, 18, 64-92.

Coase, R.H., 1937, The Nature of the Firm, Economica, 4, 386-405.

Jensen, M.C. and W.H. Meckling, 1976, Theory of the Firm: Managerial Behavior, Agency Costs and Ownership Structure, Journal of Financial Economics, 3:4, 305-360.

Mason, E.S., 1939, Price and Production Policies of Large Scale Enterprises, American Economic Review, 29, 61-74.

Porter, M.E., 1980, Competitive Strategy: Techniques for Analyzing Industries and Competitors, (New-York, Free Press).

Tirole, J., 1988, The Theory of Industrial Organization, (Cambridge, Mass., MIT Press).

Williamson, O.E., 1975, Markets and Hierarchies: Analysis and Antitrust Implications, (New-York, Free Press).

PART ONE

STRATEGIC ECONOMICS

MICROECONOMIC CONTRIBUTIONS TO STRATEGIC MANAGEMENT
J. Thépot and R.-A. Thiétart
© 1991 Elsevier Science Publishers B.V. All rights reserved.

CHAPTER 1

A DUOPOLY MODEL SUGGESTING A TAXONOMY OF COMPETITIVE SITUATIONS

G. DEMANGE   and   J.P. PONSSARD
DELTA,   CNRS and
Ecoles des Hautes Etudes   Laboratoire d'Econométrie
en Sciences Sociales   de l'Ecole Polytechnique

Abstract

A simple duopoly model is extensively analyzed. The result of this analysis is that qualitatively distinct competitive situations can be identified. This theoretical approach is then related to the taxonomy of competitive strategies that has progressively emerged from empirical studies.

1. Introduction

One major issue of business strategy is to provide clear and simple ways to characterize a competitive situation. This approach may be linked to the well known Boston Consulting Group matrices (BCG, 1981). Expressions like "fragmented industries", "stuck in the middle", "a focus strategy" have been popularized (Kiechel, 1981) and are often used in practice to capture the most relevant features of an empirical situation. For a competitor this is often suggestive of potential challenges as well as of innovative strategies designed to face these challenges. These ideas generated what could be called a taxonomy of business situations. It has been used for various developments.

A typical way of using it is in the definition of generic strategies which for example may be cost and volume oriented versus quality and market oriented. This idea has been repeatedly used for the dead-locked industries (Harrigan, 1979; Hamermesh and Silk, 1979; Frost and Thiétart, 1981; Collomb and Ponssard, 1984).

Another way of using it consists in analyzing the impact of a changing environment on the positioning of an industry. For instance the forthcoming European market may significantly and differently affect the various national sectors of the EEC depending on their underlying characteristics. An important question is to determine whether, in this new context, a given sector is or not a volume industry (Boston Consulting Group, 1985; Buigues and Jacquemin, 1989).

Finally, this taxonomy is often used to illustrate how a specific firm has been able to change the rules of the game to its own advantage. For instance Porter (1980) argues that a firm like Mc Donald moved its way from a fragmented business (restaurants) to a specialized one (fast food).

The whole idea of defining generic strategies or generic situations can also be traced back to strategic groups (Caves and Porter, 1977), a notion that has progressively emerged in industrial organization introducing more subtlety than was suggested by the original paradigm (Bain, 1956). Empirical studies now benefit from this large taxonomy of competitive situations which is continuously enriched.

This chapter addresses this question of taxonomy from a theoretic angle. Can a purely formal approach generate a meaningful taxonomy of competitive situations ? If this is so, how could one single out the essential ingredients of each case ? Could they be related to business strategy approaches ? Can such an investigation contribute to a better understanding of empirical situations ?

To investigate these questions a simple duopoly model is analyzed. In this framework, the firms compete in prices. Three parameters are introduced. They are respectively associated with relative cost advantages, with the degree of homogeneity of the market both internally and with respect to substitutes, and with specific marketing advantages. For a given context, i.e. for given values of the parameters, the corresponding game has a unique Nash outcome. This outcome may considerably vary. Yet it turns out that simple and significantly different qualitative configurations can be associated to specific ranges of the parameters.It is interesting to compare these configurations with the more pragmatic taxonomy originating from the business strategy literature. This chapter illustrates the kind of insights that results from such cross-fertilization.

The chapter is organized in two sections. The model is defined and is analyzed in section 2. The relationship with the empirical taxonomy of competitive situations is discussed in section 3.

2. The duoply model

2.1. Assumptions

We consider a duopoly model where firms compete in prices. Firm i, i = 1, 2, identifies anyone of them. Prices, p_i, are set simultaneously.

Chapter 1 - A Duopoly Model

Once the prices are set, each firm i produces a quantity derived from the demand functions:
$q_i = q_i (p_1, p_2)$
and obtains a profit, π_i, given its own cost function $c_i(q_i)$:
$\pi_i = q_i p_i - c_i (q_i)$;

Cost functions are linear without fixed costs: $c_i(q_i) = c_i q_i$ with $0 \leq c_1 \leq c_2$, namely firm 1 is the most efficient firm.

Depending on the prices set, both demands are positive, or only one of them, or none at all. In the first case, both firms are active and they face a "duopoly demand". In the second case, the active firm faces a "monopoly demand". These demand functions are defined as follows.

(i) The duopoly demands (zone A figure 1).

They are assumed to be linear and given by:

$d_1 (p_1, p_2) = N_1 - \beta p_1 + \omega (p_2 - p_1)$,
$d_2 (p_1, p_2) = N_2 - \beta p_2 + \omega (p_1 - p_2)$.

Consider figure 1. Clearly these demands are valid in zone A, which corresponds to $d_i (p_1, p_2) \geq 0$ for i = 1 and 2.

The parameters, which are assumed to be non negative, are easy to interpret.

Remark that the total market demand is equal to
$N_1 + N_2 - \beta (p_1 + p_2)$.

It does not depend on ω which only affects the splitting of this total demand between the two firms. Thus:
- β reflects the elasticity of the total market demand with respect to the "rest of the world";
- ω measures the cross-price effects between the two products. For $\omega = 0$ the products are completely independent; for a large ω, the products are close substitute to each other. One may also refer to ω as a mobility barrier between the two products;
- if there were no cross-elasticity considerations, N_1 and N_2 would be indicators of the respective natural markets accessible to each firm; a high natural market is potentially good but if the degree of homogeneity is high, it may have to be defended and relative cost positions may matter.

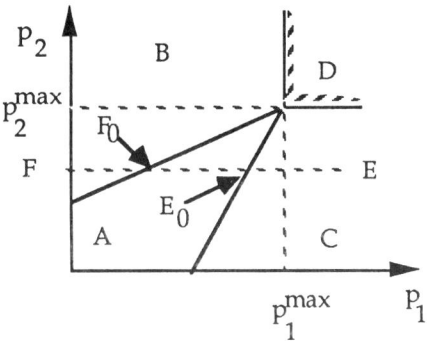

Figure 1:
Defining the demand functions

(ii) The monopoly demands (zones B and C figure 1).

Consider 1's duopoly demand when prices move from F_0 to E_0 (so that p_2 is constant). It decreases and just vanishes at E_0. It is natural to assume that when p_1 still increases and prices enter zone C, 1's demand remains null. Thus p_1 becomes irrelevant and firm 2's demand is identical to its demand at E_0. Formally :

at E_0 we have $d_1(p_1,p_2) = 0$, or:

$$0 = N_1 - \beta p_1 + \omega (p_2 - p_1)$$

that is,
$$p_1 = (N_1 + \omega p_2) / (\omega + \beta).$$

So that through straightforward calculations firm 2's demand at E_0 is equal to:
$$m_2(p_2) = N_2 + \omega N_1 / (\omega + \beta) - \beta (2\omega + \beta) p_2 / (\omega + \beta).$$

Thus $m_2(p_2)$ is also firm 2's demand at point E. This defines 2's monopoly demand which is valid in zone C. Similarly in zone B firm 1 faces a monopoly demand given by:

$$m_1(p_1) = N_1 + \omega N_2 / (\omega + \beta) - \beta (2\omega + \beta) p_1 / (\omega + \beta).$$

Finally, denote by (p^{max}_1, p^{max}_2) the prices at which $d_1(p_1,p_2)$ and $d_2(p_1,p_2)$ intersect. Remark that $p^{max}_i = ((\omega + \beta) N_i + \omega N_j) / \beta (2\omega + \beta)$ and that the monopoly demand can be simply written as:

Chapter 1 - A Duopoly Model

$m_i(p_i) = k(p^{max}_i - p_i)$
with $k = \beta(2\omega + \beta)/(\omega + \beta)$.

Clearly, in zone D, both prices satisfy $p_i \geq p^{max}_i$, and both demands should be zero.

Altogether firm i's demand on a line such as FE is depicted figure 2. Observe the kinked, but nevertheless continuous, nature of these demand functions. For each p_j denote by $p^l_i(p_j)$ the point at which the kink is obtained, $p^l_i(p_j)$ will be refered to as the limit price that triggers firm j's entry.

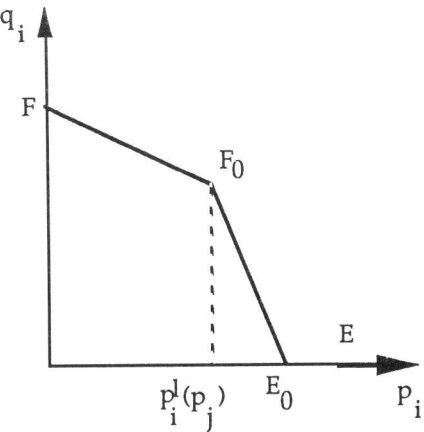

Figure 2:
Firm 1's demand for a given p_2

Remark that the duopoly demand is steeper than the monopoly one. This is indeed plausible : an increase of p_i when both firms produce discourages to buy from the other firm: an increase of the price of a firm when both produce encourages to buy to the other firm.

To sum up, firm i's demand q_i is equal to d_i in the duopoly zone A, m_i in the duopoly zone and zero elsewhere (see Table 1).

At this point the model is well defined. It is one of the simplest price competition model that one can find in the literature and many variants of it have been studied (see Shubik, 1980 for further references). Yet it is the first time that the extensive analysis of this model is carried on (for a preliminary work see Demange and Ponssard (1986)). The fact that this analysis is already quite complex may explain why most previous works concentrate on comparative statics around one or two of the parameters rather than on the whole set (for specific studies in that direction see for instance Gabszewicz, Thisse, Fujita and Schweizer, 1986).

$d_1(p_1, p_2)$	$N_1 - \beta p_1 + \omega(p_2 - p_1)$
$m_1(p_1)$	$\beta(2\omega + \beta)(p^{max}_1 - p_1)/(\omega + \beta)$
p^{max}_1	$((\omega + \beta)N_1 + \omega N_2)/\beta(2\omega + \beta)$

Table 1:
The demand functions

2.2. Existence and nature of the equilibrium

For given values of the parameters N_i, ω, β, c_i, the assumptions detailed in section 2.1. generate a game in normal form: the strategic variables are the prices, $p_i \geq 0$ for $i = 1$ and 2, and the payoff functions are the respective profits of the two firms. In this section a game theoretic analysis of this model is carried on.

Recall that prices (p^*_1, p^*_2) form a Nash equilibrium if

$\pi_1(p^*_1, p^*_2) \geq \pi_1(p_1, p^*_2)$ for any price p_1,
$\pi_2(p^*_1, p^*_2) \geq \pi_2(p^*_1, p_2)$ for any price p_2.

The most important results may be summarized as follows:
- this game has a unique Nash equilibrium outcome for all parameter values;
- the equilibrium can be of different types: a duopoly, a monopoly of either firm 1 or 2 with limit pricing, a blockaded monopoly of either firm 1 or 2 and a no-production equilibrium;
- the type of this Nash equilibrium outcome can be identified through a simple test in which each firm investigates its competitor's best response to average cost pricing.
These points will now be detailed by looking at a firm's best response curve.

Firm 1's best response curve to p_2, denoted by $p_1(p_2)$, is computed through the maximization of

$\pi_1(p_1, p_2) = (p_1 - c_1) q_1(p_1, p_2)$

Chapter 1 - A Duopoly Model

where $q_1(p_1, p_2)$ is the demand addressed to firm 1, namely it is equal to 0, $d_1(p_1, p_2)$ or $m_1(p_1)$ depending on the position of (p_1, p_2).

Some values which play a key role are given in the table 2. Their interpretations are as follows :

- $p^d_1(p_2)$ denotes the duopoly best response that is, it maximizes 1's profit $(p_1 - c_1) d_1(p_1, p_2)$. Of course it is valid only if prices $(p^d_1(p_2), p_2)$ are indeed in the duopoly zone A. In figure 3, it is given by the segment ab. At point a, the duopoly best response is just equal to the cost c_1.
- $p^l_1(p_2)$ is a limit price: it is 1's highest price which makes 2's demand null, it was already defined in section 2.1.
- p^m_1 is the monopoly price: it maximizes the monopoly profit $(p_1 - c_1) m_1(p_1)$. Remark that firm 1 produces at this price only if $p^m_1 \leq p^{max}_1$, that is if $c_1 \leq p^{max}_1$. We then say that the firm is *viable* and consider only such cases in what follows. When a firm is not viable it never produces, whatever its opponent price.

$p^l_1(p_2)$	$(N_2 - (\beta + \omega) p_2) / \omega$
$p^d_1(p_2)$	$(N_1 + \omega p_2) / 2(\beta + \omega) + c_1/2$
p^m_1	$(p^{max}_1 + c_1) / 2$

Table 2:
Key values for the best response curve

We can now describe the best response correspondance which is made of four parts depending on the values of p_2 (see figure 3):

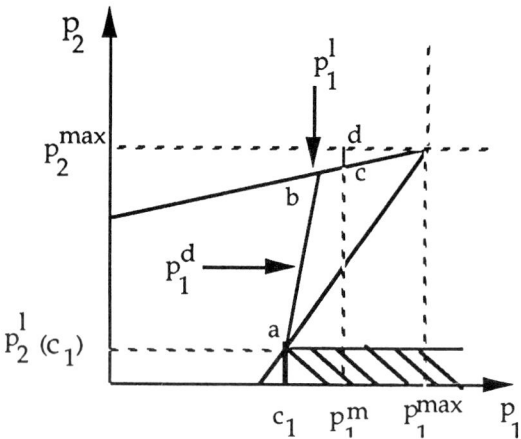

Figure 3:
Firm 1's best response curve

(1) no production (the hatched area).

Indeed, if $p_2 \leq p^l_2(c_1)$, 1's demand is positive only if it charges a price smaller than its cost. Its best response is then not to produce: it gives the hatched area. This part is of course vacuous if $p^l_2(c_1) \leq 0$ which occurs when $N_1 - (\omega + \beta) c_1 \leq 0$.

(2) duopoly pricing (segment ab)

When p_2 is a little higher than $p^l_2(c_1)$, then 1 can make profit by producing. But p_2 is small enough so that charging a limit price to eliminate firm 2 would be too costly: the best response is duopoly pricing $p^d_1(p_2)$.

(3) limit pricing (segment bc)

This part is characterized by:
$$p^d_1(p_2) \leq p^l_1(p_2) \leq p^m_1.$$

It is easy to understand why limit pricing is indeed a best response: for any price p_1 smaller than $p^l_1(p_2)$, firm 1 faces the monopoly demand. Its profit, the monopoly profit, is on its increasing part since $p_1 \leq p^m_1$. On the contrary, when p_1 is higher than $p^l_1(p_2)$ firm 1 faces the duopoly demand. It's profit, the duopoly profit, is on its

Chapter 1 - A Duopoly Model

decreasing part since its maximum $p^d{}_1(p_2)$ is smaller than $p^l{}_1(p_2)$. Thus 1's overall profit increases up to the limit price and then decreases.

(4) monopoly pricing $p^m{}_1$

Here the monopoly price $p^m{}_1$ deters 2's entry ($p^m{}_1 \leq p^l{}_1(p_2)$) and it clearly maximizes 1's profit.

The Nash equilibria are obtained by intersecting the two best response curves. This intersection may be between c and d, between c and b between b and a or below a. Assume that both firms are viable and consider different values for c_2. We now show that the type of equilibrium depends only on the the best reply of each firm to the cost of the other firm.

If c_2 is sufficiently high, the best response of firm 1 to c_2 is to exclude it. Then it is a *fortiori* true when firm 2 charges any price above its cost. Thus an equilibrium is necessarily a monopoly for firm 1. The type of this monopoly depends on 1's best reply to c_2, which is either limit or monopoly pricing. If it is limit pricing then $(p^l{}_1(c_2), c_2)$, which is clearly an equilibrium, is the unique one. Indeed, if firm 2 charges a price strictly above c_2, by reaction firm 1 increases its price, which is then higher than $p^l{}_1(c_2)$ and makes entry profitable for firm 2. If 1's best reply to c_2 is monopoly pricing, it is still the case for any $p_2 \geq c_2$: there are many equilibria, of the form $(p^m{}_1, p_2)$ where $p_2 \geq c_2$, but all yield the same outcome (i.e. same quantities and profits).

If c_2 is sufficiently low, more precisely if the best response of firm 2 to the cost c_1 prevents firm 1 from producing, a similar argument applies by exchanging the roles of the firms: the equilibrium outcome is unique. It is a monopoly but this time in favor of firm 2.

We are left with the case where the best response of each firm i to the cost of the other firm j does not exclude it: it is above $p^l{}_i(c_j)$. Since the best response curve is then an increasing function, firm i's best response is above $p^l{}_i(c_j)$ for any $p_j \geq c_j$: surely in an equilibrium both firm produce. We are back to the standard unique duopoly equilibrium usually analyzed in the literature. The prices $(p^*{}_1, p^*{}_2)$ as such that :

$$p^*{}_i = (2(\omega + \beta) N_i + \omega N_j + 2(\omega + \beta)^2 c_i + \omega(\omega + \beta) c_j) / (4(\omega + \beta)^2 - \omega^2)$$

Thus depending on the values of the parameters six types of equilibria may emerge:

(i) firm i uses its unconstrained monopoly price, the existence of the other firm is irrelevant, the situation is called a blockaded monopoly for firm i;
(ii) firm i uses limit pricing to avoid entry of the other firm i: it is called a limit pricing equilibrium for firm i;
(iii) a standard duopoly emerges;
(iv) both firms are out of the market.

In spite of their complexity, analytic expressions of profits could now be derived. Since these quantities are uniquely determined a comparative static analysis is meaningful. This will now be carried on in a systematic way.

2.3 Exploring the type of equilibrium

We want to identify what kind of equilibrium occurs and why. In spite of the simplicity of the model and in spite of the above technical results qualitative judgements on the equilibrium depending on the value of the parameters are far from obvious. Consider the following questions:

(i) ω is an indicator of homogeneity between the two products; have the firms the same incentive to increase ω, to decrease it, or does this incentive depend on the relative cost difference between the two firms? What is the role of the natural market parameters N_1 and N_2 in this respect?
(ii) firm 2 is the least efficient firm, $c_2 \geq c_1$; what are the conditions under which it could survive?
(iii) competition is formulated in terms of prices; what is the impact of price competition on profits? Would there be any incentives to collude on prices and, would that make any difference?

It turns out that global answers can be given to these questions. In a sense it is possible to propose a taxonomy such that if the values of the parameters are in some range then the situation is of a given kind, if the values are in some another range then it is globally different, etc.

Technically the set of parameters will be organized as a three dimensional space with ω ($0 \leq \omega$) referring to homogeneity, c_2 ($c_2 \geq c_1$) referring to the cost disadvantage of the least efficient firm, N_1 and N_2 referring to natural markets and being normalized as percentage of a constant. As for ß, which represents substituability with respect to other products it only plays an indirect role. Indeed suppose ß is changed to 2 ß then the equilibrium is unaffected as long as c_1 and c_2 are divided by 2 and ω is multiplied by 2. Yet the profits are divided by 2. Using this observation an increase in substitution is equivalent to an increase in internal competition (ω is changed to 2 ω) compensated by an increase in terms of efficiency (costs are divided

Chapter 1 - A Duopoly Model

by 2). The overall effect is a decrease in profits, but relative positions (market share, prices) remain the same.

Consider now in this three dimensional space a symmetrical position such as ω close to zero, $N_1 = N_2$, and c_2 close to c_1. It is clear that this position can only be associated with a standard duopoly or no entry at all. Suppose it is a duopoly. Now as ω increases the price competition becomes more severe and the cost disadvantage may become a crucial variable to determine the type of equilibrium that emerges.

At the limit, when ω goes to infinity, it can easily be seen that q_1 goes to

$N_1 + N_2 - 2\beta p_1$

so that $p^m{}_1$ goes to

$(c_1 + (N_1+N_2)/2\beta)/2$

Call $p^m{}_1(\infty)$ this value. Depending on the position of c_2 with respect to $p^m{}_1(\infty)$ one has either a limit pricing or a blockaded monopoly for firm 1 with very different profits. If $c_2 > p^m{}_1(\infty)$, firm 1 gets its full monopoly profit, this is an excellent position. If $c_2 < p^m{}_1(\infty)$, the impact of potential competition may completely destroy firm 1's profit.

What is the impact of N_1 and N_2 on this analysis ? It requires some computations to study this question but the results can nevertheless be nicely interpreted. They are depicted in figures 4 and 5 for the two extreme cases $N_1 = 0$ and $N_2 = 0$ respectively. Observe that the six types of equilibria may be obtained when $N_1 = 0$ and only three when $N_2 = 0$. This is because $c_2 \geq c_1$, which gives a definite advantage to firm 1.

It is rather surprising that even with such a simple model the analytical expressions that delimit each zone are very messy. Yet a singular point $(c^*{}_2, \omega^*)$ plays a crucial role (see figure 4). It is a situation where both firms are just viable. At this point $c_1 = p^{max}{}_1$ and $c_2 = p^{max}{}_2$. Then the equilibrium is (c_1, c_2). There is no production, profits are null and moreover duopoly pricing $(p^d{}_i(c_j))$, limit pricing $(p^l{}_i(c_j))$ and monopoly pricing $(p^m{}_i)$ are all equal to cost c_i. Thus the equilibrium is of any type so that the point $(c^*{}_2, \omega^*)$ is at the boundary of any zone. Furthermore since $c_2 \geq c_1$, such a situation arises only when $p^{max}{}_2 \geq p^{max}{}_1$ namely when $N_2 > N_1$. The identification of such a point greatly facilitates the comparate static analysis through organizing the zones around it.

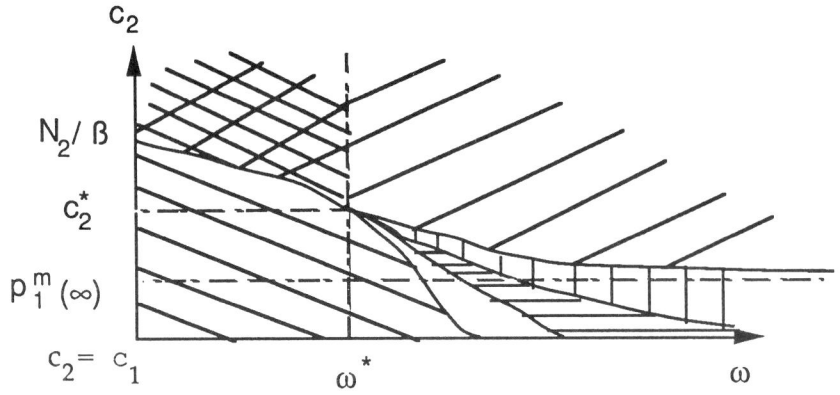

Figure 4:
The case $N_1 = 0, N_2 = 1$

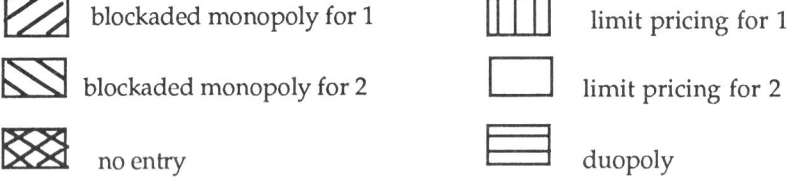

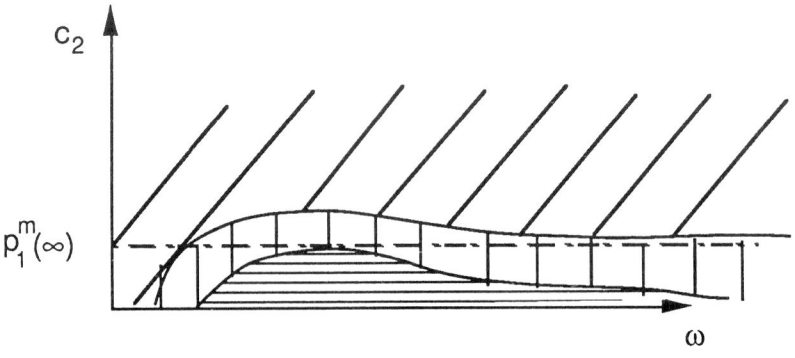

Figure 5:
The case $N_1 = 1, N_2 = 0$

Chapter 1 - A Duopoly Model 19

3. The suggested taxonomy of competitive situations

We are now in a position to use this simple duopoly model to produce a taxonomy of competitive situations which is similar to the one used in empirical studies that is:

(i) what is the main structuring factor that shapes competition: is it the cost disadvantage, is it the natural market, is it the mobility barrier?
(ii) what is the global impact of competition on profits, are the firms close to cut-throat pricing or does one firm have a significant advantage that it should exploit through price competition?
(iii) are there generic strategies that could be suggested in case of a low profit situation?

The idea is not to propose a new taxonomy and to contrast it with the empirical approach. In fact it is exactly the reverse. It will be argued that within this simple model one can already capture much of the existing taxonomy and thus provide a theoretical basis for its enrichment.

The discussion is organized along four cases which correspond to different ranges for the set of parameters.

Case 1: Firm 2's monopoly zone

Recall that firm 2 is the least efficient firm. To benefit from a monopoly situation it has to be located close to $N_2 = 1$, and $\omega = 0$. That is, it should have a good natural market associated with low market mobility. If it moves away from this location the monopoly benefit will be lost and the quicker the higher the cost disadvantage. This very limited zone is suggestive of what is called a "niche": a market segment in which the firm is protected from competition in spite of its relative cost inefficiency. The niche disappears either because the cost of firm 2 is too high relative to the size of the market ($c_2 > N_2 /ß$ and firm 2 is no longer viable on its natural market) or because the mobility barrier with respect to direct competitors on their natural markets disappears (ω increases). It may come from changes in technical norms, legal aspects, innovations, shifts in demand, etc.

Case 2: The duopoly zone

Such a zone is associated with the fact that both firms are independently viable for $\omega = 0$. This implies $c_i \leq N_i/ß$.

It is possible to investigate each firm's incentives relative to ω. At first sight one may expect that they both want lower competition. This is clearly the case for $N_1 =$

N_2 and $c_1 = c_2$. If ω is small enough this may characterize what is called "specialized industries". Each firm has its own natural market and seeks to maintain the mobility barrier. Under these conditions whether the firms collude or not when setting prices is irrelevant since duopoly prices are close to their monopoly prices anyway.

The situation becomes very different if $N_i \gg N_j$. Then the firms' incentives are antagonistic but for different reasons. If $N_2 \gg N_1$, firm 2 wants by all means to protect itself from an efficient competitor; technical norms, legal barriers, captivity of demand are typical. If $N_1 \gg N_2$ firm 1 wants to protect itself from "imitation": it has to fight an inefficient rival with a poor substitute that nevertheless captures some market. In this latter case the incentives are rather tricky and numerical calculation shows that firms 1's profit is U-shaped as a function of ω: it wants to avoid being "stuck in the middle". Indeed it faces a dilemma: more differentiation to protect its high potential market or more homogeneity to increase price competition and to take full advantage of its cost efficiency. It can choose either a "cost" strategy or a "focus" strategy. On the contrary, firm 2's profit is bell-shaped because of the narrow window within which it can operate profitably.

Case 3: Firm 1's monopoly zone

Firm 1 can enjoy a monopoly situation either through a cost advantage only or through both a cost advantage and a natural market advantage. In the first case, it has to care about its relative cost position. Indeed, if its cost advantage is sufficiently high, its incentives are clearly to increase price competition since it can capture the whole potential market at its monopoly price. This is typical of the "volume industries" where profits are high because of a substantial cost advantage over competitors. In the case of an efficient firm with a high natural market we are back to the dilemma discussed for case 2.

Case 4: Other industry types

We conclude our taxonomy by identifying two zones illustrative of the "fragmented industries" and "dead-locked industries" as used by the BCG. They are both low profit structures contrary to the volume and specialized industries.

In the fragmented industries, sources of differentiation are numerous so that the potential market of each firm is rather low and cost efficiency is not a great advantage. Many entries and exits are typical. In this simple model this means that either firm 1 or firm 2 or both firms or no firm at all may be present. Indeed such a zone exists in which all configurations are feasible within very small changes of the parameters. This corresponds to the small line segment associated with the singular point (c^*_2, ω^*). Now, as would be expected from a fragmented industry case, the profits around that segment are very low. Let us recall why this is true. The potential market for firm 1 is relatively low (N_1 close to 0) and it cannot penetrate in firm 2's market because of a low cross-price elasticity (ω^* is low). This implies a low profit for firm 1. Profit of firm 2 is also low because of its high cost relative to its potential market (c_2 is close to $N_2 / ß$). The stability of specialized industries can be contrasted with this case: high profits nearly independent of the competitor's price, similar incentives to maintain a mobility barrier (decrease ω) as opposed to a chaotic situation without profits.

The dead-locked industries are usually characterized by homogeneous products and minor cost disadvantages: they can be associated with a high ω and small differences between costs ($c_2 = c_1$). The most efficient firm, even if it is a monopoly, charges a limit price close to its cost and profits are low. Not surprisingly it is the case where collusion would be the most beneficial. This is sometimes advocated in terms of restructuring to reduce the number of players and to induce a more "responsible" behavior.

References

Bain, J., 1956, Barriers to New Competition, (Cambridge, Mass., Harvard University Press).

Boston Consulting Group, 1981, Perspectives and Strategies, The Boston Consulting Group.

Boston Consulting Group, 1985, Strategic Study of the Machine Tool Industry, (Brussels, EEC).

Buigues, P., and A. Jacquemin, 1989, Strategies of Firms and Structural Environments in the Large Internal Market, Journal of Common Market Studies, 28: 1, 261-275.

Caves, R., and M.E. Porter, 1977, From Entry Barriers to Mobility Barriers, Q. Journl. of Economics, 91.

Collomb, B., and J.P. Ponssard, 1984, Creative Management in Mature Capital Intensive Industries: the Case of Ciment, in A. Charnes and W.W. Cooper (Eds.), Creative and Innovative Management, (Cambridge, Mass. Ballinger).

Demange, G., and J.P. Ponssard, 1986, Barrière de Mobilité et Concurrence dans un Duopole, Annales d'Economie et de Statistiques, 1, 35-53.

Frost, W.H., and R.A. Thietart, 1981, Des Stratégies pour les Secteurs en Déclin, Revue Française de Gestion, March, 4-12.

Gabszewicz, J.J., J.F. Thisse, M. Fujita and U. Schweizer, 1986, Location Theory, Harwood Academic Publishers.

Hamermesh, R.G., and S.B. Silk, 1979, How to Compete in Stagnant Industries, Harvard Business Review, Sep-Oct., 61-68.

Harrigan, K.R., 1979, Strategies for Declining Industries, DBA dissertation, Harvard Business School.

Kiechel, W., 1981, Series on New Management Strategies, Fortune.

Nash, J., 1951, Non Cooperative Games, Annals of Mathematics, 54: 2, 286-295.

Porter, M.E., 1980, Competitive Strategy, (New-York, Free Press).

Shubik, M., 1980, Market Structure and Behavior, (Cambridge, Mass., Harvard University Press).

CHAPTER 2

BRAND LOYALTY AND ADVERTISING: A NOTE

D. NEVEN
Université Libre de Bruxelles
and INSEAD

and

J.-F. THISSE
CORE,
Université Catholique de Louvain

Abstract

In this chapter, we analyse price competition between firms which benefit from customers' loyalty. We assume that there is a distribution of loyalty across consumers. We show that, in equilibrium, brands with little loyalty can survive because of the variety in consumer attitude. Next, we analyse the effect of advertising on the equilibrium, presuming that advertising will affect the distribution of consumers' loyalty. We show that advertising campaigns which increase the variance of consensus attitude can backfire. Advertising campaigns should aim at raising average loyalty without exacerbating attitudes.

1. Introduction

Brand loyalty has long been a major concern for both marketing executives and marketing scholars. The interaction between marketing strategies and brand loyalty has also received particular attention. In this vein, the present chapter analyses some aspects of the interaction between price competition and advertising when brand loyalty is prevalent.

Formal analyses of competition between firms in the presence of brand loyalty have recently been proposed; for example Raju, Shranivasan and Lal (1990) have analysed price competition between firms selling differentiated products to which consumers display some loyalty. They show that the intensity of promotion is affected by the degree of brand loyalty; strong brands will resort less frequently to price promotions.

In the analysis of Raju et al. (1990), a brand loyalty is operationalised as the price differential needed to make consumers who prefer that brand switch to some competing brand. They assume that each brand has a stock of loyal customers and that the degree of loyalty, captioned by the absolute value of the price differential that make them switch, is the same across customers. As a result, there is a particular price for which a brand loses all customers. In this context, there is therefore a strong discontinuity in the demand for the brands. It is then hardly a surprise that a non-cooperative game where firms choose their price does not have any equilibrium in pure strategies. The authors then investigate equilibria in mixed strategies and interpret the equilibrium probability attached to particular strategies as frequencies of use of these strategies over time.

In the present chapter, we adopt the same modelling strategy as Raju et al. (1990), in that brand loyalty is captured by "monetary metric" (as introduced initially by Pessemier (1959)). Yet, we assume that the degree of loyalty varies across consumers; we consider an interval of "pivot" prices, that make particular customers switch, and assume that there is a continuous distribution of customers over this support. It seems that some realism is gained by assuming a distribution of loyalty rather than a uniform attitude across customers. Indeed, it accords with intuition and casual observations that consumers respond differently to price differentials.

There is a second benefit which arises from introducing a distribution of loyalty; the demand faced by each brand will be sufficiently smoothed out that an equilibrium in pure strategies exists. In turn, this enables us to characterise the equilibrium more fully and to analyse the effect of advertising on equilibrium configurations.

The chapter proceeds as follows. Our basic model is outlined in section 2 and the Nash equilibrium identified in section 3. Section 4 is concerned with the interpretation and comparative statics of the Nash equilibria.

2. The model

We consider a market with two firms $(i = 1, 2)$ selling a functionally identical product.

Production is characterised by economies of scale, with production costs given by:

$$C_i = F_i + m_i Q_i, \ i = 1, 2 \tag{1}$$

where, as usual, F_i is a fixed cost and m_i the (constant) marginal cost of production for firm i.

Each consumer is assumed to purchase exactly one unit of the product provided that price is less than some reservation price. We assume that the reservation price constraint is not binding in equilibrium.

Chapter 2 - Brand Loyalty and Advertising

Even though the two brands are functionally identical, consumers have different degrees of loyalty towards them. Differences in brand loyalty are described by a parameter θ which expresses the premium (when positive) or the discount (when negative) that will make a consumer switch from one brand to another. We assume that the parameter θ is uniformly distributed over the support $[\underline{\theta}, \overline{\theta}]$. Following Lancaster, we would contend that "the uniformity assumption provides the background of regularity against which variations in parameters of more immediate interest and importance can be investigated" (Lancaster, 1979, p. 47).

Three prices can be distinguished:

(i) P_i $(i = 1, 2)$

is the price quoted by firm i.

(ii) $P_i - m_i$ $(i = 1, 2)$

is the *net price* (or absolute margin) received by firm i from the sale of one unit.

(iii) $P_i + \theta$ $(i = 1, 2)$

is the product j equivalent price of product i for a consumer of type θ $(i \neq j)$.

In this formulation, θ measures brand loyalty as the difference in price that makes the consumer θ indifferent between brand i and j. Since no restriction is imposed on the upper and lower bounds $\overline{\theta}$ and $\underline{\theta}$, our model can accommodate several interpretations regarding consumers' attitudes toward both brands. In particular, when both $\overline{\theta}$ and $\underline{\theta}$ are positive, all consumers are loyal to the same product, albeit to a different extent. In such a case, any consumer faced with both brands offered at the same price will opt for the brand i. By contrast, when $\overline{\theta}$ and $\underline{\theta}$ are both negative, all consumers are loyal to brand j. In those circumstances, brand j is chosen unanimously when both products are offered at the same price. Finally, if the support spans zero, the population is split between the consumers who are loyal to brand i and those who are loyal to brand j. In this case, when products are offered at the same price, they both capture a positive market share. Hence, when the support of θ does not span zero, our model is akin to a model of *vertical* product differentiation, in which one of the two products dominates. On the other hand, when zero is included in the interior of the support, our model belongs to the family of *horizontal* product differentiation (see Phlips and Thisse (1982) for a discussion of various models of product differentiation and Neven (1986) for a typology of those models).

Demand can be described as follows. We can identify the *marginal consumer* who is indifferent between firm i and firm j by the condition:

$\hat{\theta}$ such that $P_i = P_j + \theta$ (2)

That is: $\hat{\theta} = P_i - P_j$ (3)

Demand for firm i is [1]:

$$D_i = \bar{\theta} - \hat{\theta}$$ (4)

i.e., the set of consumers for whom the degree of loyalty exceeds the price difference.

Demand for firm j is

$$D_j = \hat{\theta} - \underline{\theta}$$ (5)

i.e., those whom loyalty to firm i is more than compensated by the price differences.

Without loss of generality, let firm i be the low cost firm and set $m_i = 0$ so that m_j now stands for the cost differential. Profits to firm i and j (gross of fixed costs) are respectively (using (3)-(5)):

$$\pi_i = P_i (\bar{\theta} - P_i + P_j)$$ (6)
$$\pi_j = (P_j - m_j)(P_i - P_j - \underline{\theta})$$ (7)

The Nash equilibrium of the price game is a pair of prices $P^* = \{P_i^*, P_j^*\}$, such that for $i, j = 1, 2$ and $j \neq i$:

$\pi_i(P^*) \geq \pi_i(P_i, P_j^*)$ for all $P_i \geq 0$.

For an enlightening discussion of the Nash equilibrium concept, see Johanssen (1982).

3. Analysis

There are four steps to identify the Nash equilibrium of the price game:

(i) Identify the prices that satisfy the first order conditions for the maximisation of the profit functions (6)-(7), with respect to own price.

(ii) Check that these prices lead to interior solutions, i.e., that $\hat{\theta} \in \,]\underline{\theta}, \bar{\theta}\,[$.

(iii) Ensure that each firm's price exceeds its marginal production cost.

(iv) Check that no firm has an incentive to undercut its competitor.

Chapter 2 - Brand Loyalty and Advertising

Proposition. The Nash equilibrium of the price game is:

(i) $P_i^* = m_j + \underline{\theta}$ if $m_j \geq \overline{\theta} - 2\underline{\theta}$ (A)

     $P_j^* = m_j$;

(ii) $P_i^* = (2\overline{\theta} - \underline{\theta} + m_j)/3$ if $\overline{\theta} - 2\underline{\theta} > m_j > \underline{\theta} - 2\overline{\theta}$ (B)

     $P_j^* = (\overline{\theta} - 2\underline{\theta} + 2m_j)/3$;

(iii) $P_i^* = 0$ if $\underline{\theta} - 2\overline{\theta} \geq m_j$ (C)

     $P_j^* = -\underline{\theta}$.

We shall prove this proposition in three steps.

Lemma 1. If condition (B) holds, there is a unique price equilibrium given by:

$$P_i^* = (2\overline{\theta} - \underline{\theta} + m_j)/3$$

$$P_j^* = (\overline{\theta} - 2\underline{\theta} + 2m_j)/3.$$

Proof: First note that the first order conditions derived from the profit functions (6)-(7) are:

$$\overline{\theta} - 2P_i + P_j = 0 \qquad (8)$$
$$-\underline{\theta} + P_i - 2P_j + m_j = 0 \qquad (9)$$

from which we derive:

$$P_i^* = (2\overline{\theta} - \underline{\theta} + m_j)/3 \qquad (10)$$

$$P_j^* = (\overline{\theta} - 2\underline{\theta} + 2m_j)/3. \qquad (11)$$

The second order conditions are trivially satisfied. Next, we check that the prices given in (10) and (11) will lead to an interior solution. For this, we need

$$\overline{\theta} > \hat{\theta}(P^*) > \underline{\theta}. \qquad (12)$$

Substituting (3), (10) and (11) in (12) yields:

$$3\overline{\theta} > \overline{\theta} + \underline{\theta} - m_j > 3\underline{\theta}$$

which is the same as condition (B). An interior solution also requires that $P_i^* \geq 0$ and $P_j^* \geq m_j$. The former is obtained from the right hand side inequality of (B) and the latter from the left hand side inequality. Furthermore, as the demand functions are continuous and piecewise linear with a kink pointing inwards, undercutting is never profitable for either firm if condition B holds. Hence, when condition *(B)* is satisfied, the prices given in *(10)-(11)* are equilibrium prices. Q.E.D.

Now, assume that the right hand side of condition *(B)* does not hold. Then, we derive Lemma 2.

<u>Lemma 2</u>. If condition *(A)* holds, there is a unique price equilibrium given by:
$$P_i^* = m_j + \underline{\theta} \text{ and } P_j^* = m_j.$$

<u>Proof</u>: Assume that firm j charges $P_j^* = m_j$. Then firm i responds by charging $P_i^* = m_j + \underline{\theta}$. This price is positive because *(A)* is satisfied and $\overline{\theta} - \underline{\theta} > 0$.

(i) A lower price than this will lead to a lower profit since firm i secures the whole market for $P_i = m_j + \underline{\theta}$.

(ii) Any price higher than $m_j + \underline{\theta}$ gives a profit function for firm i written as:
$$\pi_i = P_i (\overline{\theta} - P_i + m_j)$$

with the solution to the first order condition: $\hat{P}_i = (\overline{\theta} + m_j)/2$.

By assumption, condition *(A)* holds. Hence, $\overline{\theta} \leq 2\underline{\theta} + m_j$ and accordingly:
$$\hat{P}_i \leq m_j + \underline{\theta}.$$

Consequently, since the profit function is concave, the best reply of firm i is given by the "boundary" price, i.e., $P_i^* = m_j + \underline{\theta}$.

(iii) A standard Bertrand argument indicates that firm j can charge no higher price than $P_j^* = m_j$. Q.E.D.

We need a final lemma.

<u>Lemma 3</u>. If condition *(C)* holds, there is a unique price equilibrium given by: $P_i^* = 0$ and $P_j^* = -\overline{\theta}$.[2]

<u>Proof</u>: Assume that firm i charges $P_i^* = 0$. Then firm j responds by setting $P_j^* = -\overline{\theta}$. Given *(C)* and $\overline{\theta} - \underline{\theta} > 0$, this price is larger than m_j.

(i) As in Lemma 2, charging a lower price would not be profitable.

ii) Any price higher than $-\overline{\theta}$ leads to a profit function for firm j given by:

Chapter 2 - Brand Loyalty and Advertising

$$\pi_j = (P_j - m_j)(-P_j - \theta)$$

with solution to the first order condition: $\hat{P}_j = (m_j - \theta)/2$.

By assumption, condition (C) holds. Hence, $-2\overline{\theta} > m_j - \overline{\theta} > -\underline{\theta}$ and accordingly, we have that $\hat{P}_j \leq -\overline{\theta}$.

As in Lemma 2, the best reply of firm 2 is given by the price at the boundary, i.e., $P_j^* = -\overline{\theta}$.

(iii) The argument is similar to that of Lemma 2. Q.E.D.

4. Interpretation and comparative statics

Clearly, according to our proposition, a necessary and sufficient condition for both firms to sell is that $\overline{\theta} - 2\underline{\theta} > m_j > \underline{\theta} - 2\overline{\theta}$. What then happens is that in equilibrium brand i is purchased by the consumers with a high degree of loyalty (in algebraic terms). Brand j captures consumers with low θ. Yet, for both brands to be sold, brand loyalty has to be "sufficiently widely spread" in the well-defined sense of condition (B). In the special case where there is unanimous loyalty towards brand i, ($\overline{\theta}, \underline{\theta} \geq 0$), if there were a very narrow support on θ, there would be no penetration of the market by firm j. It is the fact that certain groups of consumers are strongly loyal to brand i which permits brand j to be sold in the market. Similarly, when consumers are unanimously biased in favour of brand j, it is the existence of some consumers with strong preferences for this brand which enables firm i to survive. At the same time, as expected, both firms are more likely to operate simultaneously if the cost differential m_j is low.

Let us now compare equilibrium prices for different configurations of the θ-support.

First, when there is unanimous loyalty to brand i ($\overline{\theta}, \underline{\theta} > 0$), it follows immediately from condition (B) that the price of firm i exceeds that of firm j ($P_i^* > P_j^*$). This will still hold even if there is no consensus in favour of brand i ($\overline{\theta} > 0$ and $\underline{\theta} < 0$) provided that the mass of consumers with a negative bias is not too large ($-\underline{\theta} \leq \overline{\theta} - m_j$).

We now consider the market configuration when condition *(A)* or *(C)* holds. When condition *(A)* is satisfied, the combination of production costs and consumers' attitudes is such that the brand *j* is not sold. In this case, firm *i* charges a *limit price* which prevents penetration of the market. However, it is worth noticing that this price is not chosen on the basis of an ad hoc assumption but, rather, results from the equilibrium conditions. We observe a similar configuration, mutatis mutandis, when condition *(C)* holds. This condition, which ensures that firm *j* captures the whole market is, however, more stringent than the condition *(A)* because firm *j* has to overcome its cost disadvantage.

The comparative statics of the Nash equilibria are summarised in Table 1 when condition *(B)* holds. Comparative statics at the other two equilibria is straightforward. Specifically, we study the impact of an increase in the mean of the distribution while keeping the variance constant and, conversely, of an increase in the variance which leaves the mean unaffected[3]. It is well known that, for uniform distributions, the mean and variance are respectively given by:

$$\mu = (\bar{\theta} + \underline{\theta})/2 \qquad (13)$$

$$\sigma^2 = (\bar{\theta} - \underline{\theta})^2/12. \qquad (14)$$

We observe that an increase in μ, with constant variance, reduces the price of brand *j* and increases the price of brand *i* as well as its market share. This is so because, the diversity of consumers being unchanged, an increase in the average loyalty to firm *i* makes market penetration by the other firm more difficult. As a result, firm *j* lowers its price but its market share still shrinks.

By contrast, an increase in the diversity of consumers' attitudes, which does not affect the average bias, will raise both prices. Such an increase in the diversity of consumers' attitudes is akin to an enlargement in the scope for product differentiation. As a consequence, both firms have more market power, which is reflected in the increase of the prices. The increase in the diversity of consumers' attitudes has, however, an ambiguous effect on market shares. The general rule is that the firm with the larger market share will experience a reduction in its dominant position[4]. In particular, *when there is a consensus against brand j, brand i will always lose out from an increase in diversity of consumers' attitudes.* Such an increased diversity has the apparently paradoxical effect of increasing the market share of brand *j*. The reason is that brand *i* will tend to focus on consumers with high bias against brand *j*, allowing the latter to raise its price and market share. When there is a consensus in favour of brand *j* (or a diversity of attitudes), the same effect will persist provided that the production cost differential is high enough $(m_j > -(\bar{\theta} + \underline{\theta})/2)$. By contrast, when the production cost differential is relatively low and the bias against brand *i* is relatively strong - so that it has a small market share -, it will then gain customers as a result of a larger diversity.

Chapter 2 - Brand Loyalty and Advertising

The analysis presented above regarding the changes in consumers' attitudes towards competing brands allows us to study the effect of advertising campaigns.

Our analysis suggests that a campaign which has the effect of increasing the average loyalty in favour of a particular brand will raise this brand's profit. On the other hand, any campaign affecting the diversity of consumers' attitudes may not always achieve the desired objectives. More precisely, when all consumers have some loyalty towards brand i, a campaign which increases the diversity of loyalty will lead to a fall in profit. In these circumstances, a successful campaign should aim to foster a greater consensus of attitudes. By contrast, when loyalty is weak (negative θ) an effective campaign will have to widen the spectrum of attitudes. These results provide a warning that the effectiveness of an advertising campaign depends crucially on how it affects the dispersion of consumers' loyalty and upon the precise nature of the consumers' initial attitudes.

Effect of an Increase in:	μ	σ^2	m_j
P^*_i	+	+	+
P^*_j	−	+	+
$MS_i^{(a)}$	+	?	+

Table 1:

Comparative Statics of the Nash Equilibrium

(a) Firm i's market share is defined as $MS_i = (\bar{\theta} - \hat{\theta}) / (\bar{\theta} - \underline{\theta})$.

Substitution for the equilibrium prices gives:

$$MS_i = [\, 2\bar{\theta} - \underline{\theta} + m_j \,] / [\, 3(\bar{\theta} - \underline{\theta}) \,].$$

Notes

1 Demand is specified up to a multiplicative positive constant $1/(\bar{\theta} - \underline{\theta})$ which can be ignored in subsequent analysis.

2 Note that $\bar{\theta}$ is negative when (C) holds.

3 In that case, given that the lenght of the support changes, the consumer density has to be adjusted in order to keep total population constant.

4 An increase in variance raises both prices at the same rate, thereby leaving the marginal consumer unaffected. Given that an increase in variance amounts to a symmetric enlargement of the support, this implies that a firm will gain market share if and only if its market share is originally smaller than one half.

References

Johanssen, L., 1982, On the Status of the Nash Type of Non-Cooperative Equilibrium in Economic Theory, Scandinavian Journal of Economics, 84, 421-441.

Lancaster, K., 1979, Variety, Equity and Efficiency, (Oxford, Basil Blackwell).

Neven, D.J., 1986, Address Models of Differentiation, in G. Norman, (Ed.), Spatial Pricing and Differentiated Markets, (London, Pion), 5-18.

Pessemier, E., 1959, A New Way to Determine Buying Decisions, Journal of Marketing, 24, 41-46.

Phlips, L., and J.-F. Thisse, 1982, Spatial Competition and the Theory of Differentiated Markets: an Introduction, Journal of Industrial Economics, 31, 1-9.

Raju, J., V. Srinivasan, and R. Lal, 1990, The effects of Brand Loyalty on Competitive Price Promotional Strategies, Management Science, 36, 276-304.

MICROECONOMIC CONTRIBUTIONS TO STRATEGIC MANAGEMENT
J. Thépot and R.-A. Thiétart
© 1991 Elsevier Science Publishers B.V. All rights reserved.

CHAPTER 3

COST-REDUCING STRATEGIES WITH SPILLOVERS

R. DE BONDT
Katholieke Universiteit Leuven

Abstract

Investment in research and development that lowers unit production costs may also benefit rival producers because of technology spillovers. The impact of such knowledge leakages on strategic investment incentives is shown to depend on the interaction between the magnitude of the spillover and the degree of differentiation of the marketed products.

1. Introduction

Business firms often improve on their competitive advantage through strategic investments in research and development that allow to reduce cost or enhance demand. These investments typically constitute competitive moves by which firms incite actual or potential rivals to certain responses that are more advantageous to the firm than other rival strategies would be. In addition they involve resource commitments that to a large degree are sunk and are therefore costly to reverse. The appropriability of such innovative commitments may however be limited because of spillovers from one rival to another, that are realized through various formal and informal mechanisms of leakage and exchange of information. Possibly firms may seek ways to better internalize side effects through a coordination of innovative investments within a strategic alliance or joint venture.

---

* The author gratefully acknowledges the comments of R. Veugelers and an anonymous referee, as well as the assistance of C. Vlasselaer and P. Slaets and the support from the Belgian National Science Foundation and the Research Fund of the K.U. Leuven (OT/89/5).

Especially global and high-tech markets show a variety of competitive and cooperative settings in which firms improve on their competitive position through cost reducing (or demand enhancing) development activities (Lewis (1990)). A somewhat deeper understanding of the resulting fairly complex strategic interactions may be useful in inspiring and guiding their managerial design and implementation. Although modern industrial organisation analysis can highlight some of the most fundamental tendencies, it can only, at best, support the practically relevant analysis of strategic management.

Innovative strategies are embedded in the competitive environment reflected in, among others, the similarity or the differentiation of the rival products, the spillovers of the created knowledge to actual or potential competitors and the rivalrous or cooperative conduct between the current suppliers. Some of the main implications of structural and conduct characteristics for strategies and profitability can be detailed in a simple setting with linear demand and production costs.

The setting and the competitive and coordinated strategies are detailed next. This allows to explain the incentives within a strategic taxonomy, after which some observations on the magnitude of the differences and final conclusions are given.

2. A duopoly setting

Two symmetric firms are envisaged that play an innovative investment game, while producing differentiated or homogeneous products. Both firms produce with constant unit costs c_i and face a linear demand:

$$p_i = a - bq_i - dq_j \tag{1}$$

with p_i prices and q_i and q_j quantities, i, j=1,2, i ≠ j and $b \geq d \geq 0$. The degree of product differentiation is captured by d/b that attains its maximum value of 1 when rival products are similar (homogeneous for b=d), and its minimum value of 0, say when the products of both firms are positioned in completely different market segments (d=0). Product rivalry can be thought of to be more competitive as d/b increases from zero to one.

The innovative investments concern so-called process oriented research and development expenditures that lower own production costs but at the same time may lower the production costs of other firms because of the positive spillovers of the developed knowledge (d'Aspremont and Jacquemin, 1988; De Bondt and Veugelers, 1991). Formally speaking the resource commitments allow to decrease the unit cost with a spillover ß from the other firm's investment [1], or :

$$c_i = A - (x_i + ßx_j) \quad \text{and} \quad 0 \leq ß \leq 1 \tag{2}$$

Chapter 3 - Cost Reducing Strategies

Without any investments the duopolists would operate with a unit cost level equal to A>0 (difference of demand and cost intercept equal to (a-A)>0). The innovative output is the total amount of cost reduction that equals the own efforts x_i plus the spillover from the rivals βx_j. (The level of cost improvement is sometimes called the effective R&D (Kamien, Muller and Zang (1990), since it is the investment that each firm would have to make to get a given cost reduction, if it could not have benefited from spillovers). The parameter ß reflects the extent to which knowledge leaks to rivals as well as the productivity of the acquired knowledge in lowering rivals production costs. It is thought to be mainly determined by technological and organisational characteristics of the firms.

The cost-reducing investments are envisaged to be made with diminishing returns that are reflected in a quadratic cost function $(\Gamma/2)x_i^2$, $i = 1, 2$, with the parameter Γ, being inversely related to the efficiency of the innovative activities. Firms compete on investment and on quantity 2 with payoffs V_i,

$$V_i = \pi_i - (\Gamma/2)x_i^2 \tag{3}$$

with $\pi_i = (p_i - c_i)q_i$. Discounting is ignored for reasons of exposition.

3. Computing strategies

3.1. Competitive strategies

Two information settings can be looked at involving a simultaneous-move and a sequential-move setting. In the **simultaneous** Nash equilibrium both firms decide independently from each other on both the investment and production levels with complete information on the payoff functions of each other. This simulates situations when prohibitive adjustment costs require firms to plan simultaneously on development and production. In the **sequential** Nash equilibrium firms decide on quantities contingent on the own and observed rival investment decisions, which themselves are chosen in perfect anticipation of this response.

The computation of these Nash equilibria is straightforward. The simultaneous-moves $x_i°$ and $q_i°$ solve the system of equations :

$$\frac{\partial V_i}{\partial q_i} = \frac{\partial \pi_i}{\partial q_i} = 0 \quad \frac{\partial V_i}{\partial x_i} = \frac{\partial \pi_i}{\partial x_i} - \Gamma x_i° = 0 \quad i=1,2 \tag{4}$$

The sequential Nash equilibrium is subgame perfect and is computed through backward induction. In the second stage quantity competition prevails given the earlier chosen investment strategies. The Nash equilibrium of that period solves ∂V_i

$\partial q_i = 0$, yielding:

$$q_i = \frac{a-A}{2b+d} + x_i \frac{2b-\beta d}{4b^2-d^2} + x_j \frac{2b\beta-d}{4b^2-d^2} \quad i,j=1,2 \quad i \neq j \tag{5}$$

In the first stage the competitive investment strategies are chosen with perfect foresight of the output decision rules given above. The Nash strategies solve the following system of equations:

$$\frac{\partial V_i}{\partial x_i} = \frac{\partial \pi_i}{\partial q_j} \cdot \frac{\partial q_j}{\partial x_i} + \frac{\partial \pi_i}{\partial x_i} - \Gamma x_i = 0 \quad i,j=1,2 \quad i \neq j \tag{6}$$

A stable symmetric equilibrium with investment and output levels $x_i{}^s$ and $q_i{}^s$ solving both (5) and (6), will apply for a wide range of parameter values [3], see Table I.

	Ω^*	x^*	V^*
Simultaneous Nash $* = o$	Γ		
Sequential Nash $* = s$	$\dfrac{\Gamma(2b-d)(2b+d)}{2b(2b-\beta d)}$	$\dfrac{(a-A)}{\Omega^*(2b+d) - (1+\beta)}$	$x^{*2}(b\Omega^{*2} - \Gamma/2)$
Pre-competitive cooperation $* = c$	$\dfrac{\Gamma(2b+d)}{2b(1+\beta)}$		

In all settings $q^* = \Omega^* x^*$ and $\pi^* = bq^{*2}$. Ω^* allows to write short expressions, and facilitates making comparisons.

Table I:
Equilibrium values under various behavioral scenarios

3.2. Coordinated investments

Firms may seek to coordinate the strategic investments, while continuing to choose independently their other (output) strategies. This could be achieved, for example, by a joint venture (with equal ownership shares) in which the long-run innovative commitments are coordinated while the managers of each of the products continue to act independently. In any case it is supposed here that the coordinated choices can be implemented and enforced.

The coordinated choices $x_i{}^c$ anticipate the product Nash equilibrium given by the strategy rules of equation (5) and seek to maximize total profits $V_1 + V_2$, a natural objective given the symmetry of the duopolists. The investment strategies therefore solve:

$$\frac{\partial V_i}{\partial x_i} + \frac{\partial V_j}{\partial x_i} = \frac{\partial \pi_i}{\partial q_j} \cdot \frac{\partial q_j}{\partial x_i} + \frac{\partial \pi_i}{\partial x_i} - \Gamma x_i{}^c + \frac{\partial \pi_j}{\partial q_i} \cdot \frac{\partial q_i}{\partial x_i} + \frac{\partial \pi_j}{\partial x_i} = 0 \qquad (7)$$

The research joint venture (rjv) takes into account not only the impact on own profits ($\partial \pi_i/\partial x_i - \Gamma x_i{}^c$), but also the competitive effect because of the reaction of the other partner ($\partial \pi_i/\partial q_j . \partial q_j/\partial x_i$), as well as the effect on the other firms product profitability ($\partial \pi_j/\partial q_i . \partial q_i/\partial x_i + \partial \pi_j/\partial x_i = dV_j /dx_i = d\pi_j/dx_i$). See Table I for the resulting symmetric values and profits.

4. A strategic taxonomy

With sequential strategies both firms have an incentive to make a competitive move, that is to incite rivals to make an output (or price) decision that is more advantageous to each of them than another rival's decision would be. This effect is formally captured by the "strategic term":

$$\frac{\partial \pi_i}{\partial q_j} \cdot \frac{\partial q_i}{\partial x_i} = - q_i . d . \frac{(2b\beta - d)}{(2b-d)(2b+d)} \qquad i,j=1,2 \qquad i \neq j \qquad (8)$$

which may have a positive or negative sign or may also be zero.

A positive sign means that an increase in investment is a beneficial competitive move, a negative sign implies the opposite. In the simultaneous move setting the opportunity for a strategic move is not present, since firms cannot or prefer not to wait with their output (or price) decisions until they observe the other firm's investment decisions. From the computed equilibria in Table I it follows immediately that:

$$\text{sign } (x_s - x_o) = -\text{ sign } (\Omega_s - \Omega_o) \qquad (9)$$
$$= -\text{ sign } [d(2b\beta-d)] = \text{sign strategic term (8)}.$$

The over- or underinvestment with the sequential moves, relative to the simultaneous strategies, thus depends crucially on the spillovers and on the nature and the degree of differentiation of the marketed products (see Figure 1). With a small level of spillovers ($\beta<d/2b$) overinvestment occurs and with a large level of leakage ($\beta>d/2b$), underinvestment applies. The critical treshold spillover level $\beta=d/2b$ corresponds to a razor's edge case where all strategic interactions cancel and a decision theoretic solution applies. This level equals one half if the products are perfect substitutes and it becomes smaller as the products are more differentiated.

The under- or overinvestment outcomes are also related to the tough or soft nature of the strategic investments (Fudenberg and Tirole (1984)). In line with general economic intuition "tough" simply means that the competitive move creates a negative externality to the other firm, since it reduces the profits of that firm. "Soft" can then be associated with a positive externality. In the present setting the tough or soft nature of the investments coincides with the incentives towards over- or underinvestment, since it can be shown that :

$$\text{sign (strategic term (8))} = -\text{ sign } (d\pi_j/dx_i)$$

with $(d\pi_j/dx_i)$ indicating the impact of the strategic investment on the other firm's profitability[4]. Note that the externality on the second stage profits coincides with the effect on the value of the firm, since $dV_j/dx_i = d\pi_j/dx_i$.

As long as a competitive move makes a firm tough, that is as long as it inflicts a negative externality upon the other firm, the internalization of this effect in a research joint venture, should result in a smaller level of the investment than would result with competitive (Nash) strategic behavior. Likewise should a larger investment result from such coordination, if the independent moves were to inflict positive externalities, i.e. when they make firms so called soft. This intuition corresponds to general economic insights on the consequences of externalities and it is indeed confirmed in the present framework, since it can easily be established from Table I and (9) :

$$\text{sign } (x^c - x^s) = -\text{ sign } (\Omega_c - \Omega_s) = \text{sign } (2b\beta - d) \qquad (10)$$
$$= \text{sign } (d\pi_j/dx_i)$$

Chapter 3 - Cost Reducing Strategies 39

Product differentiation

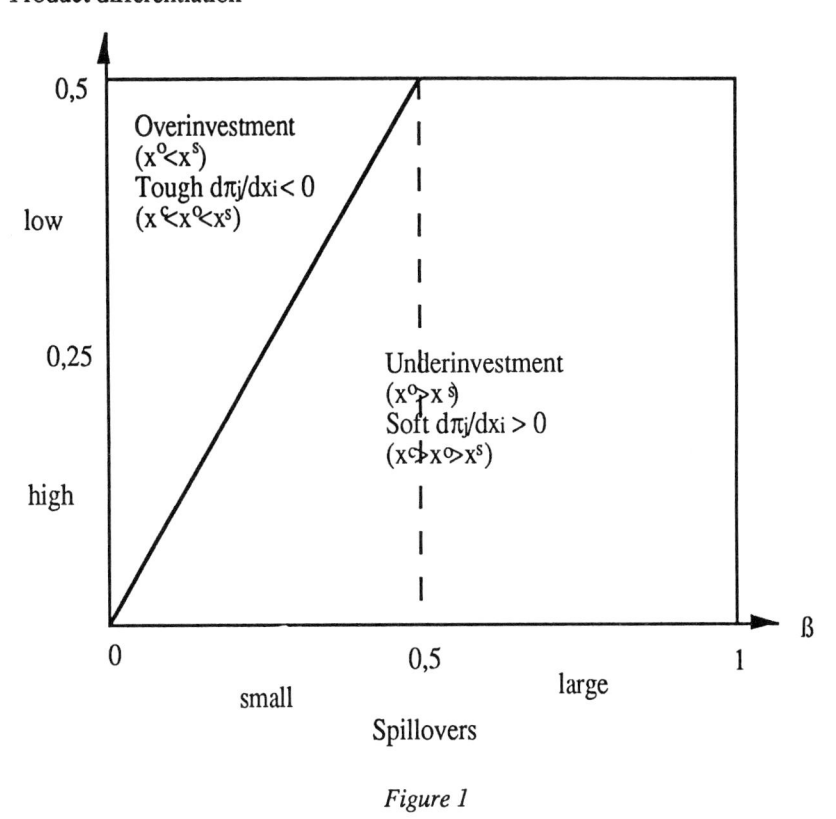

```
0,5 ┤
     │ Overinvestment
     │ (x°<xˢ)
     │ Tough dπj/dxi< 0
low  │ (xᶜ<x°<xˢ)
     │
0,25 │
     │         Underinvestment
     │         (x°>xˢ)
     │         Soft dπj/dxi > 0
     │         (xᶜ>x°>xˢ)
high │
     │
   0 └─────────┬──────────┬──→ ß
   0         0,5          1
       small        large
           Spillovers
```

Figure 1

Comparison of competitive investments x° (simultaneous move), xˢ (sequential move), and coordinated commitments xᶜ.

The research joint venture hence reduces the tough overinvestments and increases the soft underinvestments (see Figure 1). This will typically result in higher profits than would apply with independent competitive moves [5].

5. Understanding the strategic incentives

The above taxonomy highlights the importance of the interaction between the strategic moves and the subsequent product competition. A somewhat deeper understanding can be given with the aid of the reaction curves, that indicate the best output response of the producers. Tough overinvestment occurs in a sequential equilibrium, given zero spillovers and regardless of the degree of product differentiation. The larger cost-reducing investment is a move that incites the firm itself to produce more and rivals to market less (Brander and Spencer, 1984). It is a tough move, since it reduces rivals profits. This incentive is visualized in figure 2c for a duopoly with a moderate degree of product differentiation and zero spillovers.

Figure 2 shows the profit and reaction curve consequences for both firms. Only the firm that produces output q_1 is envisaged to make an investment to reduce its costs from a value of zero to one, although the actual equilibria also involve a move by the second firm. This is not shown since the only intention of the figure is to highlight the importance of the interactions between the spillovers and product differentiation for the nature and the extent of the competitive moves.

With positive spillovers the strategic move shifts the rival's reaction curve, even before it has made a move itself. The rival also benefits directly from the received knowledge and will plan for a larger production and this tends to offset the gains from the strategic investment. Because of this the incentives towards tough overinvestment are only preserved with ß < d/2b : small spillovers and a relatively intense product rivalry, because of little product differentiation (Figure 2a and 2e).

Soft underinvestment applies with ß > d/2b : moderate spillovers (ß < 1/2) and sufficient differentiation (Figure 2d) or extensive spillovers (ß > 1/2) with any kind of product rivalry (Figure 2b en 2c). In the case of extensive leakage rivals benefit a lot from cost-reducing efforts and increase their output in response. As a consequence the profits of the investing firm at best only moderately increase and it becomes more likely that this does not justify large investment, or in other words only a more limited investment is warranted. With moderate spillovers and important differentiation, a too large investment will likewise fail to generate a sufficient reduction in rival output (and profit) and increase in own profits, see Figure 2d. More product differentiation tends to segment the markets and creates less room for gaining a competitive advantage. Formally this can be seen in the previous figures, because more differentiation means a lower d/b and hence a flatter reaction curve of the rival (dq_2/dq_1 = -d/2b in the figure becomes less negative), so that it is "harder" to incite that rival to a smaller output. Spillovers of even a moderate magnitude, further reduce the competitive possibilities and profitability of the strategic activities.

Chapter 3 - Cost Reducing Strategies 41

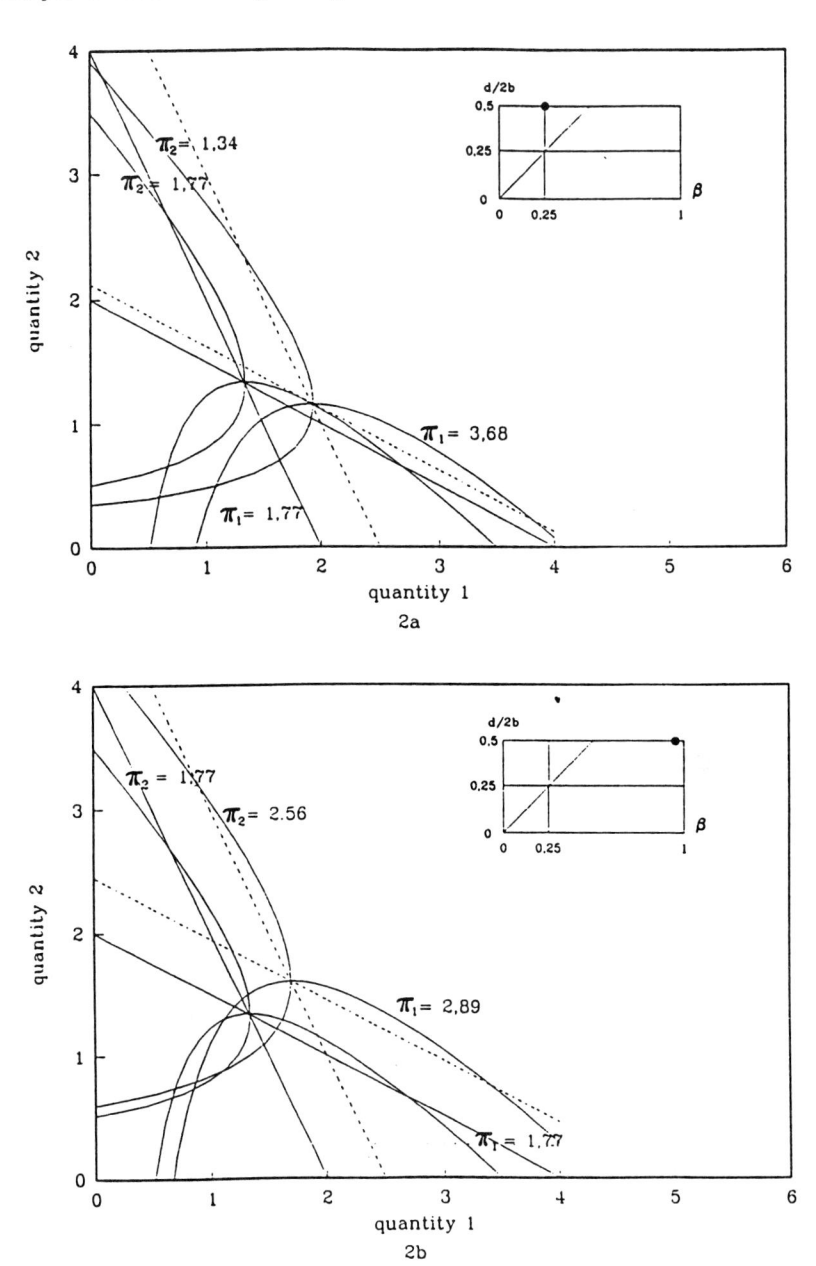

Figure 2
Consequences for outputs, profits and reaction curves of a cost-reducing investment by firm one [6]

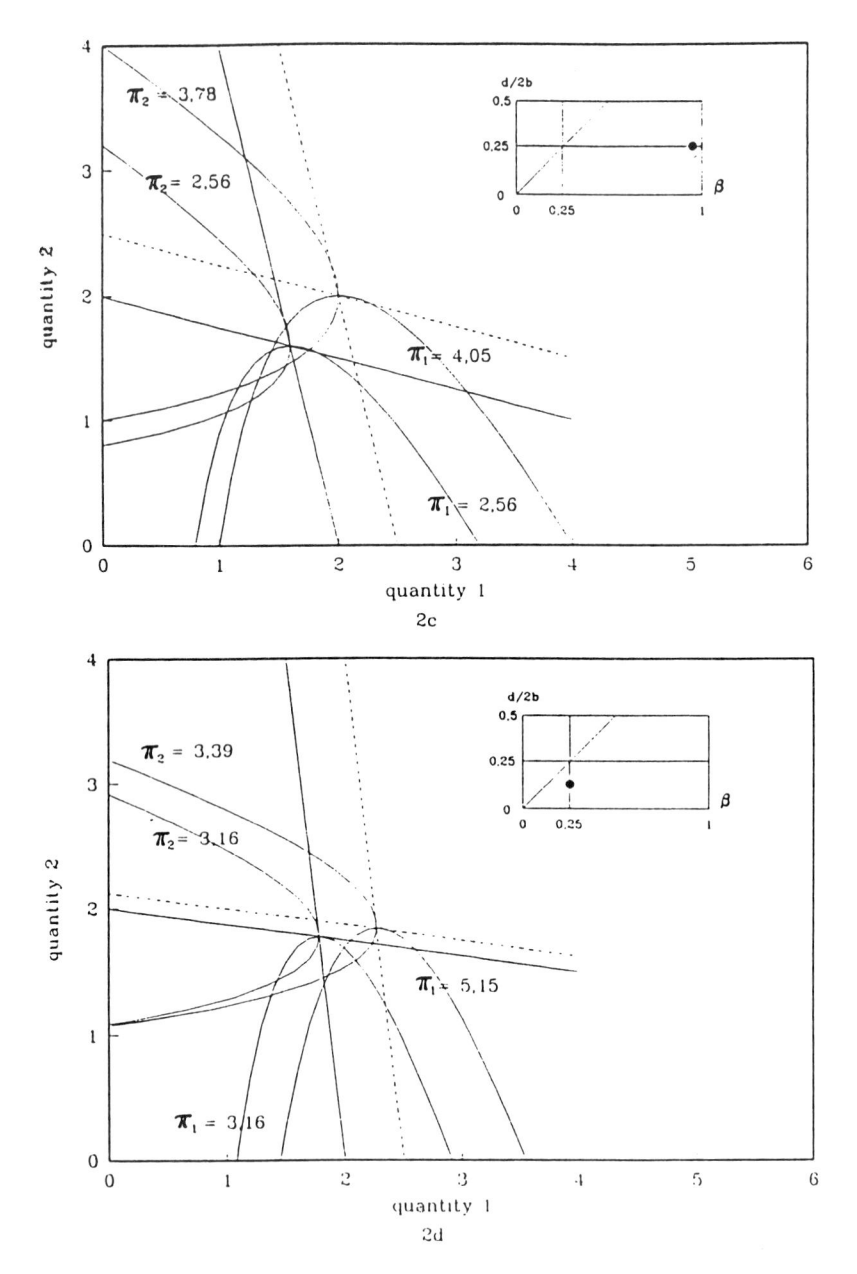

Figure 2 (cont.)
Consequences for outputs, profits and reaction curves of a cost-reducing investment by firm one [6]

Chapter 3 - Cost Reducing Strategies 43

Figure 2 (cont.)
Consequences for outputs, profits and reaction curves of a cost-reducing investment by firm one [6]

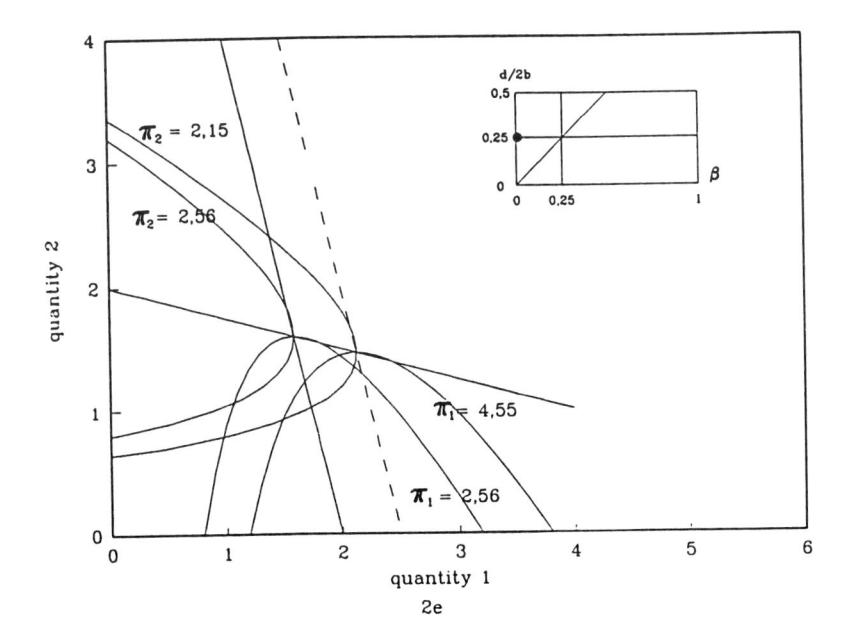

6. Magnitude of differences

The differences in magnitude of the strategies and profits are also important and some tendencies in this regard can be obtained using numerical analysis. The investment levels and the consequent differences in profitability are dependent on the spillovers and the degree of product differentiation as Figure 3 illustrates.

The magnitude of the simultaneous strategies (very slightly) increases as the spillovers augment. But exactly the reverse tends to apply for sequential competitive moves that are made with not too high R&D efficiency (De Bondt, Slaets, Cassiman, 1990). Positive spillovers prevent the internalisation of the benefits of individual efforts and with low R&D efficiency, the synergies of information leakage are not strong enough to compensate this disincentive effect. In such situations the innovative investments decrease as this leaking of knowledge becomes more important (there exist levels of high R&D efficiency for which individual efforts increase with spillovers). The coordinated investments internalize the externalities and will in the present setting always increase as the spillovers become more important. All levels are positively affected by an increase in product differentiation.

The profitability of the various behavioral scenario's in a duopoly tend to improve as the spillovers increase. But note that the profits with simultaneous, investments are higher than those that are realized with (sequential) competitive moves. The strategic incentives appear to trap both players in a kind of prisoners' dilemma situation : both firms could gain by simultaneously restraining their desire for a competitive move and sticking to the simultaneous Nash values. The analysis here would predict that the advantages of a commitment to simultaneous R&D tend to be larger in settings with important information exchange. The move towards a research joint venture in any case is even better for profitability (except in the razor's edge case of $\beta = d/2b$ in case of which there is no difference).

The examples suggest that in a duopoly, the profit advantages of a rjv:
- may decrease as the spillovers increase for tough investments that will occur with relatively homogeneous products and moderate spillovers ($\beta < d/2b$);
- increase as the spillovers augment for soft investments that are likely to accompany large spillovers and moderate leakage and important product differentiation ($\beta > d/2b$).

The profit advantages of the rjv thus necessarily increase as the spillovers increase, if innovative investments are made by a few rivals that operate in relatively segmented markets with sufficiently important technological information transfers. And such advantages tend to be less pronounced if a few firms market very similar products. The differences in profitability that are visualized in Figure 3 reflect the differences in the investment levels. The reason is that differences in efforts are translated into differences in innovative output and consequently profitability.

In industries with more than two firms additional effects may lead firms to form a rjv. It can be shown that the profitability of the competitive scenario (Vs) in industries with "many" rivals may also deteriorate with extensive spillovers ($\beta > 1/2$) (De Bondt, Slaets and Cassiman (1990)). For most levels of (not too extreme) differentiation "many" means a number of firms larger than 5. Too many rivals combined with large leakage means that the amount of cost-reduction tends to get smaller as spillovers increase, and limiting the information transfer could benefit the firms. And if this is not practical, firms have an even stronger incentive to make the best of the large information flows and seek ways to coordinate the investments say in a research joint venture[7].

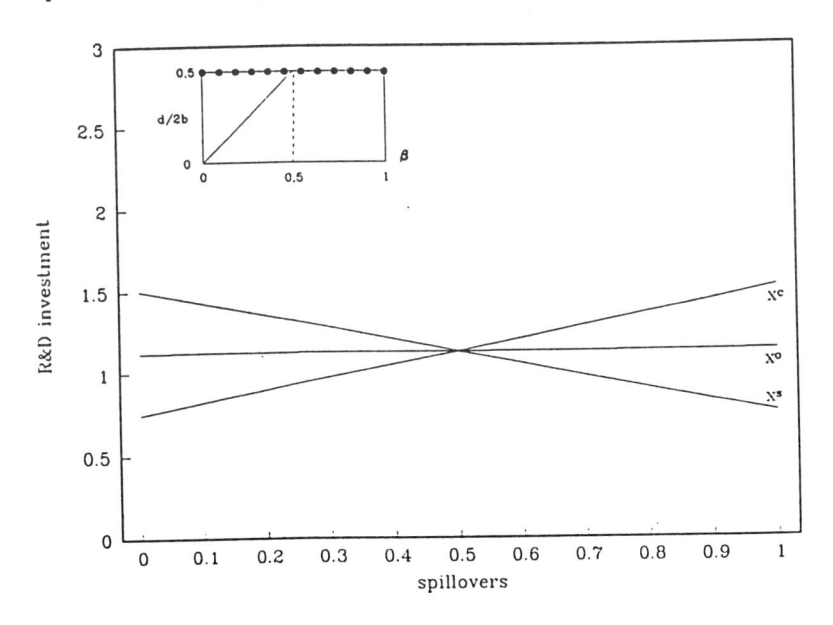

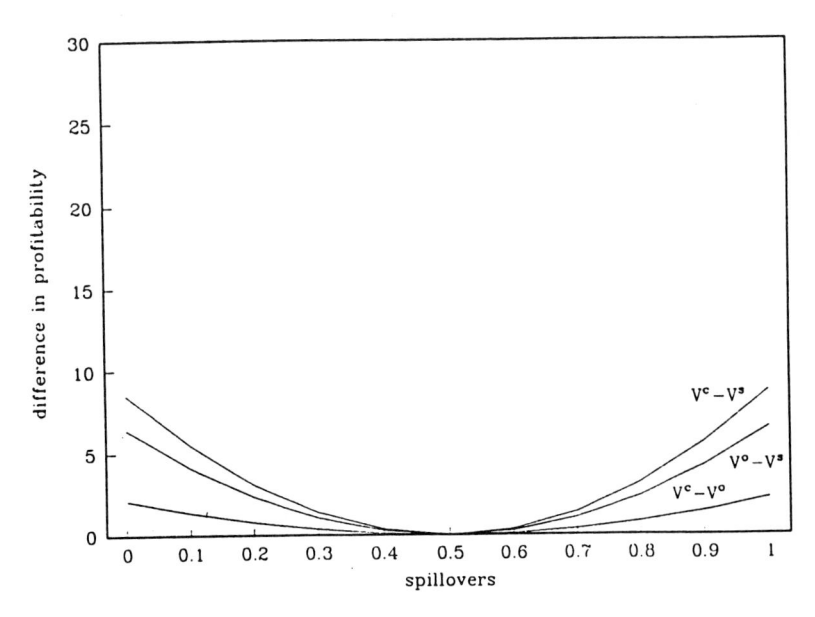

Chapter 3 - Cost Reducing Strategies 45

Figure 3
Cost-reducing strategies with competitive simultaneous (x^o) and sequential choices (x^s) and with coordinated commitments (x^c) as a function of spillovers. Consequent profit levels are V^o, V^s and V^c [8].

Figure 3 (cont.)
Cost-reducing strategies with competitive simultaneous (x^o) and sequential choices (x^s) and with coordinated commitments (x^c) as a function of spillovers. Consequent profit levels are V^o, V^s and V^c [8].

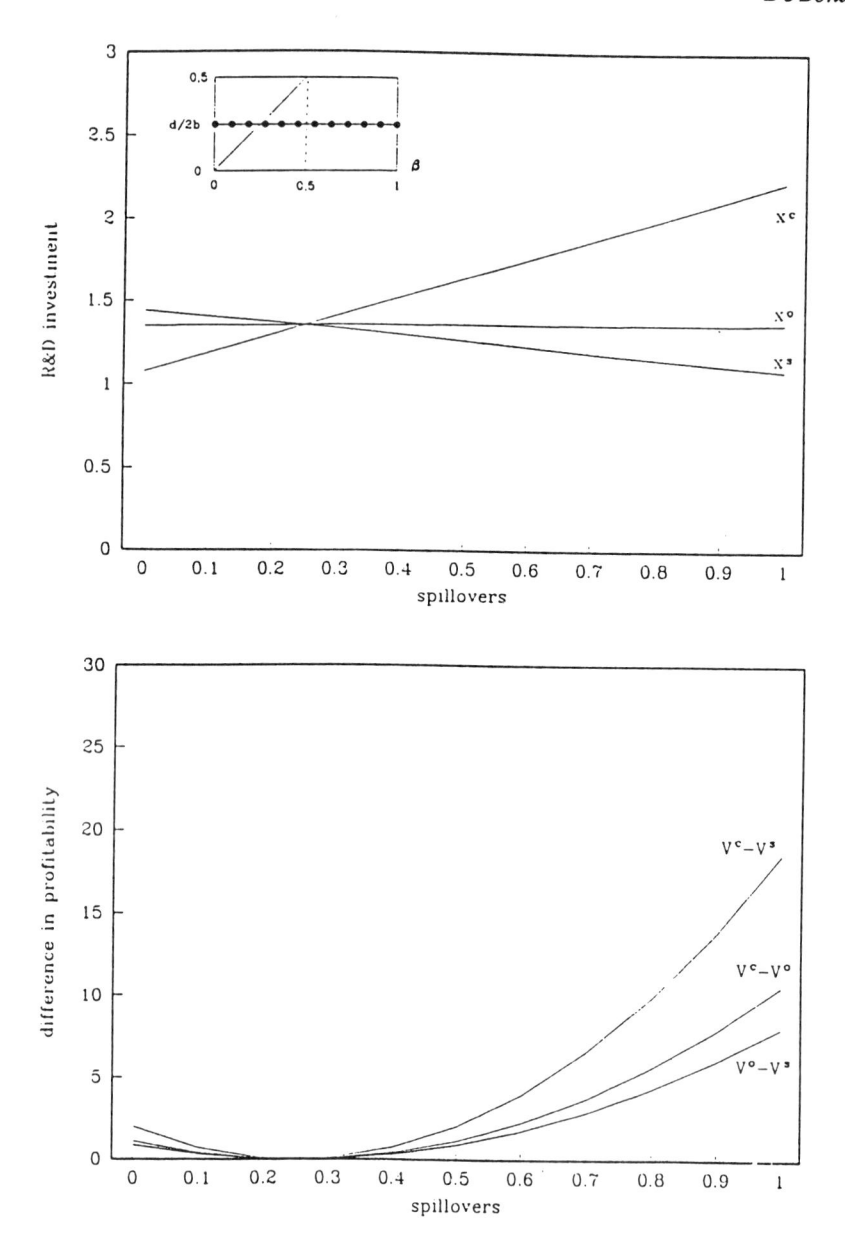

Chapter 3 - Cost Reducing Strategies 47

Figure 3 (cont.)
Cost-reducing strategies with competitive simultaneous (x^o) and sequential choices (x^s) and with coordinated commitments (x^c) as a function of spillovers. Consequent profit levels are V^o, V^s and V^c [8].

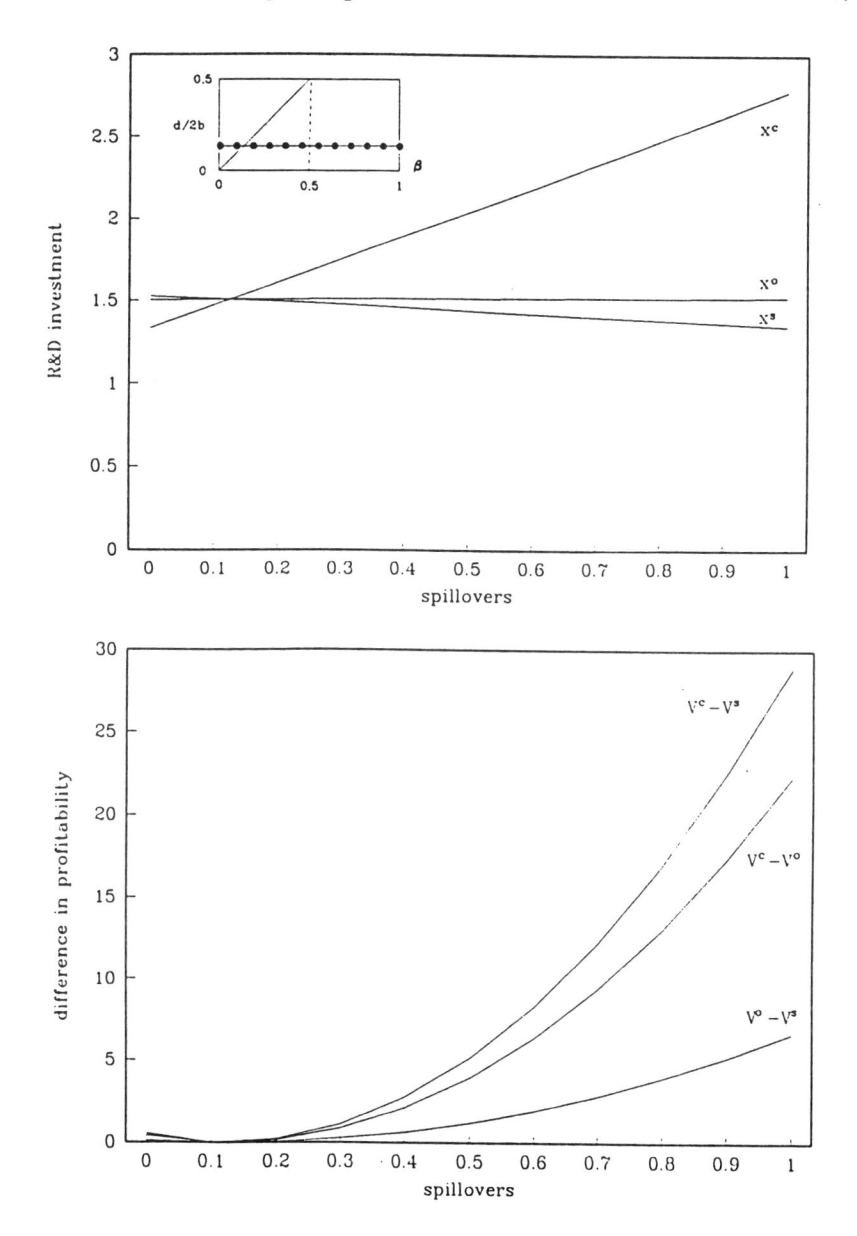

All of this calls for a more detailed investigation of the conduct aspects of the information transfers that occur in competitive and cooperative environments (Kamien, Muller and Zang, 1990). The present setting can also be used to analyse the implications of various spillover scenarios in different conduct environments, but a full endogenisation and explanation of the spillover mechanisms observed in reality still needs to be accomplished.

7. Conclusions

Situations leading firms to strategically over- or underinvest in research and development that lowers costs (or enhances demand), are examined to take into account the spillovers that typically accompany these commitments. The computation and comparison of explicit equilibria for a duopoly with quadratic payoffs allows to clarify the underlying economics in a comprehensive way.

Firms that compete with relatively homogeneous substitutes tend to strategically overinvest, provided that zero or moderate positive spillovers accompany such tough commitments. Pre-competitive coordination of these investments tends to neutralize the overinvestment incentive and results in lower levels and higher profitability. Important positive spillovers or small leakage and differentiated substitutes, however, imply incentives towards soft underinvestments. The coordination of these investments will internalize the positive externalities and result in more investment and higher profits.

Non-segmented or homogeneous markets, spillovers and rivals tend to limit the possibilities of appropriation of benefits of innovative (cost-reducing) activities. Real industrial organisations have each of these ingredients in various combinations and it therefore appears useful to inquire on their impact on such competitive moves. The above analysis intended to clarify how the extent of product differentiation and information leakage may interact in a simple way to determine strategic incentives. Hopefully it can inspire further research along these lines and analytical thinking in applied work.

Notes

1 Since demand is shifting in a parallel fashion the model cannot pretend to capture all of the specifics of product innovation. The spillovers as thought of here, are mainly determined by technological characteristics, while absorption capacity of the firms is supposed to be the result of previously acquired knowledge and know-how. Different treatments of these aspects can be found in Levin and Reiss (1988) and Cohen and Levinthal (1989).

2 As is well known there is a relation with price competition (reaction curves are

Chapter 3 - Cost Reducing Strategies

upward sloping, instead of downward), and this could be used to translate the results to such a setting (Singh and Vives, 1984).

3 The restrictions for second-order conditions and stability tend to create little restrictions on admissable spillovers if R&D efficiency is not too important (Γ large, De Bondt and Veugelers, 1989; De Bondt a.o. (1990).

4 $\frac{d\pi_j}{dx_i} = \frac{\partial \pi_j}{\partial x_i} + \frac{\partial \pi_j}{\partial q_i} \cdot \frac{\partial q_i}{\partial x_i} = ßq_j - dq_j \frac{2b-ßd}{(2b-d)(2b+d)}$

$= q_j \cdot 2b \cdot \frac{2bß-d}{(2b-d)(2b+d)} = -$ sign (strategic term (8)).

5 As long as ß ≠ d/2b, (De Bondt and Veugelers, 1991).

6 The figures are drawn with (a-A)=4 and b=1. The dots in the small inserts allow to infer the employed d and ß values.

7 Setting up a separate firm could be one mechanism for controlling information flows. This means that a somewhat different competitive scenario applies, elements of which have been looked at by Veugelers and De Bondt (1991).

8 The employed parameter values are (a-A)=100, b=1 and Γ=30. The dots in the inserts allow to infer the d values.

References

Brander, J., and B. Spencer, 1984, Strategic Commitment with R&D : the Symmetric Case, The Bell Journal of Economics, 14, 225-235.

Cohen, W.M., and D.A. Levinthal, 1989, Innovation and Learning: The Two Faces of R&D, The Economic Journal, 99, 569-596.

De Bondt, R., and R. Veugelers, 1989, Strategic Investment with Spillovers, European Journal of Political Economy, forthcoming.

De Bondt, R., P. Slaets and B. Cassiman, 1990, The Degree of Spillovers and the Number of Rivals for Maximum Effective R&D, Onderzoeksrapport 9025, (Leuven, Katholieke Universiteit Leuven).

D'Aspremont, C., and A. Jacquemin, 1988, Cooperative and Noncooperative R&D in Duopoly with Spillovers, American Economic Review, 78, 1133-1137.

Fudenberg, D., and J. Tirole, 1984, The Fat-cat Effect, the Puppy-dog Ploy and the Lean and Hungry Look, American Economic Review, 74, 361-366.

Kamien, M.I., E., Muller and I. Zang, 1990, Research Joint Ventures and R&D Cartels, Northwestern University.

Levin, R., and P. Reiss, 1989, Cost Reducing and Demand Creating R&D with Spillovers, The Rand Journal of Economics, 19, 538-556.

Lewis, J.D., 1990, Partnerships for Profit, (New York, The Free Press).

Singh, N., and X. Vives, 1984, Price and Quantity Competition in a Differentiated Duopoly, The Rand Journal of Economics, 15, 546-554.

Veugelers, R., and R. De Bondt, 1991, Cooperative Innovative Activities, in C. Antonelli (Ed), The Economics of Information Networks, (Amsterdam, North-Holland Elsevier Science Publishers).

MICROECONOMIC CONTRIBUTIONS TO STRATEGIC MANAGEMENT
J. Thépot and R.-A. Thiétart
© 1991 Elsevier Science Publishers B.V. All rights reserved.

CHAPTER 4

BARRIERS TO ENTRY AND STRATEGIC MARKETING INVESTMENTS

J. K. KARLSEN
Centre for Research in Economics
and Business Administration

and

K. GRØNHAUG
Norwegian School of
Business Administration

Abstract

The purpose of this paper is to enhance our understanding of the relationship between barriers to entry, the derived concepts mobility barriers and strategic groups, and strategic marketing investments. Entry barriers are dealt with in the traditional, or "structuralist", industrial organization literature. As both marketing and strategy research to a large extent borrows from the structuralist tradition, many of the inherent assumptions in the structuralist paradigm has become deeply embedded in strategy and marketing literature. We briefly review the structuralist tradition in order to identify these underlying assumptions. The "new" industrial organization in many respects represents a better theoretical foundation for the analysis of strategic action. As an example, a well-known two-stage model, focusing on opitmal entry-deterring or accomodating strategies, is presented, including examples of strategic marketing investments. This is contrasted with the traditional approach, and theoretical advances and recommendations for empirical strategy research are highlighted. Important implications for aspects of empirical strategy research are discussed, and recommendations for future research suggested.

1. Introduction

In disciplines like corporate strategy and marketing, the strategic aspects of marketing activities has more recently gained widespread interest. It should be noted, however, that these disciplines in their approach to this topic mainly has been *borrowing* disciplines (Myers et al., 1980), with elements from traditional industrial organization as important input. Today the textbook by Porter (1980), aslo building on traditional industrial organization, is probably the most quoted source. In addition, it has been claimed that marketing is limited in scope, as the focus has mainly been on the buyers, with modest explicit attention to competitive forces (Day and Wensley, 1983), and with more focus on tactics than strategy (Wind and Robertson, 1983). More recently it has been claimed that marketing activities should be treated as investments, by focusing on the long term nature of such activities, indicating that such investments are crucial to both profitability and the ability to survive in the long run (Johansson and Mattson, 1985). When treating marketing activities as investments, marketing research, however, gives almost no explicit attention to competitor´s reactions, an element of analysis which is central to the "new" industrial organization literature. An interesting observation is that prominent industrial economist besides having explicitly analyzed marketing related research questions also have published their findings in marketing and strategy journals (Schmalensee and Thisse, 1988). This may indicate that a lowering of disciplinary borders is taking place.

The benefits of marketing exchanges, however, depend on the firm´s ability to create and sustain a competitive advantage over its competitors. Sustainable competitive advantages are related to barriers of some sort. When no such barriers exist, when nothing distinguishes the firm from its competitors, it (the firm) has no specific competitive advantages allowing for protection and surplus profit.

The concept of barriers to entry plays an important role both in industrial organization and in the strategy discipline to which it has contributed. Application of this concept - originally developed for normative analysis of industries - in positive analysis at the firm level (Teece, 1984), is, however, not without ambiguities. The purpose of this paper is to focus on barriers to entry in relation to firm specific, *strategic* actions.

The papers is organized as follows: First, the background for analysis of entry barriers from traditional industrial theory is sketched. Second, relevant aspects (for the present purpose) from the strategic management literature is briefly reviewed. In this section we introduce the concepts of mobility barriers and strategic groups. Third, the research agenda inherent in the orginal analysis of entry barriers is discussed. Here some very basic assumptions in the original theory of industrial organization, not explicitly dealt with in the strategy literature, are identified. In using the prior sections as point of departure, we fourth present a well-known game-theoretical model focusing on optimal entry-deterring or accommodating reponses to the threat of potential entry. Examples of market-related strategies are given. We, fifth, apply this model to the analysis/understanding of mobility barriers and strategic groups. Basic research questions and assumptions for strategic analysis are derived and contrasted with research hypotheses concerning mobility and strategic groups as dealt with in the strategic management literature. Finally, the results are summarized and implications for empirical research highlighted.

2. Entry barriers in the structure-conduct paradigm

Caves (1984) has characterized "the concepts of strategic groups and mobility barriers" as "a dynamized add-on to the traditional structure-conduct-performance paradigm" (p. 130). After the introduction of the concepts of "strategic groups" and

Chapter 4 - Barriers to Entry 53

"mobility barriers", these concepts have become central to much of the subsequent strategy and marketing research. We claim that important aspects of the structuralist paradigm has become deeply embedded in strategy and marketing research. We proceed to take a closer look at the structure-conduct paradigm, in order to enhance our understanding of the structuralist influence.

The first in depth treatment of *entry barriers* is attributed to Bain (1956). He worked within the structure-conduct model of the original Harvard industrial organization school, often called the Mason-Bain paradigm, and greatly influenced subsequent analysis in the field. To gain an understanding of how this effort has influenced the discipline of strategy, we will look into both Bain's research program as well as some of the basic assumptions in his approach to industrial organization research.

In his approach, Bain emphasized the formulation of *direct* empirical links between structure and performance, while the element of conduct was de-emphasized. His perspective was *static*. Three assumptions were important in his approach (Scherer, 1980).
First, conduct variables were unimportant to industrial organization theory as it was assumed that acceptable levels of prediction of performance could be made by using structural explanatory variables.
Second, he found theorizing over conduct of little value as predictions would become ambiguous.
Third, even if a satisfactory structure-performance theory could be established, theory testing was assumed to be hindered by lack of reliable data at the firm or business level.

Shepherd (1976) in reviewing Bain's contribution, states that "Bain used the industry as the basic unit of analysis" (p. 13). This, of course, implies that an industry *can* be defined, implying that industry boundaries can be drawn, i.e. insiders and outsiders identified. Bain saw entry barriers and industry-internal structural characteristics (e.g. concentration) as determinants of industry profitability. He also hypothesized that existence of barriers and degree of concentration would be highly correlated. An implication of this perspective is that the distinction between barriers and internal structural elements becomes ambiguous, which also is reflected in his ".. remarkably long taxonomic lists" when describing sources of barriers to entry (Shepherd, 1976 p. 9).

Jaquemin (1987) also claims that the structuralist paradigm has ignored to place the analysis within the context of a well-defined micro-economic model. The form of oligopolistic interdependence is not explicitly defined, and the role of agents' behaviour is thus de-emphasized.

Inclusion or exclusion of explanatory variables are often done in an ad hoc manner by researchers subscribing to the structuralist perspective. Empirical research is mainly based on case-studies and cross-sectional data. Schmalensee (1982) has characterized this research in the following way: "One also finds very little explicit theorizing in the cross-section literature; a priori arguments are typically limited to verbal justifications for the inclusion or the exclusion of particular variables on the right-hand side of a single linear equation" (p. 255). An implicit assumption in this paradigm is also that theoretical understanding is less important than establishing stable empirical relations, believed to possess great external validity applicable in a wide range of empirical settings.

To sum up, in this tradition the unit of analysis is clearly the industry. Entry barriers are industry-specific, influencing the, presumably homogenous, industry incumbents in a symmetrical manner. This brief review isn't included for the purpose of devaluing Bain's work as we fully recognize the importance of his contributions. It is, however, important to identify the basic elements in the approach which has inspired the corresponding analysis within the field of strategy.

3. Barriers in the strategic management literature

Caves and Porter (1977) suggested that Bain's concept of barriers to entry should be applied to subgroup structures within industries, i.e. groups of firms similar along specific structural dimensions. They also introduced the term *mobility barriers* to denote restricted entry into and movement between groups. In their original formulation, entry and mobility barriers are conceptually the same. Hunt (1972), in his doctoral dissertation, coined the term *strategic groups*. In his analysis of the U.S. white good industry he found three stratifying dimensions, used as basis for four strategic groups. In Hunt's view such grouping lead to ".. minimized economic asymmetry in each group ..", and his purpose was to describe ".. barriers to entry to each strategic group .." (p. 57).

In accordance with the prevailing industrial organization literature at that time, Caves and Porter (1977) emphasized structural factors in explaining the existence of entry barriers. The emphasis on structural factors is not only illustrated through their reference to Bain's long taxonomic list of sources of entry barriers, also the analysis of entry barriers created through limit pricing, e.g. Modigliani (1958) and Sylos-Labini (1962), relied on the existence of exogenously given scale or cost advantages for the incumbent firm. Caves and Porter (1977) wanted to make entry barriers *endogenous*, i.e. results of firm actions, and not only a structural element as treated in the industrial organization theory. They claimed that "firms' investments in entry barriers play a role in defining and differentiating the groups" (op.cit. p. 253). Among the important inferences drawn by Caves and Porter (1977), is the one that industry incumbents will differ along structural traits (other than size), contributing to subgroup definition in the industry, and that subgroupmembers are similar, or symmetrical, along these structural traits. Mobility barriers are assumed created by the same sources which create entry barriers. From this follows that mobility barriers, restricting movement between groups, also define strategic groups.

Porter (1979) further elaborated these concepts. In his view this approach could provide an explanation for differences in profitability (among groups), and for stable differences in competitive strategies among firms within an industry, e.g.: ".. some groups may have superior bargaining power with suppliers and buyers .." (p. 215), implying that the group of firms as such behaves collectively, i.e. as an economic agent in its own right. From his (Porter 1979) discussion follows that the meaning of strategy is "what firms do". Description and analysis of firms´ strategies then become a mapping of the firms´ activities as group members follow similar strategies. It is assumed that irreversible investments, e.g. investments in R&D and advertising, are used to build mobility barriers, contributing to define strategic groups. As firms strive for competitive strategic advantages they will race for attractive strategic group membership. This implies first-mover advantage in gaining strategic group membership, *asymmetry* between firms in different groups, and *symmetry* in terms of structural traits, strategy choices (i.e. activities) and the level of profitability between members of the same group is assumed. It also seems to be assumed that firms, at least at the business unit level, can belong to one group only. Much like in Bain´s original analysis, the height of mobility barriers is seen as an indicator of potential differences in profitability. Porter (1979) also claims that rank- ordering of strategic groups is possible, where high levels of profitability is a necessary, but not a sufficient condition for supernormal profits in lower ranking groups. Specifically, he hypothesizes that "warfare" in a group "sours profits for all other directly or indirectly market interdependent groups ranking lower on the mobility barrier hierarchy" (p. 219).

The research question at the heart of the structure-conduct paradigm, as emphasized in the industrial organization literature, is welfare effects and resulting policy implications of various structural features of an industry, while firm performance is the main focus in the strategy literature. According to Teece (1984): "The trick that has been used to apply this paradigm to strategic analysis is to treat the normative analysis of industrial organization as a positive theory of strategic management" (p. 94). Although this represents a valid procedure, we believe it is crucial to specify both the basic assumptions and the underlying hypotheses in the original paradigm, identifying the way these has been dealt - or not dealt - with in the strategic management literature and explicitly evaluate the resulting theory. We will proceed to do so.

4. Research agenda and basic assumptions

Most theoretical and empirical strategy research, though indistinguishable from other social science research in scope or methodology, has one distinguishing feature. In addition to reporting findings and conclusions, managerial implications are outlined. A prominent example of this literature is Porter's book, *Competitive Strategy*, which probably is the most quoted source in the corporate strategy and marketing strategy literature. This is especially true in the so-called "strategy content" research, aiming to develop, as Teece (1984) observed, a positive theory of strategic management from an existing, normative body of industrial organization theory. In developing such a theory, potentially valuable for managers, the question is not only one of evaluating how strategic management theory has been influenced by its theoretical ancestors, but also asking what relations such a theory *ought* to specify. We will start with an assessment of current theory elements and methodology, and then return to recommendations for strategy research.

4.1 Elements of theory

In the structure-conduct paradigm, industry is clearly an entity which logically precedes the possible existence of entry barriers. Industry is usually defined with reference to demand (products), or in some instances production (technology), and *not* by the existence of entry barriers. In the strategic management literature, mobility barriers are often cited as defining strategic groups. Whether or not one is willing to accept this as a productive way of perceiving strategic groups, it is in *conflict* with the theory which inspired it. Even more prevalent in the strategic management literature is the definition of strategic groups as firms following a common or similar strategy. Strategy is here defined as what firms do, i.e. a mapping of activities. In the literature such stategies covers the whole range from large irreversible investments to operations. Porter (1980) claims that "Competitive strategy involves positioning a business to maximize the value of the capabilities that distinguish it from its competitors" (p. 47). No attempts is made, however, to define or describe specifically what these strategic activities are. Without a proper, agreed upon, definition of which activities comprise a strategy, it is hard to see that day to day activities or operations in itself should give rise to groupings which should be difficult for outsiders to imitate and thus become members of the actual strategic group.

In Bain's original analysis, the height of entry barriers were seen as positively related to the potential for profit differentials between the industries. Existence of barriers makes it possible to exploit market power to ensure profitability, as access to the profitable market is denied for potential entrants, who would have dispersed the economic rent accruing to the incumbents. In the strategic management literature a parallel outcome is sometimes hypothesized. Undesirable strategic groups is also described, and mobility barriers to entry is sometime seen as (potenially) damaging barriers to exit (Caves and Porter, 1976). If mobility barriers protect or isolate a group of firms from other firms, *asymmetry* between groups is implied. As noted above, Hunt's original (1972) formulation of strategic groups saw the grouping as a means for minimizing intra-group asymmetry. It less clear, however, why or along which dimensions, this similarity should apply.

Chapter 4 - Barriers to Entry

There are also unresolved questions concerning the unit of analysis. Porter´s (1979) description of strategic groups indicates that they (strategic groups) act collectively. Even though strategic groups may be wieved as a valid unit of analysis, it is evident that the actors in a theory of competitive strategy should be firms, as strategic actions are primarily performed at the firm level.

In the strategy literature mobility barriers are sometimes described as structural in nature, i.e. independent of firm-specific action. When looking for sources to mobility barriers most researchers refer to Bain´s "long list" of possible, structural sources of entry barriers. The variables chosen for empirical discrimination between groups are, however, often influenced by the researchers original focus on one, or a group of variables, resulting in *ad hoc* choices. The Caves and Porter (1977) construction of the concept of mobility barriers was partly motivated by an ambition to integrate the firms actions as an endogenous source of mobility barriers. In order to do so a careful specification of sources of mobility barriers stemming from firm strategic actions is needed. Completion of such a task would be central to strategic management and represent an important contribution to strategic theory as well.

4.2 Elements of methodology

While there has been "an empirical renaissance in industrial economics" (Bresnahan and Schmalensee, 1987 ; Bresnahan, 1989), empirical strategy research is still lagging behind the rapid theoretical developments.

Above it was noted that the structure-conduct-performance paradigm emphasizes the establishment of universal and stable empirical relationships rather than constructing and testing theory. It seems fair to characterize much of the empirically oriented strategy literature in the same way. Most research on stratetegic groups is based on studies covering a range of industries where the choice of stratifying variables based on different classification schemes in most cases have been justified in an ad hoc manner. The underlying assumption is seemingly that identification of stable differences in performance among groups is an empirical question, and that theorizing is or should be based on empircal findings. As noted by Thomas and Venkatraman (1988), however: "a variety of methods have been used to derive groupings in empirical research setting, which makes the much-needed exercise at the accumulation of research findings an almost impossible task" (p. 538). In their discussion on stratetic groups they (Thomas and Venkatraman 1988) classify the literature according to whether the classification schemes are based on a priori information of groupings, or whether groupings are derived a posteriori based on empirical results. In their words "the former reflects a deductive approach to strategic group development (i.e. theory-driven), while the latter subscribes to an inductive approach (i.e. data-driven) perspective" (op.cit. p. 539). Most of the literature reviewed here apparently belong to the data-driven category.

Use of data-reducing mulivariate techniques may result in groupings reflecting nothing more than "statistical homogeneity". Within-group homogeneity in "strategy", may from a statistical point of view easily be demonstrated just by including corresponding stratifying variables. There is, however, no reason to expect similar responses to exogenous stimuli from firms within a group when the grouping is based on such procedures. Several authors have also reported that the evidence of performance differences across groups is weak.[1] To the present authors, a reemphasis of focus linking firm specific strategic action to profitability differences on the firm level seems more fruitful. To us it is preferable to interpret a strategic group as a collection of firms which have built firm specific mobility barriers of the same kind.

4.3 Recommendations

In this subsection we will give recommendations with regard to which elements and structural features a strategic theory of mobility barriers and strategic groups should contain.

First, there should be an *explicit* focus on firms, both as the unit of analysis and as the decision-making unit, as has been done in recent industrial organization literature.
Second, analysis of strategic groups should be based on sources of firm-specific mobility barriers. This includes identification of basic assumptions and elements in order to capture mobility barriers as endogenous variables.
Third, sources and explanations of profitability differences among firms should be a focus for analysis as well.

5. A model of business strategies

In the strategy literature suggestions have been made to circumvent deficiencies of the industrial organization theory. McGee and Thomas (1989) proposed strategic action in the form of "investment to create mobility barriers" (p. 106). They also hypothesized that rivalry and oligopolistic interaction reflect the resulting "asset structures" (p. 106). This way of reasoning is similar to Rumelt´s (1981) discussion of investment in "idiosyncratic capital" resulting in "isolating mechanisms". Instead of extending and reformulating the original industrial organization theory in this manner, the potential gains from returning to basic industrial organization theory will probably be greater.
Over the last two decades we have witnessed a substantial development in what Schmalensee (1982) calls "the new industrial organization theory". An important aspect of this new theory is the analysis of oligopolistic interaction, including strategic investment as firm-specific competitive actions. The use of equilibrium concepts from non-cooperative game theory is central to this analysis. We will demonstrate the usefulness of this approach for the present purpose by presenting a

Chapter 4 - Barriers to Entry

model of two-period competition with the possibility of strategic investments.[2]

To ease the discussion we will assume that there are two firms, one firm which is established in period 1, and a potential entrant, who will enter in period 2, if at all. Period 2 interaction is modelled as ordinary, static oligopoly if the new firm enters, elsewise the incumbent remains monopolist. In period 1 the established firm can make a *strategic investment*. This investment influences the optimal actions of the established firm in period 2. This is understood by the potential entrant, and thus influences the decision of whether or not to enter.

Two possible modes of competition are recognized, that of *strategic complements* and *strategic substitutes* respectively. Strategic complements normally means that the main decision variable in the oligopolistic competition is that of price, and the standard model of Bertrand-competition applies. In this case, a more aggresive decision from the established firm (i.e. a lower price) will be met with a correspondingly aggressive response from the potential entrant, i.e. a price cut. The case of strategic substitutes normally implies that the main decision variable is quantity (or capacity), and the standard model is Cournot-competition. In this case, an aggressive action from the established firm, i.e. an increase in output, will result in a less aggressive response from the potential entrant, i.e. a decrease in output.[3]

The possible strategic investments are assumed to fall into two categories; investments which "*softens*" the competition, and investments which make the competition "*tougher*". If the investment makes the incumbent firm tougher, it will make a more aggressive decision (i.e. lower price or higher output); a less aggressive decision follows investments which softens the competition. An example of an investment which makes the established firm tougher is an investment in machinery or equipment which lowers unit (and hence, marginal) costs. This makes it optimal for the established firm to claim a lower price, or increases its output in period 2, i.e. to behave more aggressively. An example of a strategic investment which softens competition could be an investment in advertising. Building brand loyalty gives the established firm an incentive to avoid price cuts or expansion of output which may hurt the possible price premium from loyal customers in an industry where price discrimination is not possible. In this case, the investment makes the established firm less aggressive.

It is central to this model that the established firm´s strategic investments influences the potential entrant only indirectly. The investment influences the choice of price or quantity for the established firm in period 2. Because oligopoly is characterized by mutual interdependence between competitors in their choice variables, investments influence the potential entrant because this firm chooses price or quantity under the consideration of the optimal choice of its competitor. The investment therefore influences the potential entrants choice because the investment will change the established firm´s own actions. This is called the *strategic effect*. For this to be the case, it is necessary that the investment in question to be *irreversible*. If the investment is reversible, the established firm can invest in equipment to allegedly deter entry, and later on resell and never use the equipment if entry was successfully deterred. The potential entrant can also be tempted to call the bluff, knowing that the established firm will rather accommodate and resell than engage in a price war. The irreversibility of the investment is ensured in the model by applying the game-theoretic concept of subgame perfect equilibrium, an equilibrium concept that in its very nature rules out non-credible threats.

The investment is evaluated on two criteria. The first is the "*direct*" effect. This effect corresponds to any normal investment evaluation, and captures the direct effect of the investment on the established firm´s profit. An obvious example is capital outlay for investment in machinery or equipment, compared to (the discounted) value of future unit cost savings. It is, however, the *strategic effect* which is of primary interest to us. This effect is (as mentioned above) a consequence of the oligopolistic interdependence between the competitors. The strategic effect of the investment influences the incumbent´s profit function[4] through changing the incumbent optimal price or quantity choice in periode 2, thereby changing the potential entrants response through the oligopolistic interdependence. It is this change in the potential entrant´s price or quantity choice which strategically influences the incumbents profit.

The model is based on *non-cooperative* game theory, which implies that we are explicitly modelling competition. Under competition, the basic condition for deterring entry is that the profit that accrues to the new entrant from entering is *negative*. This firm will then prefer not to enter, because this will result in a negative outcome. Given that it is possible for the incumbent firm to deter entry, it will choose to do so if the resulting profit is greater than the profit from accommodating. It is important to realize this realistic feature of the model, i.e. to deter entry is *not always* optimal. The incumbent may thus choose to accommodate rather than deter entry, and the strategic investment level is chosen correspondingly. If the sum of the direct and the strategic effect indicates to the established firm that it is optimal to make a sufficiently large investment as to deter entry, the firm should make a strategic *over*investment if the investment makes the incumbent firm though (i.e. more aggressive), and it should *under*invest if the strategic investment softens intrafirm competition. Over- and underinvestment is measured relative to level of investment the stablished firm would choose if the potential entrant could not observe, and hence not respond to the investment.[5] If the incumbent, however, finds that entry deterrence is not optimal, strategic investment can be used to accommodate, and thus reduce the impact of entry. In the case of strategic substitutes, which implies that incumbent aggressiveness results in a less aggressive response from the entrant, the same strategy is used as in the case of entry deterrence. If the period 2 competition is characterized by strategic complements, i.e. incumbent aggressiveness induces aggressive counteraction, the incumbent will try to soften competition by underinvesting in strategic investments which makes the incumbent though, and overinvesting in strategic investments

Chapter 4 - Barriers to Entry

which makes it soft. The optimal strategies discussed are summarized in table 1.

The table is to be read in the following manner. The top row describes the effect of strategic (marketing) investments on the incumbents (tactical) actions, making the incumbent either "though" or "soft". A "though" incumbent will lower prices or increase output, while a "soft" incumbent will increase prices or reduce output. The optimal strategies, however, is dependent on whether the tactical actions are strategic complements, normally associated with competition in prices, or strategic substitutes, associated with competition in output. If there is competition in output, aggressiveness always pays. Under price competition aggressiveness is appropriate for deterring entry, but if it is optimal to accomodate both firms benefit from "softening" the competition in period 2.

It should be noted that the incumbent generally enjoys an advantage over the potential entrant in this model, because the incumbent is the first-mover. The strategic investment in period 1, when the potential entrant is inactive, creates the asymmetry favoring the incumbent. This normally gives the incumbent an advantage *relative* to the potential entrant. In the case of preemption, however, the possible advantage following the strategic investment is exhausted by the first mover, and the potential entrant is deterred from participating. Two cases of preemption are the first firm to patent an innovation, or the first firm to move into a product niche which only sustains one supplier.

Examples of strategic marketing investments are numerous: Advertising as an investment to soften incumbent behavior has already been mentioned. For experience goods, the incumbent may enjoy an advantage when using the first period to broaden the base of customers who have tried the incumbent's product. Network economies give the same effect, when consumer utility increases with the size of the customer base, as in the case of telecommunications. Product compatibility choices can introduce consumer switching cost's increasing customer loyalty. First period preemption of attractive retail outlets or distribution channels gives incumbency advantage. Similar preemption of available product niches can be achieved through product line positioning. It is, however, necessary to carefully specify the economic content of these strategic marketing moves in terms of the elements of the above model. The stringency thus introduced into the analysis of strategic marketing is an attractive feature of this approach.

		Strategic investment makes incumbent:	
		"Tough"	"Soft"
	Strategic complements	A Under-investment -> non-aggressive	A Over-investment -> non-aggressive
Tactical actions are:		D Overinvestment -> aggressive	D Underinvestment -> aggressive
	Strategic substitutes	A and D Overinvestment -> aggressive	A and D Underinvestment -> aggressive

A = accommodation,   D = deterrence of entry

Figure 1.

Optimal business strategies for the incumbent firm[6]

Chapter 4 - Barriers to Entry

6. Contrasting the approaches

Below the new and traditional approaches are contrasted.

6.1 Theoretical improvements

Compared to the original theory of entry barriers, the new theory represents something new in the following manner.

The *firm* is the unit of analysis, and thus the theory focuses on the firm's decision making. This is supplemented by the fact that mobility barriers are seen as the outcomne of explicit, *firm-specific* strategic action.

The model is *dynamic*, first period actions have binding consequences for period two interaction.

Moreover, there is a clear distinction between strategic actions and day-to-day activities concerning price or quantity decisions, i.e. tactics. Investments are of a strategic nature because they are *irreversible* and thus bind the firm, while pricing or quantity decisions are tactical in nature because they - in principle - can be reversed or reassessed in each period. Strategic actions thus result in *firm specific, idiosyncratic* capital or assets. Firm specific strategic investments are undertaken for *profitability* reasons, and should consequently give rise to profitability differentials on a firm basis. The model which is based on a limited set of variables allow for predictions of a rich set of strategic actions. This approach also includes strategies for influencing accommodation, unlike the original theory where whether or not to deter entry are the only strategic options.

This approach has been characterized as a "very simple generic model" (Shapiro, 1989, p. 383). The distinction between strategic substitutes and complements makes it possible to apply the model in industries with differing types of oligopolistic interdependency. Strategic investments also holds great generality and can be interpreted as any fixed, irreversible factor. The analytical framework can be put to use both as a normative and a descriptive model. The structural description in the model makes it clear for which situation the model does not apply.

In contrast, the generic models associated with strategic management literature are based on a limited set of archetypal strategies. Neither the individual archetypes, nor the set of archetypes taken together are normally adaptable to different industry setting, they are believed to hold universal applicability. These theories then generally lacks criteria for falsification. An example is Porter's (1980) three generic strategies, where empirical observations not fitting any of the three archetypes conveniently are labeled "stuck in the middle" as a residual category.

6.2 Implications for empirical research

The model provides us with a set of basic building blocks of great generality. Applying these "building blocks" to understand mobility barriers have implications for appropriate empirical research. Most important is that one should start looking at the *microstructure* of the industry in question to determine the type of competition being waged. This corresponds to what we have defined as tactics. An effort should thus be made to study the history of the industry to determine the mode of competition.

Many studies in the strategy literature hold that profit maximization is not the firm objective, but rather to earn satisfactory levels of profit, or pursuing a mixture of different performance goals (Newman 1978; Galbraith and Schendel 1983). Some authors see differences in objectives as a basis for differences in strategic group membership. This clearly complicates any inferences between differences in levels of profitability and group membership. In the game-theoretic model discussed above, profit maximization is an explicit assumption.

Some comments on the existence and definition of strategic groups are also appropriate. As emphasized above entry barriers are seldom relevant for defining an industry. The corresponding concept, mobility barriers, is often regarded as defining strategic groups at the sub-industry level. Definitions of strategic groups are multiple and disparate. There are conflicting statements in the strategy literature on whether strategic groups can be overlapping, and whether members of the same strategic group can serve different customers or market niches. "Data driven" studies are common in empirical strategic research. As noted above such studies tend to produce groupings primarily representing "statistical homogeneity". Such studies often claim that the stratifying variables and resulting groupings reflect "similarities in strategies" among group members, where the conclusion seems to be based on an assumption that such groupings reflect so called "generic"[7] strategies. Galbraith and Schendel (1983), however, characterize such typological approaches as: ".. conceptual constructs derived from appropriate dimensions taken from theory without much empirical support beyond perhaps some grounding in case studies and anecdotal accounts of competitive strategy" (p. 155).

To the present authors findings regarding strategic groups based on "data driven" research are of minor both theoretical and managerial value. When subscribing to a perspective as reflected in the above model, such grouping of strategies should mainly be regarded as an instrument to enhance understanding of actual strategic behavior and as input for further analysis.[8] In sum, the concept of strategic groups seems primarily related to the design of empirical studies, and should be defined in accordance with the prime purpose of the study to be undertaken.

As mentioned earlier, there is a rapidly emerging field of empirical industrial economics research, potentially of great importance also for strategy research.

Chapter 4 - Barriers to Entry 65

Although no attempt is made here to comprehensively assess or review this literature a few important principles guiding this research is worth noting. In assessing the "new" industrial organization theory of business strategy, Shapiro (1989b) identifies as a metatheme that predictions from theoretical models is sensitive to the exact specifications of the models, e.g. the timing and sequence of moves, the definitions of tactical and strategic choice variables and the number and size of competitors. This has consequently lead the authors within this new empirical tradition to develop theoretical models tailor-made to a specific empirical setting. Testable empirical hypotheses are derived and tested on data from the actual setting. Regarding the growing collection of models of business strategy originating from industrial organization theory, Shapiro (1989b) notes that the focus is on "the dynamics of strategic action" and "the role of commitment in strategic settings", also noting that *"we should distinguish strategic desicions .. from tactical decisions"* (p. 127, italics in original), exactly the factors emphasized in the model we have presented earlier.

A noteworthy example of theory-based empirical research is provided by De Bondt et al. (1988). The authors test predictions from a formal two-stage game model regarding the existence of innovative strategic groups in multinational industries on empirical survey data using a principal component analysis. Veugelers and vanden Houte (1989) study the effect of the presence of multinational firms on domestic R&D, combining the use of a game-theoretic model with regression analysis on empirical data. In both studies, the theoretical model is developed to fit both the theoretical issues investigated and the empirical setting. Sutton (1989) contrasts the predcitions from a theoretical oligopoly model against an empirical setting, the history of the frozen food industries in the UK and the USA, by using case studies from these industries. Theory based, cross-sectional comparative empirical studies is also the theme of Suttons forthcoming book. His approach represents an attemept to generate some empirical regularities on the basis of the multitude of specific analyses within this tradition. This is the same ambition which underlies the structuralist paradigm, but Sutton´s approach is firmly based in contemporary game-theoretic industrial organization. The basic idea in Sutton´s approach can be identified with reference to the model we have presented earlier. "Strategic" or long-lasting factors is dichotomized as exogenous or endogenous, where the former can be regarded as given technological factors such as minimum efficient scale, while the latter, such as advertising or R&D are strategic commitments. Unlike the structuralist paradigm a given factor is not, however, generally believed to give rise to universal effects across industries. A given structure may have different, or even reverse effects on the level of concentration and profitability depending on the mode of the "tactical" decision making. Price competition among undifferentiated products can be cut-throat in a duopoly, while firms in a far less concentrated oligopoly structrure can attain levels of profitability close to the joint maximization of profits given repeated interaction and a stable, transparent environment. The commitment to endogenous strategic investments, will be made under consideration of the impact on the resulting tactical rivalry. Strategic choices will thus generally depend on the timing of moves, the size and number of competitors, the nature of the tactical rivalry and on the impact of the strategic investment on the tactical rivalry.

Two examples from the "new empirical industrial organization" exemplify this. In the first example Slade (1987) investigates the pricing strategies of a number of Vancouver gas stations whose demand is related as the stations are located close to each other. The stations are regarded as constituting a market. The tactical decision variable in this case is price. In this investigation there were a number of candidate factors to the identification of strategic groups. These included type of ownership, degree of horizontal and vertical integration, and the regional marketing extent. In a companion study, Slade (1986), type of ownership was identified as the most powerful explanatory stratifying variable, resulting in a dichotomous classification of the stations as belonging to two strategic groups, "major" brand companies and "independents". This should then be regarded as an exogenous factor influencing the rivalry among these gas stations. According to Slade (1987), the firms in a market producing a differentiated product can be subdivided into strategic subgroups, "where all members of a group face similar demand conditions and exhibit similar responses to rival actions" (p. 501). This initial hypotheses concerning strategic groups is then made subject to explicit testing with econometric techniques.

The second example is related to the endogenous choice of advertising level for saltine crackers in a localized retail market, as analyzed by Slade (1990). In this investigation the central question is whether advertising is predatory, merely shifting market shares, or cooperative, increasing total market demand. In the language of the model presented earlier, the impact of increased levels of advertising on rivals choices of advertising levels and price corresponds to identifying whether advertising and price are own- and cross-strategic complements and substitutes. This finally translates into the question of whether investments in goodwill make firms aggressive or accommodating. As we see, the application of the kind of theory presented gives rise to sharp-cut questions of the utmost strategic significance. The predictions made and research questions raised should in turn be made subject to empirical analysis.

The above quoted approaches to empirical industrial organization research can definitely be classified as theory-driven, and have resulted in valuable new insights. We firmly believe that such theory-driven empirical approaches will be of the utmost importance in future strategy research.

7. Concluding remarks

In reviewing the strategy literature on mobility barriers and strategic groups, largely inspired by traditional industrial organization, we have made observations similar to Montgomery (1988), i.e. ".. that the field today does not have a dominant, unique, research paradigm" (p. 3). We have also observed that much of the research is data-driven and based on the structural industrial organization theory, i.e. on the paradigm

Chapter 4 - Barriers to Entry

which originally inspired it. Research findings in the discipline of strategy are mixed, and lack of consensus is the resulting outcome.

We have suggested an alternative approach, starting with a formal, game-theoretic model borrowed from the "new" industrial organization. The suggested approach places the firm at the center of interest, both as the central decision-making unit, and as the primary unit of analysis. Mobility barriers are seen as firm-specific, resulting from strategic actions in the form of investments. A basic assymmetry between firms is then introduced, indicating first-mover advantages. As emphasized above, this gives rise to explicit hypotheses of strategic importance to the firm. We also suggest that empirical studies should start with a careful examination of the microstructure of the industry in question, i.e. identifying what sort of competition is being waged, as the type of competition determines the effect of strategic investments.

This paper also reflects the belief that theorizing which give rise to formulation of testable hypotheses allowing for rigid investigation (and thus the opportunity to potentially falsify the theory) represents an advantage over "data-driven" research mainly focusing on empirical relationship. This perspective also implies that theory and theory-development should be seen as the "driving force" in strategic empirical research.

From the above discussion also follows that day-to-day marketing activities which easily can be imitated by the firms competitors are *not* conceived as strategic actions. A variety of marketing investments may, however, be considered as strategic actions as they create strategic effects, and may give rise to sustainable competitive advantages as well. In our opinion future research on marketing strategy should focus on true strategic marketing decisions. In order to do so the underlying theoretical rationale must be developed and clarified - something which has been done only to a modest extent in the literature on strategic marketing.

Notes

1 See Cool and Schendel (1988), Lawless (1989), Thomas and Venkatrama (1988).

2 This model was independently introduced by Fudenberg and Tirole (1984) and Bulow et al. (1985). A full presentation of this model is also given by Shapiro (1989) and Tirole (1988).

3 The formal definition of strategic substitutes is that $\partial^2 \pi i / \partial S i \partial S j < 0$ and correspondingly strategic complements if $\partial^2 \pi i / \partial S i \partial S j < 0$, where π denotes profits, subscripts refer to firms, in this case i, j = (1,2), i # j, and S is defined as the firm decision variable, i.e. quantity or price, so that increased S means increased

aggressiveness (i.e. $S = q$ or $S = 1/p$). The sign of the crosspartial derivative of firm i's profit function corresponds to whether the reaction functions in the static oligopoly game is upward (> 0) or downward (< 0) sloping.

4 Formally it can be shown that the sign of the strategic effect corresponds to the sign of the expression below:

$$\partial^2 \pi_E / \partial S_E \partial K \cdot \partial^2 \pi_P / \partial S_P \partial S_E \cdot \partial \pi_E (S_E, S_P, K) / \partial S_P$$

    (i)   (ii)   (iii)

π and S are defined as in the note above, and K denotes the level of strategic investment made by the incumbent, and subscript E denotes the established (or incumbent) firm, while P denotes the potential entrant. This expression is the product of (i) the effect of the strategic investment on the incumbents price/quantity choice, (ii) the effect of the incumbents price/quantity choice on the potential entrants corresponding choice, and (iii) the effect of the potential entrants price/quantity choice on the incumbents profits. According to our prior definition (iii) is always negative, the sign of (i) corresponds to whether the strategic investment makes the incumbent "tough" (> 0), increased investments induces incumbent aggressiveness (increased quantitaty or price cuts), or "soft" (< 0), increased investment induces incumbent compliance (decreased quantity or price increases) while the sign of (ii) as before denotes strategic substitutes (< 0), incumbent agressiveness pays, or strategic complements (> 0), where incumbent compliance is the best response. This makes for the four cases recognized in Table 1.

5 This would result in a so called open-loop equilibrium. We characterize the level of strategic investment in our model relative to the investment level in this kind of equilibrium.

6 Based on Fudenberg and Tirole (1984, p. 365) and Tirole (1988, p. 327).

7 This corresponds to a typology over "archetypes" or "gestalts", strategic types recurring and observable over a wide spectrum of settings or industries, cf. Porter (1980).

8 This interpretation is discussed among others by Hatten and Hatten (1987), and is recommended by Thomas and Venkatraman (1988).

References

AMA, 1988, Developing, and Utilizing Marketing Knowledge, AMA Task Force on the Development of Marketing Thought, Journal of Marketing, 52, 1-25.

Bain, S., 1956. Barriers to New Competition, (Cambr. Mass., Harvard Univ. Press).

Bresnahan, T. F., 1989, Empirical studies of Industries with market Power, Chapter 17 in Schmalensee R. and R. Willig (Ed.), The Handbook on Industrial Organization, (Amsterdam, North-Holland), 1011-1057.

Bresnahan, T. F., and Richard Schmalensee, 1987, The Empirical Rennaisance in Industrial Economics: An Overview, The Journal of Industrial Economics, 35, 371-378.

Bulow, J., D. Geanakoplos and P.D. Klemperer, 1985, Multimarket Oligopoly: Strategic Substitutes and Complements, Journal of Political Economy, 93: 3, 488-511.

Caves, E., and M.E. Porter, 1976, Barriers to Exit, in Masson R.T. and P. Qualls (Eds.), Essay on Industrial Organization in Honor of Joe S. Bain, (Cambr. Mass., David Ballinger Publ. Co), 39-69.

Caves, E., and M.E. Porter, 1977, From Entry Barriers to Mobility Barriers: Conjectural decisions and Continued Deterence to New Competition, Quarterly J. of Economics, 91, 241-262.

Cool, K,. and D.E. Schendel, 1988, Performance Differences Among Strategic Group Members, Strategic Management Journal, 9, 207-223.

Day, G.S., and R. Wensley, 1983, Marketing Theory with a Stratetic Orientation, Journal of Marketing, 47 (Fall), 79-89.

De Bondt, R., L. Sleuwaegen and R. Veugeleres, 1989. Innovative Strategic Groups in Multinational Industries, European Economic Review, 32, 905-925.

Dess, G., and P. Davis, 1984, Porter´s, 1980, Generic Strategies as Determinants of Strategic Group Membership and Organizational Performance, Academy of Management Journal, 27, 467-488.

Fudenberg, D., and D.E. Tirole, 1984, The Fat-Cat Effect, The Puppy-Dog Ploy, and the Lean and Hungry Look, American Economic Review, 74: 2, 361-366.

Gailbraith, C., and D.E. Schendel, 1983, An Empirical Analysis of Strategy Types, Strategic Management Journal, 4: 2, 153-173.

Harrigan, K.R., 1981, Barriers to Entry and Competitive Strategies, Strategic Management Journal, 2, 395-412.

Harrigan, K.R., 1985, An Application of Clustering for Strategic Group Analysis, Strategic Management Journal, 6, 55-73.

Hatten, K.J., and M.L. Hatten, 1987, Stratetic Groups, Asymmetrical Mobility Barriers and Contestability, Strategic Management Journal, 8, 329-342.

Hatten, K.J., and D.E. Schendel, 1977, Heterogeneity within an Industry. Firm Conduct in the U.S. Brewing Industry, 52-71, The Journal of Industrial Economics, XXVI: 2, 97-113.

Hunt, M.S., 1972, Competition in the Major Home Apppliance Industry 1960-1970, Unpublished doctoral dissertation, (Boston, Harvard University).

Jaquemin, A., 1987, The New Industrial Organization. Market Forces and Strategic Behavior, (Oxford, Clarendon Press).

Johansson, J., and L.G. Mattson, 1985, Marketing Investments and Market Investments in Industrial Networks, International Journal of Research in Marketing, 2, 185-195.

Mascarenhas, B., and D.A. Aaker, 1989, Mobility Barriers and Strategic Groups, Strategic Management Journal, 10, 475-489.

McGee, J., 1985, Strategic Groups: A Bridge between Industry Structure and Strategic Management, in Thomas H. and D. Gardener (Eds.), Strategic Marketing and Management, (New York, Wiley), 293-313.

McGee, J., and H. Thomas, 1986, Strategic Groups: Theory, Research and Taxonomy, Strategic Management Journal, 7: 2, 141-160.

McGee, J. and H. Thomas, 1989, Research Notes and Communications, Strategic Groups: A Further Comment, Strategic Management Journal, 10, 105-107.

Modigliani, Franco, 1958, New Developments on the Oligopoly Front, Journal of Political Economy, 66, 215-232.

Montgomery, C. A., 1988, Guest editor's Introduction to the Special Issue on Research in the Content of Strategy, Strategic Management Journal, 10, 101-103.
Myers, J.G., W.F. Massey and S.A. Greyser, 1980, Marketing Research and Knowledge Development, (Englewood Cliffs, N.J., Prentice-Hall).

Nayyar, P., 1989, Research Notes and Communications: Strategic Groups: A Comment, Strategic Management Journal, 10, 101-103.

Newman, H.H., 1978, Strategic Groups and the Structure-Performance Relationship, Review of Economics and Statistics, LX, 417-427.

Oster, S., 1982, Intraindustry Structure and the Ease of Strategic Change, Review of Economics and Statistics, LXIV: 3, Aug, 376-384.

Porter, M.E., 1979, The Structure Within Industries and Companies Performance, Review of Economics and Statistics, LXI: 2, 214-227.

Porter, M.E., 1980, Competitive Strategy: Techniques for Analyzing Industries and Competitors, (New York, Free Press).

Rumelt, R.P., 1981, Towards a Strategic Theory of the Firm, (Univ. of Southern Calif., Conference paper).

Rumelt, R.P., 1987, Theory, Strategy and Entrepreneurship, in Teece D. (Ed.), The Competitive Challenge. Strategies for Industrial Innovation and Renewal, (Cambr. Mass., Ballinger Publish. Co), 137-158.

Scherer, F.M., 1980, Industrial Market Structure and Economic Performance, (Boston, Houghton Mifflin Co).

Schmalensee, R., 1982, The New Industrial Organization and the Economic Analysis of Modern Markets, in Hildenbrand W., (Ed.), Advances in Economic Theory, (Cambridge, Cambridge University Press), 253-285.

Schmalensee, R., and J. Thisse, 1988, Perceptual Maps and the Optimal Location of New Products. An Integrative Essay, International Journal of Research in Marketing, 5, 225-249.

Shaked, A., and J. Sutton, 1987, Product Differentiation and Industrial Structure, The Journal of Industrial Economics, 36, 131-146.

Shapiro, C., 1989, Theories of Oligopoly Behavior, in Schmalensee R. and R. Willig (Eds.), The Handbook on Industrial Organization, (Amsterdam, North-Holland), 229-414.

Shapiro, C., 1989b, The Theory of Business Strategy, Rand Journal of Economics, 20, 125-137.

Shepherd, W.G., 1976, Bain's Influence on Research into Industrial Organization, in Masson R.T. and P. Qualls (Eds.), Essays on Industrial Organization in Honor of Joe S. Bain, (Cambr. Mass., David Ballinger Publ. Co.), 1-17.

Slade, Margaret E., 1986 "Conjectures, Firm Characteristics, and Market Structure. An Empirical Assessment, International Journal of Inudstrial Organization, 4, 347-369.

Slade, Margaret E., 1987 Interfirm Rivalry in a Repeated Game: An Empirical Test of Tacit Collusion, The Journal of Industrial Economics, 35, 499-516.

Slade, Margaret E., 1990, Product Rivalry with Multiple Strategic Weapons: An Empirical Analysis of Price and Advertising Competition, (Unpublished paper).

Sutton, John, 1989, Endognenous Sunk Costs and the Structure of Advertising Intensive Industries, European Economic Review, 33, 335-344.

Sutton, John, 1990, Sunk Cost and Market Structure (book-manuscript).

Sylos-Labini, P., 1962, Oligopoly and Technical Progress, (Cambr., Mass., Harvard Univ. Press).

Teece, D.J., 1984, Economic Analysis and Strategic Management, California Management Review, XXVI: 3, 87-110.

Thomas, H., and N. Venkatraman, 1988, Research on Strategic Groups: Progress and Prognosis, Journal of Management Studies, 6, 537-556.

Tirole, J., 1988, The Theory of Industrial Organization, (Cambr. Mass., MIT Press).

Veugelers, R., and P. vanden Houte, 1990, Domestic R&D in the Presence of Multinational Enterprises, International Journal of Industrial Organization, 8, 1-15.

Wind, Y., and T.S. Robinson, 1983, Marketing Strategy: New Directions for Theory and Research, Journal of Marketing, 47 (Spring), 12-25.

MICROECONOMIC CONTRIBUTIONS TO STRATEGIC MANAGEMENT
J. Thépot and R.-A. Thiétart
© 1991 Elsevier Science Publishers B.V. All rights reserved.

CHAPTER 5

DYNAMIC DIVERSIFICATION AND LEARNING EFFECTS

J. THEPOT
LARGE,
Université Louis Pasteur

Abstract

This chapter presents a formalization of the BCG diversification problem on two business lines : the financial resource allocated in each activity is determined by the financial resources accrued by the accumulation of the past profits derived from both. The impact of learning effects on the firm's strategy is analysed on the basis of an optimal control model.

1. Introduction

In recent years, the popular approach of the Boston Consulting Group (Porter, 1980), has been a stimulating decision-making framework for top managers and CEO in their diversification strategies. It has indeed been widely applied by most of the multinational companies.

The principles of the BCG approach are well known : it relies upon the argument that learning effects in a given business activity are positively correlated with the relative market share. According to the BCG one should build a business lines portfolio with a product distribution concerning various stages of development along the PLC curve so as to use the cash generated by mature activities to support the introduction of new ones.

I should like to thank Alain Bultez for interesting comments.

Some management best-sellers pointed ont the misuses of BCG approach : "In too many instances, strategic planning degenerated into acquiring growth businesses that the buyers did not know how to manage and selling or milking to death mature ones" (Brandt, 1986). Of course, this point of view does not condemn the BCG analysis, which has been often applied to inappropriate environments and firms. (Hayes, 1985; Gray, 1986); it merely suggests that we need to further specify the theoretical roots and the robust microeconomics foundations in order to implement managerial rules deduced from BCG to real business situation.

The key element of the BCG diversification problem is mastering time. At time t, the firm faces diversification opportunities and financial resources that result from the past investments and their financial returns ; in addition the learning processes at work within the firm are not instantaneously effective.

This chapter is aimed at illustrating the dynamics inherent to product-market portfolio analyses through an optimal control model (Lesourne, 1976 ; Thépot, 1988) : we consider a monopolistic firm acting on two separate business lines, over an infinite planning horizon, [0,+∞(. The firm tries to maximize the net present value of the dividends flow ; in addition, it faces a self-financing constraint : at any point of time, the invested amount on both products cannot be higher than the current overall profit which in turn, depends on the previous investments. Then the cash generated in either activity can be devoted to investing in the other one. A specific attention is paid to the role of the learning effects, i.e. a direct cost as a function of the cumulated output of a given product.

The main result of the paper is the following: At time O, the products are differentiated as "new" or "old" according to the output capacity devoted to their production ; Through time the firm has to articulate successively two types of strategies; in a first phase, the firm gives a great emphasis on the new product, spending all the current profit to increase its production, at the expenses of the growth of the old product ; in a second phase, both products are jointly developed. When the learning effects take place, the first phase is reduced, since a more intensive investment in the old product creates a decrease of the cost and consequently generates further additional resources, which can the be used to develop more efficiently the new product.

The chapter is organized as follows: in section 2, a general model is presented ; the situation where the firm does not gain from manufacturing experience is studied in section 3, while section 4 is devoted to the learning effects case. Concluding remarks are given in section 5.

Chapter 5 - Dynamic Diversification 75

2. A Dynamic Model of Diversification

Let us consider a monopolistic firm operating on two business lines over an infinite horizon. Each is associated with one product to be sold on a specific market segment. At any point in time, the firm faces demand functions x_1 and x_2. We do not consider here saturation and diffusion effects (Rao and Bass, 1985). Demand functions of the two products are assumed only to depend on the prices : (In the following, i,j stand for i,j = 1,2, i ≠ j):

$$x_1 = x_i(p_i) \text{ with the classical assumptions :} \tag{1}$$
$$\partial x_i / \partial p_i < 0 \; ; \; \partial [p_i x_i] / \partial p_i < 0, \tag{2}$$

where $p_i(t)$ denotes the price of product i charged at time t.

2.1. Learning effects

Direct unit operating costs c_i are incurred (fixed costs are not taken into consideration). Let us define $x_i(t)$ as the accumulated sales of product i at time t :

$$\dot{X}_1 = x_i, \; X_i(0) = X_{i.}^o \tag{3}$$

where X_1^o denotes the accumulated sales before time 0. In section 4, cost c_i will be assumed to depend on accumulated sales X_i so as to take into account learning effects.

2.2. General statement of the model

$$\text{Max} \int_0^\infty [(p_1 - c_1) x_1 - (p_2 - c_2) x_2 - v (I_1 + I_2)] \tag{4}$$

$$\dot{X}_1 = x_1, \; \dot{X}_2 = x_2 ; \tag{5}$$

$$\dot{y}_1 = I_1, \; \dot{y}_2 = I_2 ; \tag{6}$$

$$y_1 \geq x_1, \; y_2 \geq x_2 ; \tag{7}$$

$$I_1 \geq 0, \; I_2 \geq 0 ; \tag{8}$$

$$v(I_1 + I_2) \leq (p_1 - c_1) x_1 + (p_2 - c_2) x_2 ; \tag{9}$$

$$y_1(0) = \xi_1, \; y_2(0) = \xi_2 \; ; \; X_1(0) = X_1^o, X_2(0) = X_2^o \quad .$$

This model is a two-product extension of a basic model studied by many authors in various contexts like Nickel (1974), Lesourne (1976), : y_i denotes the output capacity devoted to product i, I_i is the rate of investment in product i capacity, v the cost of investment which is assumed to be constant and identical for both products. Relations (7) express that demand for product i which equals the production has to remain lower than the product i capacity. Without loss of generality, depreciation of capacities is not taken here into account. Relations (8) state that the investments are irreversible because of imperfectnesses in equipment and/or labor markets. In such a simplified context, the dividend equals the operating profit minus investment cost. The firm wishes to maximize the net present value of the dividends flow on the horizon $[0 + \infty[$.

Constraint (9) plays a key role in the optimal strategy of the firm. It means that the dividend must remain nonnegative ; since neither borrowing opportunities nor capital increase are allowed, investments at date t have to be financed by the current operating profit of the firm at this date. In the two product case, such an overall constraint gives the opportunity of spending a part (or the whole) of the profit generated by a product to increase the other product capacity. This is the crucial point discussed in portfolio models.

As in previous works (Thépot, 1983; Thépot, 1988) we assume that demand functions are constant elasticity functions of the form $x_i = M_i p_i^{-\varepsilon_i}$ with $\varepsilon_i > 1$ and M_i a scaling constant. Specific price levels will play a significant part in the discussion of the results ; they are defined as follows :

- long run price of product i, $p_i^* = \varepsilon_i [c_i + rv]/(\varepsilon_i - 1)$;
- short run price of product i, $\tilde{p}_i = \varepsilon_i c_i / (\varepsilon_i - 1)$.

The interpretation of these prices is quite classical in Microeconomics.

2.3. Initial situation of the firm

In this model, we are interested in diversification problems arising in stable environments. Accordingly, there is no trend in the demands ; in addition, we assume that, at the begining, there is no excess capacity, namely $\xi_i = x_i (p_i (0))$; initial prices $p_i (0)$ are exactly determined by relation : $p_i (0) = (\xi_i / M_i)^{-1/\varepsilon_i}$; they are higher than the long run prices :

$$p_i(0) \geq p_i^*. \qquad (10)$$

Chapter 5 - Dynamic Diversification

Since the beginning, the firm faces immediate incentives to develop separately both business lines ; relation (10) amounts to say that, at time 0, the marginal profit of each product is higher than the investment cost.

At the beginning, product 2 is supposed to be newer that product 1 in the following sense :

$$[p_2(0) - \tilde{p_2}] > A [p_1(0) - \tilde{p_1}], \text{ with } A = (\varepsilon_1 - 1)\varepsilon_2 / [(\varepsilon_2 - 1)\varepsilon_1]. \tag{11}$$

The interpretation of relation (11) will be given later. When the elasticities ε_1 and ε_2 and the operating costs c_1 and c_2 are respectively equal, relation (11) means that, at time 0, capacity ξ_1 is higher than capacity ξ_2.

3. Absence of Manufacturing Experience

Hence we consider the case where $x_i = x_i(p_i)$ and c_i = constant. This case will be used as benchmark in Section 3 to define myopic strategies when learning effects between the products are neglected by the manager.

3.1. Characteristics of the strategies

The strategies to be used over the horizon are determined by the necessary conditions of the Maximum Principle. The Current Value Dualized Hamiltonian H is defined by:

$$H = (1+\beta) [(p_1-c_1)x_1 + (p_2-c_2)x_2 - v(I_1+I_2)] + (q_1 + v_1)I_1 + (q_2+v_2)I_2 + \delta_1 (y_1 - x_1) + \delta_2(y_2-x_2),$$

where q_i are the costate variables associated with differential equations (3), δ_i, n_i and β the Kuhn & Tucker multipliers associated respectively with constraints (4), (5) and (6). Necessary conditions are the following :

$$\dot{q_i} = r\, q_i - \delta_i ; \tag{12}$$

$$(1 + \beta) [(p_i - c_i) \frac{\partial x_i}{\partial p_i} + x_i] - \delta_i \frac{\partial x_i}{\partial p_i} = 0 ; \tag{13}$$

$$q_i = (1 + \beta) v - n_i ; \tag{14}$$

$$\delta_i \geq 0, \quad n_i \geq 0, \quad \beta \geq 0 ; \tag{15}$$

$$\delta_i (y_i - x_i) = n_i I_i = \beta [(p_1 - c_1) x_1 + (p_2 - c_2) x_2 - v (I_2 + I_2)] = 0 ; \quad (16)$$

$$\lim_{t \to \infty} e^{-rt} q_i(t) = 0. \quad (17)$$

The strategies the firm is liable to use along the optimal path are determined through combinations of zero and positive values of δ_i, n_i and β variables. Thanks to the initial conditions only three of them are likely to be chosen in our context.

Strategy (1/3) : ($\delta_1 > 0$, $\beta > 0$, $n_1 = 0$, $n_2 > 0$) : the firm has no excess capacity ; it uses the global operating profit to develop only product 2 while keeping product 1's sales at a constant level. Strategy (3/1) is symetrically defined.

Strategy (3) : ($\delta_1 > 0$, $\beta > 0$, $n_i = 0$) : the firm has no excess capacity ; it spends all the operating profit to develop jointly both products in a balanced way.

Strategy (2) : $\delta_1 > 0$, $\beta = 0$, $n_i = 0$) : the firm has no excess capacity ; it distributes dividends (the so-called long run strategy).

The main characteristics of the strategies are given in table 1 (for the computations see Appendix A) ;

3.2 Optimal trajectory

The optimal trajectory of the firm is a sequence of the strategies defined above. Under the assumption of continuity of costate variables q_1 and q_2 at switching dates, it is straightforward to show that the optimal planning is of the type :

P1 : (1/3) → (3) → (2).

Chapter 5 - Dynamic Diversification

Strategies	1 / 3	2	3
p_1	constant	constant$(=p_1^*)$	both decreasing with
p_2	decreasing	constant$(=p_2^*)$	$(p_2 - \tilde{p_2}) = A(p_1 - \tilde{p_1})$
y_1	constant	constant	increasing
y_2	increasing	constant	increasing
q_1	decreasing (if $p_1 > p_1^*$)	constant$(=v)$	decreasing (if $p_1 > p_1^*$)
q_2	decreasing (if $p_2 > p_2^*$)	constant$(=v)$	decreasing (if $p_2 > p_2^*$)

Table 1 :

Main characteristics of the strategies

Figure 1 represents the firm's optimal pricing behavior in the p1, p2 space.

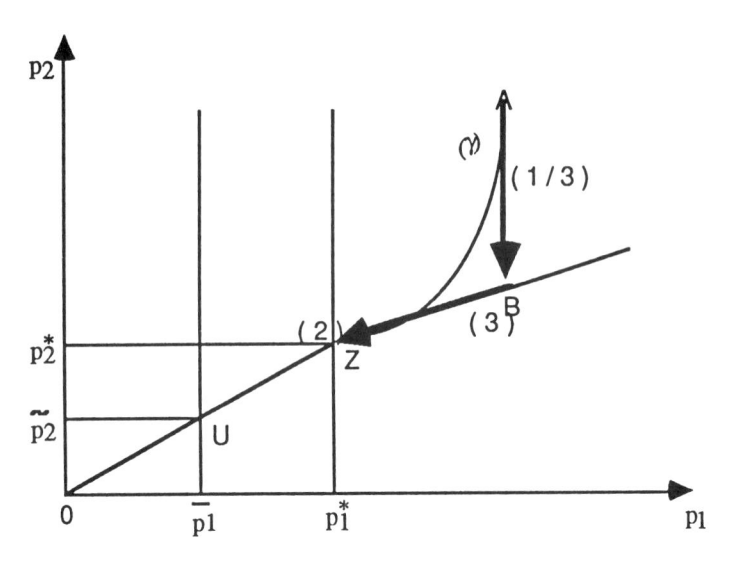

Figure 1 :
Optimal price paths

Initial conditions are represented by point A of coordinates $(p_1(0), p_2(0))$. Using strategy (1/3), the firm only invests in product 2 ; it keeps price p_1 constant while decreasing price p_2.

Once lince UZ of equation $(p_2 - \tilde{p}_2) = A(p_1 - \tilde{p}_1)$ is reached in point B at time $\bar{t}$, the firm uses strategy 3, investing in both products, decreasing the prices until time t^* when point Z of coordinates (p_1^*, p_2^*) is reached. Strategy 2 is then used up to infinity. Figure 2 depicts the sales evolutions of the products.

Chapter 5 - Dynamic Diversification

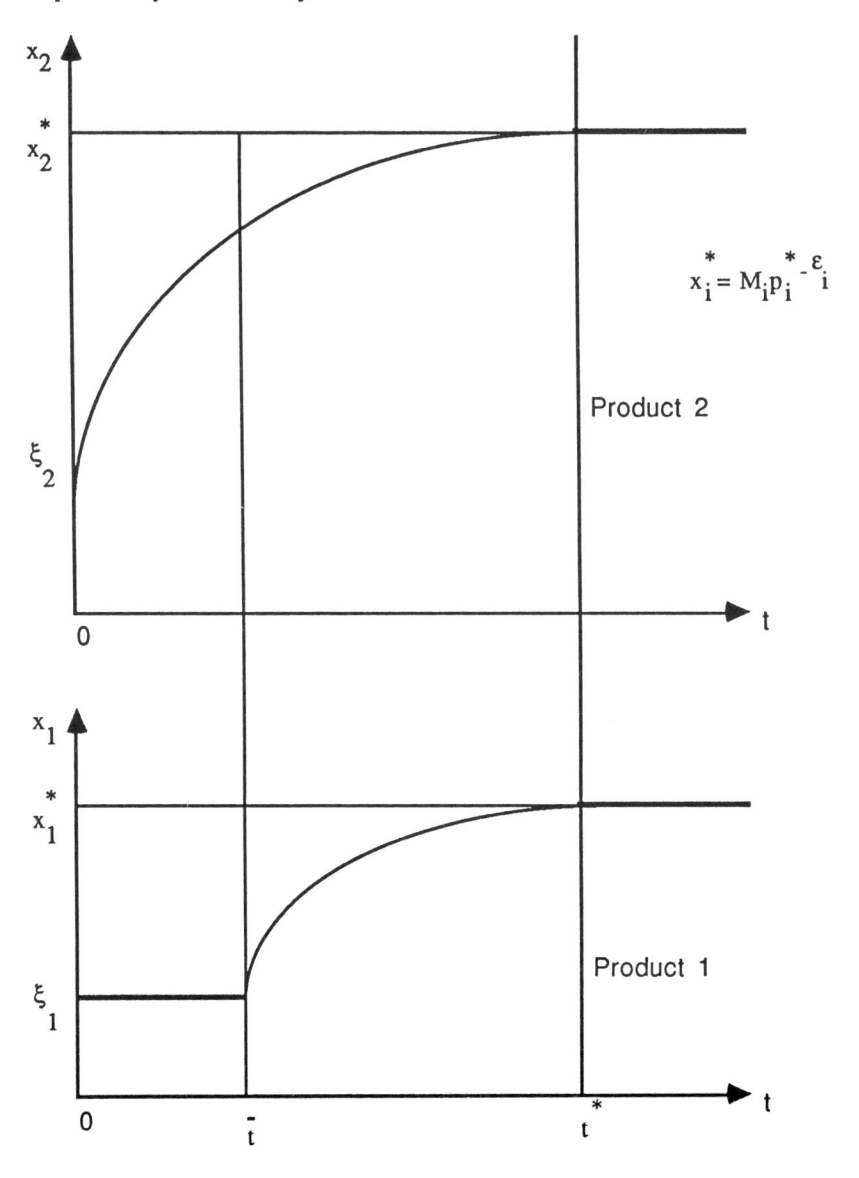

$$x_i^* = M_i p_i^{*-\varepsilon_i}$$

Figure 2 :

Sales evolution of the products

In words, priority is given, at the begining, to the newer product at the expenses of the older the production of which is temporarly blocked at the initial level. Of course, applying such a result would induce a strange behavior for firms launching several products sequentially over time : all the financial resources of the firm is instantaneously shifted towards the latest product the profitability of which has urgently to be enhanced. This is typically a sort of "stop and go" marketing policy likely to create troubles and discrepancies in the production planning as well as within the sales force, the distribution networks and - last but not least - cause of confusions in the customers minds. In practice, any shift of strategy is not costless. At time t (and 0 according to the past) fixed costs should be incurred so that the firm is deterred to stop investing in product 1. Taking into account such fixed costs would result in a smoother optimal path like curve (γ) on figure 1. A more general model is needed to study such a phenomenon.

4. The Learning Effects Case

Let us consider situations when the operating costs depend on the cumulative output i.e. $c_i(X_i)$. Costs are decreasing with the experience of the firm in product i, as related to the total quantity sold since the introduction of the product. Hence we assume that :

$$c_i'(X_i) \leq 0, \quad \lim_{X_i \to \infty} c_i(X_i) = \gamma_i > 0 \text{ and } c_i(X_i) = c_i^o \text{ for } X_i \leq X_i^o \quad (18)$$

The unit cost function c_i is depicted in figure 3.

Chapter 5 - Dynamic Diversification 83

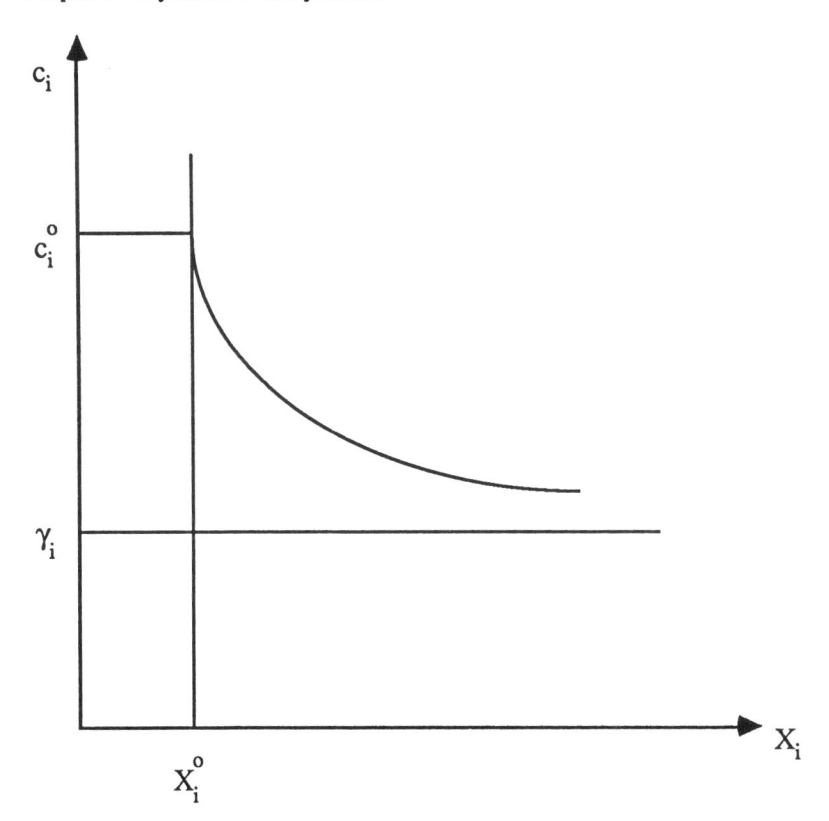

Figure 3 :
Unit cost function.

Necessary optimality conditions are modified by adding state variables X_i and adjoint variables ϕ_i such that :

$$\dot{\phi}_i = r\,\dot{\phi}_i + (1 + \beta)\, x_i\, c'_i(X_i), \tag{19}$$

$$\lim_{X_i \to \infty} e^{-rt}\phi_i(t) = 0 \; ; \tag{20}$$

Relations (13) become :

$$(1+\beta)\,[(p_i - c_i)\frac{\partial x_i}{\partial p_i} + x_i] - (\delta_i - \phi_i)\frac{\partial x_i}{\partial p_i} = 0. \tag{21}$$

To evaluate the specific influence of learning effects on the "stop and go" phenomenon previously identified, we restrict the analysis to situations where learning effects only affect the operating cost of product 1 which was supposed to be the earliest introduced in the market, as indicated by a relatively higher initial production capacity. Consequently,

$$c_2(X_2) = c_2^o = \gamma_2, \phi_2 = 0.$$

4.1 Characteristics of the strategies

The three types of strategies defined in the previous case are still candidates to be used along the optimal path. Major changes affect strategies (2) and (3).

Strategy (2) :

Relation (19) can be written in a well known form (Bass & Bultez, 1982) :

$$\phi_1(t) = -(1+\beta) \int_t^{+\infty} x_1(p_1(\theta)) c_1'(X_1(\theta)) e^{-r(\theta-\upsilon)} d q. \quad (22)$$

In words, costate variable ϕ_1 measures the current value of the marginal costs incured in the future when strategy (2) is used. As a result, ϕ_1 is a decreasing and positive function of t :

$$\phi_1(t) \geq 0, \dot{\phi}_1(t) \leq 0. \quad (23)$$

Of course, strategy 2 is used with price p_2 constant and equal to long run price p_2^*. Relation (19) gives :

$$p_i = \varepsilon_1 [c_1(X_1) + r v - \dot{\phi}_1] / \varepsilon_1 - 1). \quad (24)$$

Differentiating relation (24) and using relation (19) results in :

$$\dot{p}_1 = -\varepsilon_1 \phi_1 / (\varepsilon_1 - 1) \leq 0. \quad (25)$$

Consequently price p is decreasing when strategy (2) is used.

Strategy (3)

Chapter 5 - Dynamic Diversification

As in the constant costs case, we have $\delta_1 = \delta_2$. Relations (21) give:

$$(p_2 - \widetilde{p_2}) = A(p_1 - \widetilde{p_1}(X_1)) + G(t)\phi_1(t) \quad \text{with:}$$
$$\widetilde{p_1}(X_1) = \varepsilon_1 c_1(X_1)/(\varepsilon_1 - 1) \text{ and } G(t) = \varepsilon_2/[(\varepsilon_2 - 1)(1+\beta(t))] \geq 0. \quad (26)$$

These optimal strategies have to be compared with the myopic ones which are used when the firm does not take into account the learning effects. In this situation, the firm acts as if the costs were constant. Clearly the myopic strategies derive from the optimal strategies by letting:

$\phi_1 = 0$. The basic changes are the following:

Myopic strategy (2): Price p_2 is kept constant and equal to p^*_2 while

$$p_1 = \varepsilon_1[c_1(X_1) + rv]/(\varepsilon_1 - 1) \text{ is decreasing [cf. relation (18)]}.$$

Myopic strategy (3): Price p_1 and p_2 satisfy the relation:

$$(p_2 - \widetilde{p_2}) = A(p_1 - \widetilde{p_1}(X_1)). \quad (27)$$

4.2 Optimal versus myopic trajectory

Let us compare the optimal and the myopic trajectories so as to evaluate the changes induced by the ability of the firm to incorporate the learning effects in the definition of its policy. Some important technicalities due to function $c_1(X_1)$ do not yield analytical results as in the previous case since the relations depend on X_1 (namely the past) and ϕ_1 (the future). However, it is possible to have some idea of the evolution by drawing roughly the paths in the plane $\{p_1, p_2\}$.

Product 2 is still assumed to be newer than product 1 in the following sense:

$$p_2(0) - \widetilde{p_2} \geq A(p_1(0) - \widetilde{p_1}(0)). \quad (28)$$

Two situations may occur according to whether product 2 is significantly newer than product 1 or not.

4.2.1. Product 2 significantly newer than product 1

Figure 4 depicts the optimal and the myopic path starting from a given initial

86   Thépot

position in the plane $\{p_1, p_2\}$.

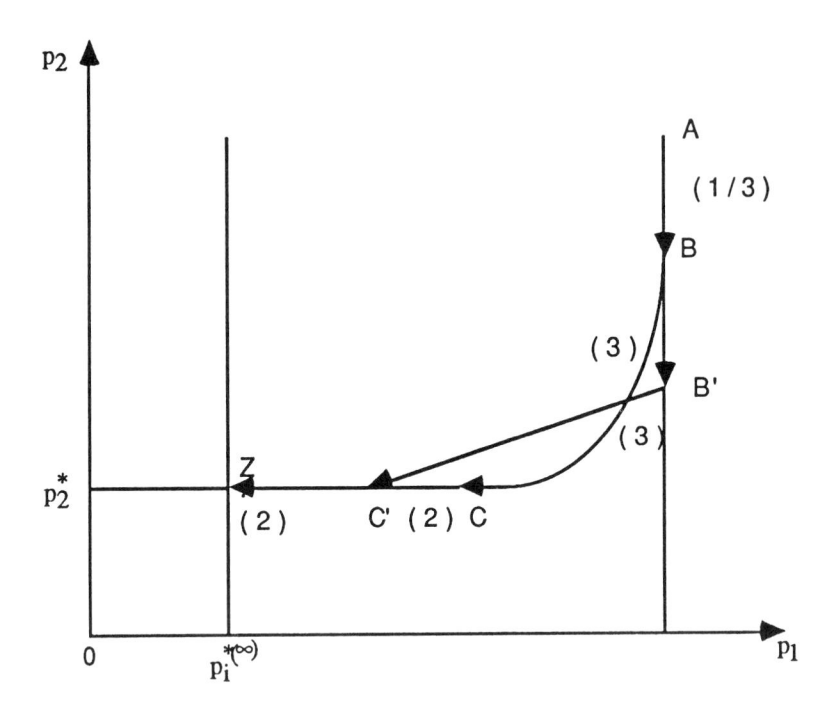

Figure 4 :

Optimal and myopic pathes

The optimal path is represented by the continous line (A B C Z) while the myopic path is represented by the line (A B' C' Z). From A to B (B') the firm uses strategy (1/3), spending all the cash flow to develop product 2. At point B the optimal path diverges from the myopic path. For the sake of optimality, the firm has to benefit from the learning effects of product 1 ; the stop of investment period of product 1 is therefore shorter. Figure 5 depicts the sales evolution of the products.

Chapter 5 - Dynamic Diversification

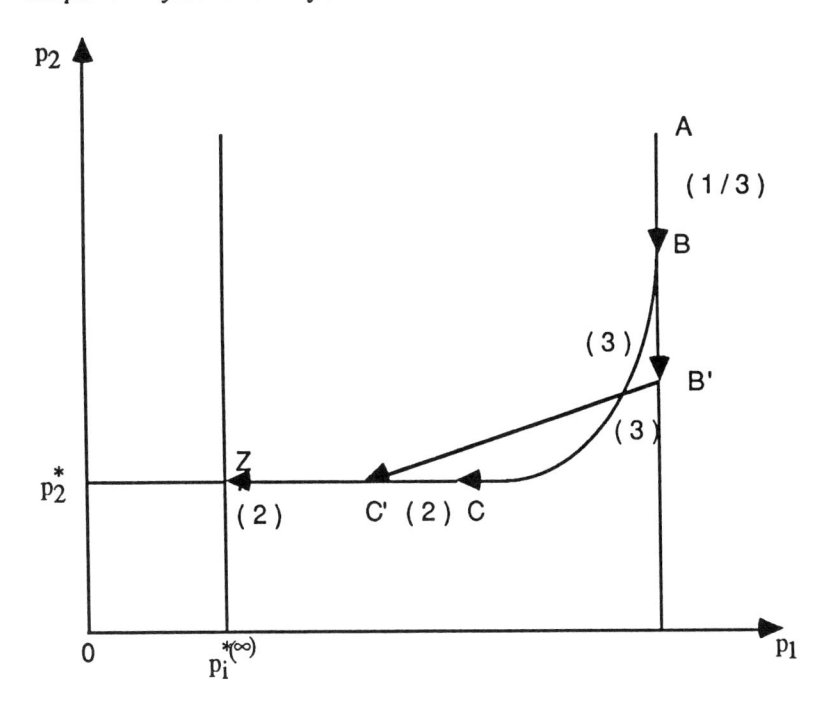

Figure 5 :
Roduct lige cycles with learning effects

$\overline{t_o}$ and t_o^* (resp. $\overline{t_m}$ and t_m^*) are the switching dates of the strategies along the optimal (resp. myopic) path. The optimal sales curves of product 1 is higher than the myopic one since the firm wants to benefit from the learning effects. The sales curve of product 2 illustrates the dynamic consequences of the learning effects : in an early phase $([t_0, \theta])$ the optimal sales curve is lower than the myopic one : increasing the sales of product 1 to ripe the learning effects induces a slower growth of the sales of product 1 because of the financial limitations. In a subsequent period $([\theta, t_m^*])$, the reduction of cost c_1, due to the learning effects improves the financial resources of the firm which can in turn be invested in the development of product 2 ; consequently, the optimal curve is higher than the myopic one.

4.2.2. Product 2 hardly newer than product 1

In this case, the optimal and the myopic sequences of strategies are qualitatively different from the beginning. According to the optimal rule, the firm begins to develop product 1 and not product 2 (strategy 3/1) while, the myopic behavior implies exactly the opposite (strategy 1/3). Figure 6 depicts the optimal and the and the myopic curves in plane $\{p_1, p_2\}$.

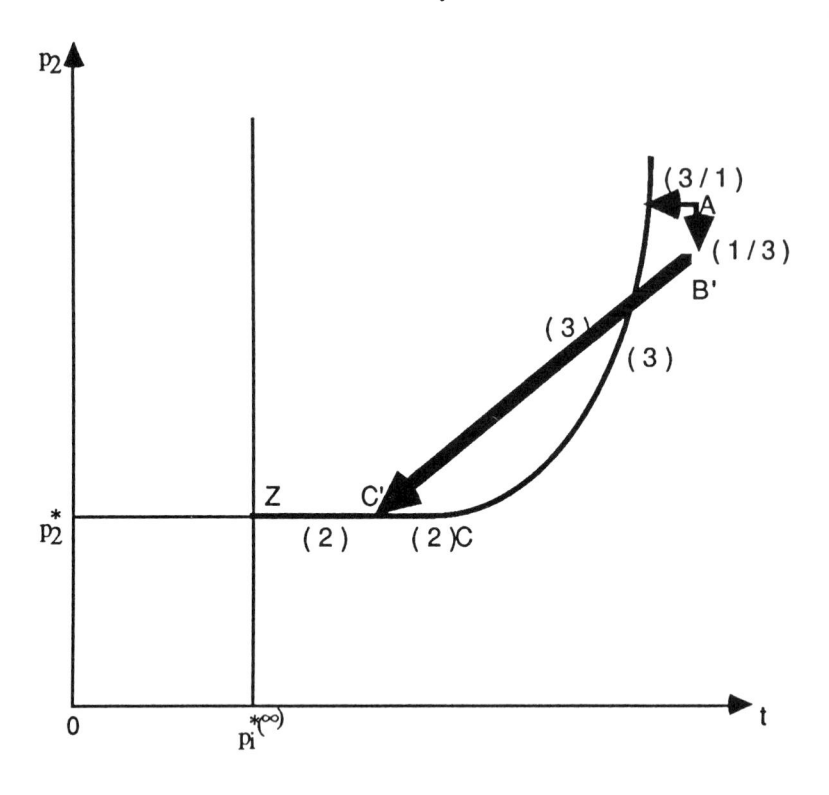

Figure 6 :
Optimal and myopic pathes

Chapter 5 - Dynamic Diversification 89

Figure 7 depicts the sales evolution of the products.

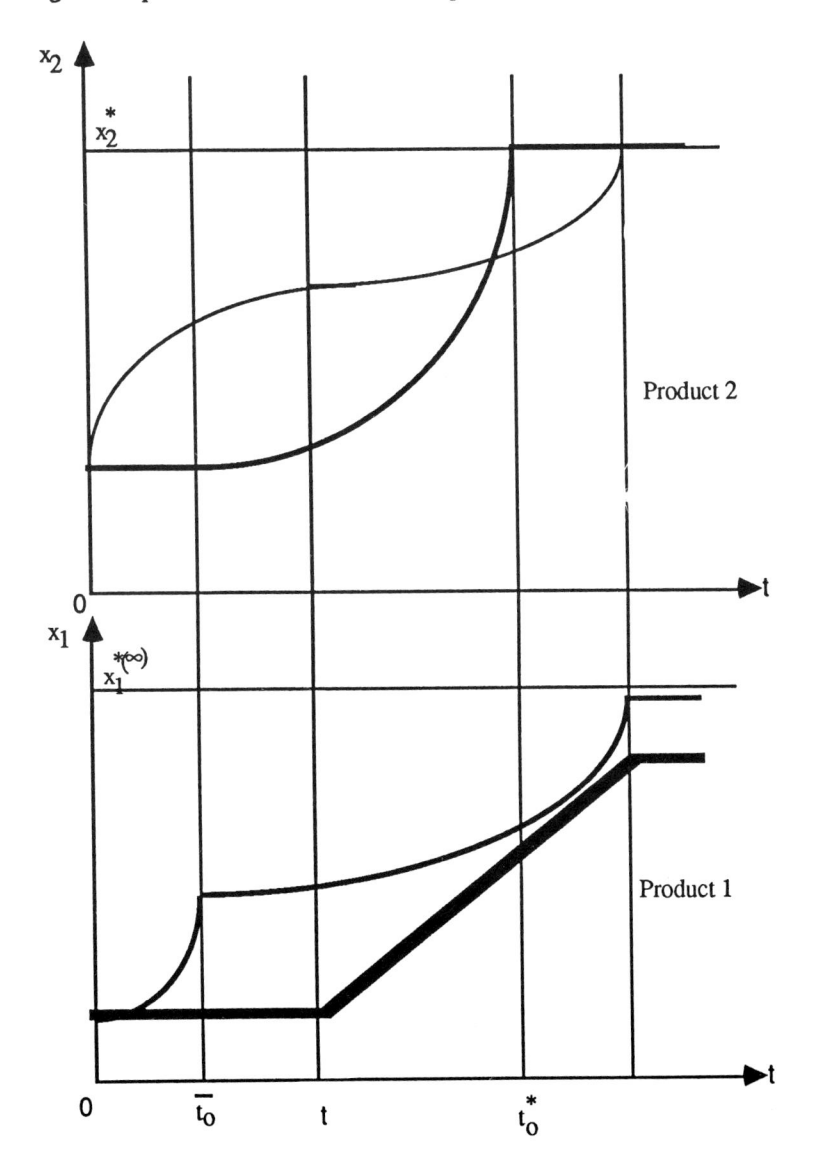

Figure 7 : Sales evolutions

The sales curves clearly indicate the shift of strategies due to the myopic behavior. The interpretation of the curves is anallogons it the previous one.

5. Conclusion

This chapter presents a dynamic model of a firm facing a diversification problem among two activities in a self-financing situation. When there are no learning effects, the optimal planning consists in giving the priority, at the beginning, to the new product, in order to get as soon as possible a balanced portfolio of business lines. When learning effects take place, the priority is not systematically given to the new product, so as to benefit from the learning effects which reduce the costs and increase the current profit to be further invested in both business lines.

In this approach two major ingredients of the diversification problem are neglected : (i) risk, which is inherent to the portfolio management (ii) competition, which induces strategic interactions between the firms operating on both activities. Along these research lines, substantial efforts are to be made in further contributions.

APPENDIX 1 Characteristics of the strategies

Strategy (1/3)

$I_1 = 0$, then $\dot{y}_1 = \dot{x}_1 = 0$ hence price p_1 is kept constant.
$I_2 = [(p_1 - c_1) x_1 + (p_2 - c_2) x_2] / v$; then :

$$-\dot{p}_2 / p_2 = [N(p_1) p_2^{+\varepsilon_2} + (p_2 - c_2)] , \qquad (A.1)$$

with $N(p_1) = (p_1 - c_1) M_1 p_1^{-\varepsilon_1} / M_2$. With $p_2 > p_2^*$, price p_2

decreases through time, leading to a finite value lower than c_2 when $t \to \infty$ Relation (11) gives :

$$\delta_i = (1 + \beta) (\varepsilon_i - 1) (p_i - \tilde{p}_i) \varepsilon_i . \qquad (A.2)$$ Hence, via relations (12)

$$(A.3) \qquad \dot{q}_1 = (1 + \beta) [(\varepsilon_1 - 1) (p_1^* - p_1) / \varepsilon_1] - r v_1 ,$$

Chapter 5 - Dynamic Diversification 91

(A.4) $\qquad \dot{q}_2 = (1+\beta)[(\varepsilon_2 - 1)](p_2^* - p_2)/\varepsilon_2$.

Hence q_1 and q_2 are decreasing functions of time for $p_i > p_i^*$.

Strategy (3)

I_1 and $I_2 > 0$ then $q_1 = (1+\beta)v = q_2$ and $\dot{q}_1 = \dot{q}_2$; relations (10) give :

(A.5) $\qquad \delta_1 = \delta_2$.

Thanks to relation (A.2), we have :

(A.6) $\qquad (p_2 - \tilde{p}_2) = A(p_1 - \tilde{p}_1)$, with $A = (\varepsilon_2 - 1)\varepsilon_1 / (\varepsilon_1 - 1)\varepsilon_2$.

Since $\qquad v(I_1 + I_2) = [(p_1 - c_1)x_1 + (p_2 - c_2)x_2]$,

(A.7) $\qquad (\varepsilon_1 y_1 \dot{p}_1 / p_1) + (\varepsilon_2 y_2 \dot{p}_2 / p_2) = -[(p_1 - c_1)y_1 + (p_2 - c_2)y_2]/v$.

Substituting (A.6) in (A.7) results in :

(A.8) $\qquad \dot{p}_i [\varepsilon_1 y_i / p_1 + \varepsilon_j^A y_j / \tilde{p}_j + A(p_i - \tilde{p}_i)] =$
$\qquad \qquad - [(p_1 - c_1)y_i + (\tilde{p}_j - c_j) + A(p_i - \tilde{p}_i))y_j]/v$.

Clearly the prices are decreasing through time leading to finite values lower than c_i when $t \to \infty$.

Costate variables q_i are governed by relations of (A.4) types : accordingly, they are decreasing for $p_i > p_i^*$

Strategy (2)

I_1 and $I_2 > 0$, $\beta = 0$, then $q_i = v$ and $p_i = p_i^*$. Note that relation (A.6) is satisfied with $p_i = p_i^*$

References

Bass, F.M., and A. Bultez, 1982, A note on Optimal Strategic Pricing of Technological Innovations, Marketing Science, 1, 371-378.

Brandt, S.C., 1986, Entrepreneuring in Established Companies, New York, (Dow Jones-Irwin).

Gray, D.H., 1986, Uses and Misuses of Strategic Planning, Harvard Business Review, Jan-Feb., 89-97.

Hayes, R.H., 1985, Strategic Planning Forward in Reverse, Harvard Business Review, Nov-Dec., 111-119.

Lesourne, J., 1976, Optimal Growth of the Firm in a Growing Environment, Journal of Economic Theory ,13, 118-137.

Nickell, S., 1974, On the Role of Expectations in Pure Theory of Investment, Review of Economic Studies, 41, 1-19.

Porter, M., 1980, Competitive Strategy, New York, (Mc Millan),

Rao, D.R., and F.M. Bass, 1985, Competition, Strategy and Price Dynamics : a Theoritical and Empirical Investigation, Journal of Marketing Research, 22, 283-296.

Thépot, J., 1983, Marketing and Investment Policies of Duopolists in a Growing Industry, Journal of Economic Dynamics and Control, 5, 387-404.

Thépot, J., 1988, An Optimal Control Contribution to Product Life Cycle Theory, International Journal of Research in Marketing, 5, 271-288.

MICROECONOMIC CONTRIBUTIONS TO STRATEGIC MANAGEMENT
J. Thépot and R.-A. Thiétart
© 1991 Elsevier Science Publishers B.V. All rights reserved.

CHAPTER 6

MULTIMARKET COMPETITION:
Entry Strategies and Entry Deterrence When the Entrant Has a Home Market

M. van WEGBERG   and   A. van WITTELOOSTUIJN
University of Limburg   University of Limburg

Abstract

The multimarket perspective identifies potential entrants as existing firms in related markets, which may be regional markets of a homogeneous good or different product markets that are related technically or by goodwill. The chapter uses this framework to analyze entry strategies and entry deterrence. Successful entry and entry-deterring strategies require understanding of the feedbacks from the entry market to the home market and *vice versa*. In order to deter entry an incumbent firm may, for example, shift the battleground from his own home market to the entrant's. The multimarket perspective pulls together insights from industrial organization and strategic management.

1. Introduction

Potential entry is a challenge to strategic management (SM) as it raises issues such as the identification of potential entrants, the selection of entry markets and the scale of entry. SM theory recognizes the key importance of potential entry (Porter, 1980; Watson, 1982; Yip, 1982). This is an area where industrial organization (IO) has made many useful contributions, beginning with Bain (1956) and Sylos-Labini (1962). Yet it can be argued that the mainstream of IO centers on entry by new firms (Kottke, 1962). If, however, potential entrants are existing firms, their home market can be of crucial importance to their entry strategies. There is a steady flow of literature within IO and SM which emphasizes this point. This literature, however, is scattered and no consistent terminology is used. The aim of this chapter

---

The authors are grateful for the comments of an anonymous referee. Of course, the usual disclaimer applies.

is to discuss concepts and insights that may help to integrate this field. Thus the chapter contributes to the exploration of the IO - SM interface, following the advice of Porter (1981), Caves (1984), Teece (1984), Camerer (1985), Shapiro (1989) and Thépot and Thiétart (1991).

The *ease of entry* approach emphasizes the advantages which an existing firm entrant derives from her home market (Andrews, 1949, 1964; Hines, 1957; Brunner, 1961; Kottke, 1962; Yip, 1982). Intangible assets which the firm has developed or acquired in her home market, can be transferred at low extra cost to an entry market. Examples are R&D know how, patents, and goodwill. Moreover, idle productive resources can be transferred to an entry market. In both cases the firm economizes on entry costs relative to a new or unrelated firm entrant, who has to start up an entry activity from scratch. Thus existing firms with related resources have a competitive advantage over other potential entrants. They can enter a market even if entry barriers exist which deter entry by others. They exert a competitive pressure on incumbent firms which is more intense than can be expected from new or unrelated firms.

The aim of this chapter is to pull together these and other disparate insights. The theory of multimarket competition which emerges, informs IO and SM alike (Van Witteloostuijn and Van Wegberg, 1991a, 1991b). The key feature of multimarket competition is that *inside* (that is, from within the set of related markets) rivals are able to (relatively quickly) overcome barriers which are unsurmountable to *outside* (that is, from outside the set of related markets) entrants. The perspectives opened up by this literature are, as we will point out, relevant for decision making by multinational, diversified and integrated enterprises.

The chapter is organized as follows. First the chapter reviews pieces of multimarket theory within IO and SM. Next we review empirical evidence. SM theorists discuss illuminating case studies: we also present a new, tentative case study. This confirms the relevance of the models of multimarket competition to SM. Finally, the chapter presents a conceptual framework for entry deterrence and entry strategies. The conclusion identifies adjacent literature. Following current practice, we refer to the incumbent firm with 'he' and to a potential entrant with 'she'.

2. Competition in a multimarket environment

2.1. Multiple markets

Porter's (1980) famous schedule of 'Forces Driving Industry Competition' identifies five sources of (potential) competition. His concept of *extended rivalry* encompasses rivalry with other incumbent firms, threats of substitutes, potential entry and bargaining power of suppliers and buyers. These sources refer to markets in which

Chapter 6 - Multimarket Competition 95

firms operate. Each incumbent firm buys inputs in input markets and sells output in output markets. The firm's suppliers and buyers not only exert bargaining power, but they are also potential entrants if they can consider to integrate forward or backward. Substitutes can be demand substitutes, if a technically different product serves similar needs, or technical substitutes, if an existing supplier can switch production from the substitute to the incumbent firm's product. The latter activity is a form of entry. Thus the forces of potential competition which an incumbent firm faces are related to the constellation of markets in which he operates. Figure 1 illustrates this.

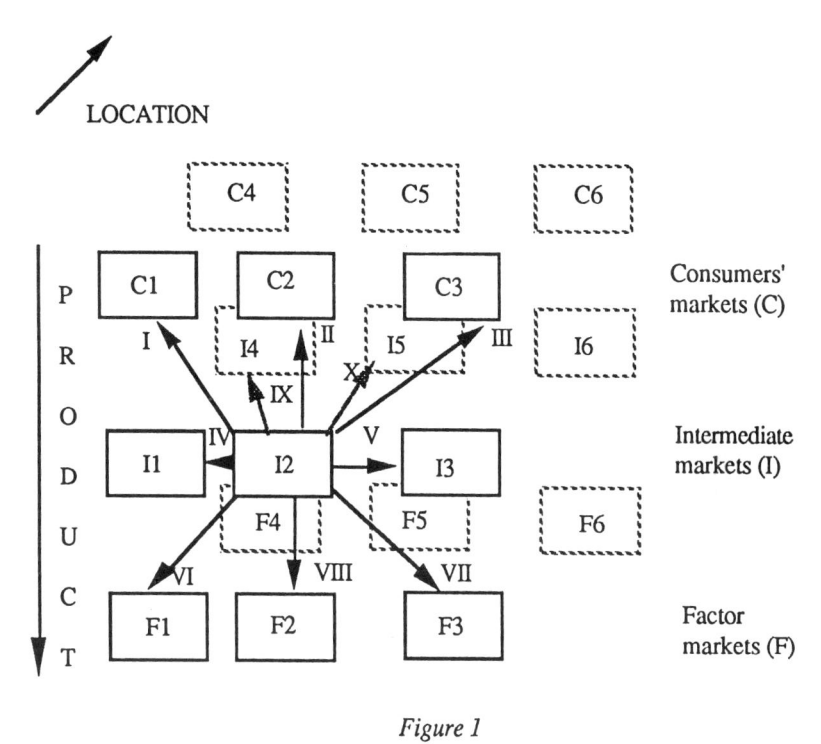

Figure 1

Multiple Markets

Figure 1 assumes that multimarket strategies (diversification and integration) and multimarket spillovers can be defined in terms of location and product. For example, I1, I2 and I3 indicate different product markets (IV and V depict horizontal product diversification and/or spillover), whereas I2, I4 and I5 are different geographical markets (IX and X denote horizontal geographical diversification and/or spillover). Broadly speaking, from the viewpoint of a firm in an intermediate market I2 five categories of multimarket strategies/spillovers can be distinguished: (1) forward diversifying integration/spillover (I and III), (2) forward downstream integration/spillover (II), (3) horizontal diversification/ spillover (IV and V), (4) backward diversifying integration/spillover (VI and VII) and backward upstream integration/spillover (VIII). The five broad categories of strategies and spillovers can be used as a heuristic device so as to distinguish pure cases.

Figure 1 makes clear that multimarket competition is related to many different branches of literature. Worthy of mention is the literature on diversification (Ramanujam and Varadarajan, 1989; Thépot, 1991), integration (Caves and Bradburd, 1988; Krickx, 1991), multiproduct firms (Teece, 1982; Shaked and Sutton, 1990), multimarket oligoply (Bulow, Geanakoplos and Klemperer, 1985; Lal and Matutes, 1990), multinational enterprise (Caves, 1982; Dunning, 1989), interbrand competition (Judd, 1985; Sullivan, 1990), transaction costs (Williamson, 1989; Boone and Verbeke, 1991) and international trade (Brander and Krugman, 1983; Venables, 1990). This chapter can of course only refer to illustrative examples. To support the argument, a selection of exemplary pieces of literature is mentioned when convenient. By and large, this chapter's argument on strategy is concentrated on horizontal multimarket competition that ensues from diversification.

2.2. Multiple games

Competition can be associated with three categories of games. Figure 2 depicts the three games.

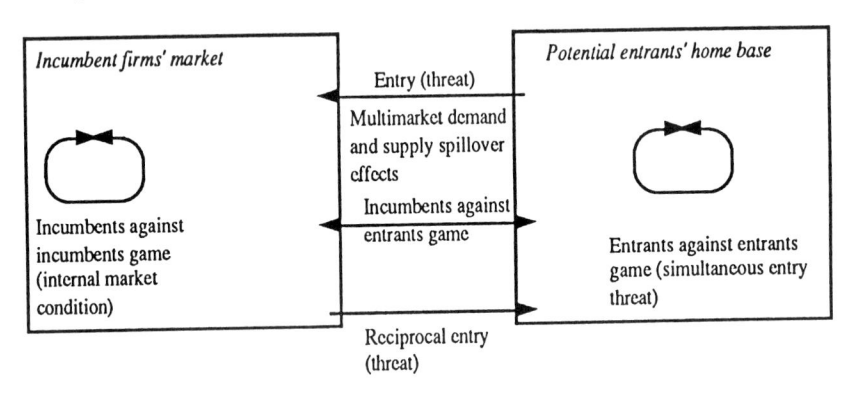

Figure 2

Multimarket Competition

First, incumbent firms play an incumbents against incumbents game: only internal market conditions determine competition (actual rivalry). This type of game is studied in the well-established theories of (im)perfect competition without (free) entry (Shapiro, 1989b). Second, incumbent firms and potential entrants are engaged

Chapter 6 - Multimarket Competition

in an incumbents against entrants game: external conditions dominate over internal competition (potential rivalry). The entry (deterrence) literature focuses on the features and implications of this category of games (Gilbert, 1989). Third, potential rivals are the players in an entrants against entrants game: multiple potential entrants have to coordinate (implicitly or explicitly) simultaneous entry decisions (entry rivalry). This game is explored only sporadically (Nti, 1989). This chapter focuses on the incumbents against entrants game, where multimarket competition is in force if the entrant is an existing firm.

2.3. Scale and mode of entry

Two important determinants of the force of potential competition are the scale and mode of entry. *Large-scale* (or total) entry occurs if the entrant underprices (and, in the limit, threatens to fully replace) the incumbent firm, which triggers retaliation strategies by the incumbent firm such that his post-entry behavior differs qualitatively from his pre-entry conduct. *Small-scale* (or partial) entry indicates that the entrant merely disposes part of her excess capacity by temporary or niche entry without inducing a significant threat to the incumbent firm's market share. The dynamic features of the process follow from the response lags of firms. The entry process involves lags: particularly worth noting are the entry lag and the incumbent firm's response lags in his own home market respectively the entrant's home market (the reciprocal entry lag).

Porter (1980) distinguishes two modes of entry for an existing firm. In the case of *internal entry* the entrant brings new production capacity, distribution networks, and know how to the market. In the case of *entry by acquisition*, the entrant uses productive and other resources which are already there: the entrant may instead contribute financial means and general managerial skills. In this chapter we focus on internal, large-scale entry by firms who introduce their own resources and skills into the entry market. This entry confronts the potential entrant with four types of feedback between her home and entry market.

2.4. Resource economizing entry

The prime feedback from entry on home market is that both markets compete for the entrant's resources. An existing firm owns resources, which she can divert from her home market to the entry market. The *pro* of this strategy is that by using existing resources, she economizes on entry costs[1]. This entails a competitive advantage relative to a new firm entrant. Using existing resources, however, does involve costs. First of all there are adjustment costs in production when switching from the current good to a technical substitute to be sold in a different product market. Alternatively, there can be transport costs in exporting the product from the home base to another region or country. Entry is *easy* if the adjustment or transport cost is low (Calem, 1988). Diverting productive resources away from the home market also entails a cost in the sense of home market profits foregone. This is the opportunity cost of entry. The case with a binding capacity constraint offers an example. With binding capacity, goods exported to an entry market are withheld from the home market. The home market revenues foregone constitute the opportunity cost of entry (Bulow et al., 1985; Calem, 1988). The opportunity cost depends on, first, the scale at which resources are diverted and, second, the profitability of using these resources in the home market. Home market profitability, in turn, follows from many conditions. Competition is one of them. For example, entry into the home market changes home market revenues and so affects the level of home market profits foregone if the incumbent firm enters into another market. All this is to say that the *opportunity cost of entry* is *endogenous*.

A usual assumption within IO is that the opportunity cost of entry is zero. In our context (existing firm entry) that means that no home market profits are foregone for the sake of entry. This is the case where excess resources are used. Since they are not being utilized for the home market, using excess resources for an entry project does not inflict a loss upon the entrant's home market (Cairns and Mahabir, 1988). Another case is where resources have a public good character. Intangible assets, such as know how, consumer goodwill and management skills, may have this characteristic (Teece, 1980, 1982). For example, using R&D know how for an entry market does not diminish *per se* the amount of know how available for the home market. These competitive advantages point to cases where the most credible entry threat comes from existing rather than new firms[2].

2.5. Multimarket spillovers

A second major feedback from entry on the home market is that the entry activities can be associated with positive and/or negative multimarket spillovers. Multimarket spillovers are defined as externalities between two or more markets: that is, the payoffs in market A have an impact on the payoffs in market B and *vice versa*[3]. Note that positive (negative) multimarket spillovers, as opposed to economized entry cost, increase (decrease) the overall profit of the entrant *beyond* (*below*) the entry profit *per se* (Porter, 1980). The key point is that multimarket spillovers can exert influence on strategy choice. To be precise, the opportunity to exploit (or danger to incur) multimarket spillovers can be an important motive for (refraining from) entry. For example, positive spillovers, *ceteris paribus*, lower entry barriers to inside firms (but increase outside firm barriers). This observation is also recognized in literature on diversification, multiproduct firm, integration and multinational enterprise. An early example of a list of sources of multimarket spillovers is Hines (1957). Table 1 lists illuminating examples.

Chapter 6 - Multimarket Competition

Spillover	Positive	Negative
Demand	. Goodwill . Complements	. Badwill . Substitute
Supply	. Scale economies . Scope economies	. Scale diseconomies . Scope diseconomies

Table 1

Multimarket Spillovers

Bulow *et al.* (1985) distinguish two multimarket spillover effects. *Multimarket supply spillovers* include (dis)economies of scale or scope between products in separate markets. Joint economies imply that a firm can decrease unit production cost of product A in market 1 by increasing supply of product A (scale economies) or B (scope economies) in market 2. Integration advantages are a second example where operating in two separate (vertically integrated) markets conveys positive spillovers between both activities (Brunner, 1961).

Multimarket demand spillovers include goodwill in the home market which carries over to the entry market. These spillovers arise if the same buyers are active in several product markets[4]. The strategy of firms in market 2 influences the scale of demand in market 1 (and *vice versa*) due to a nonzero cross-elasticity of demand. The multimarket demand spillover

'is positive if a firm's demand in one market is complementary to its demand in the second ... and would be negative if selling more in one market hurts prospects in the other' (Bulow *et al.*, 1985).

That is, complements are associated with a positive demand dependency (video recorders and cassettes) whereas the demands of substitutes are negatively correlated (public and private transport). If positive multimarket spillovers dominate, entry increases the overall profits of the entrant beyond the entry profits *per se* (Porter, 1980).

The key point is that multimarket spillover effects can have important implications for multimarket competition. Table 1's list of examples is of course not exhaustive. For instance, Caves (1982) summarizes spillovers in the context of multinational enterprise and Teece (1982) lists multimarket externalities which diversified firms can exploit. A key argument in this literature points to exploitation of (excess) fungible and *intangible* assets as an explanation of (international) diversification (for example, R&D capabilities, marketing facilities, know how, managerial skills, *etcetera*). An illustrative example in the IO-tradition is the impact of imputation spillovers (Dranove and Tan, 1990; Green and Laffont, 1990). This indicates that multimarket spillover effects need not to be restricted to tangible factors.

2.5. One-sided and reciprocal entry

Calem (1988) explicitly offers two economic rationales for one-sided entry. First, the incumbent firm's entry cost is sufficiently large to trigger his decision to refrain from entering the potential entrant's market (Calem, 1988). Second, legal or regulatory barriers exist which prevent incumbent firms from being potential entrant into the rival's market (Calem, 1988). However, one-sided entry is far from the only plausible case (Venables 1990). Inside firms can exert a *reciprocal entry* threat (Porter, 1980; Calem, 1988). So, a third feedback arises if the incumbent firm in the entry market retaliates in the entrant's home market. Attempts in this direction are key elements in understanding strategic behavior in multimarket competition. Porter (1980) summarizes the strategic implications by arguing that

'multiple markets provide a way in which one firm can reward another for not attacking it, or conversely, provide a way of disciplining a renegade.'

The impact of reciprocal entry is particularly studied in the literature on intra-industry trade and reciprocal dumping (Brander and Krugman, 1983; Calem, 1988; Dei, 1990; Salvatore, 1990; Venables, 1990).

Reciprocal entry is a response to initial entry. Bulow *et al.* (1985) illustrate this as follows. Suppose that entry from market 1 into market 2 reduces sales of the incumbent firm in market 2. The latter firm now faces (increased) excess capacity. Since the opportunity cost of unused capacity is less than the opportunity cost of used capacity, the initial entry reduces his opportunity cost of entry. If his expected entry profit exceeds the reduced opportunity cost, the incumbent firm will enter market 1. Hence, entry into market 2 elicits reciprocal entry into market 1. Three assumptions drive this result. First, capacity can be used for production in both markets. For example, low transport costs allow the product to be sold in both (country) markets or low switching costs permit the same capacity to be used for different products. The second assumption is a capacity constraint. Excess capacity in the home market can be used to produce goods for an entry market. If the scale of entry is insufficient to recover entry costs, entry does not occur. If the incumbent firm, however, faces entry, his home market sales fall and excess capacity increases. Consequentially, the scale of entry may increase up to a level which does allow the firm to recover entry costs. Reciprocal entry then occurs as a consequence of initial entry. Third, Bulow *et al.*'s (1985) argument also implicitly assumes the existence of insurmountable exit barriers to third markets. If exit is free, the incumbent can decide to accommodate entry by (partial) exit toward another market (Judd, 1985). If, however, he faces insurmountable exit barriers to third markets, he only has one entry market - the entrant's home market.

Three examples illustrate reciprocal entry (threats). First, incumbent firms in the entry market may decide to retaliate in the entrant's home market (Calem, 1988). This strategy of counter-attack is a parry to the potential entrant's entry attack (Yip, 1989). Second, Watson (1982) identifies counter-competitive strategies which anticipate the potential rivals' entry move: counter-competition entails actions (for example, entry into the potential entrants' home market) that force the potential entrant to tie resources to her home market. Third, hostage or foothold strategies can be employed so as to keep potential entrants in check (Caves, 1982). A foothold in the potential entrants' home market signals the ability to immediately respond to the potential entrants' entry strategy by retaliation in her home market (Karnani and Wernerfelt, 1985).

2.6. Multimarket collusion

The outcome of multimarket competition (after, for example, a series of entry and reciprocal entry moves) may well be a reduction in competition. Edwards (1955) proposed the hypothesis that

'when sellers meet in several markets, their recognition of the interdependence of their operations may blunt the vigor of their competition with each other' (Scott, 1982).

Feinberg (1985) specifies Edwards' hypothesis by arguing that

'companies meeting rivals in more than one market will be able to facilitate collusion in one or all of those markets.'

Harrington (1987), Kantarelis and Veendorp (1988) and Bernheim and Whinston (1990) provide a theoretical foundation of the multimarket collusion hypothesis.

Companies with multimarket encounters are inclined to facilitate collusion if the payoff of the cooperative outcome exceeds the competitive profit. This phenomenon is also recognized in the literature on international trade (Jacquemin, 1989). For example, reciprocal dumping is the worst of both worlds (or, to be precise, four worlds in a Prisoners' Dilemma): if both parties agree upon refraining from dumping, joint profit is maximized (Pinto, 1986). The key point is however that cheating must be unattractive. Bernheim and Whinston (1990) formally show

'that multimarket contact relaxes the incentive constraints governing the implicit agreements between firms, and that this has the potential to improve firms' abilities to sustain collusive outcomes.'

3. Current evidence

3.1. Existing firm entry and multimarket spillovers

Our analysis indicates that existing (related) firm entry differs qualitatively from new or unrelated firm entry. Empirical evidence supports this view. The high incidence of existing firm entry is confirmed by empirical figures on international trade. The post-war historical trend towards increased intra-industry trade, though weakened in the 1980s, is particularly illustrative (Globerman and Dean, 1990). Existing firms tend to enter at a much larger scale than new firms (Hause and Du Rietz, 1984) and to encroach on the market share of the leading incumbent firms (Berry, 1974). Existing firms in related markets seem to have a higher speed of entry than unrelated firms with few related skills and assets (Lambkin, 1988). In the Japanese semiconductor industry firms with strategic advantages in terms of tangible and intangible assets (*i.e.*, technological innovation, broad product line and vertical linkages) develop higher rates of foreign direct investments (Kimura, 1990). Existing (diversifying) firm entry does not seem to be responsive to barriers to entry, while the opposite holds for new (or small) firm entry (Gorecki, 1975).

The argument underlying these findings is that a successful entry strategy may build upon the entrant's home market. Sullivan (1990) reports evidence on the importance of brand image spillovers. Moreover, the crucial role of synergies is emphasized in the empirical literature on related diversification (Chatterjee, 1986; Seth, 1990). If positive spillovers exist between related markets, an efficiency motive makes firms enter all of these markets. If they do so, they tend to develop high multimarket contact. Scott (1982) presents a test of the hypothesis that multimarket contact is too high to be random. His sample contains 437 of the 1000 largest U.S. manufacturers in 1974. He concludes that multimarket contact among these manufacturers far exceeds the level that would occur by chance. Thus systematic forces make firms tend to group in the same markets. This indicates the relevance of multimarket spillovers (or multimarket economies, in his words) to firm's decision making.

3.2. Protected markets and one-sided entry

Kottke (1962) observes that

'food distributors' entry into the bread industry illustrate the mixed results of "countervailing power". The conventional method of wholesaling bread through route salesmen absorbs about 30 percent of the price. Here chain food stores can make a large saving. But where food chains have established their own bakeries they may be tempted to go a step further, selling bread below cost and recouping on other merchandise. For the retailer who employs it, a loss leader is simply a special form

Chapter 6 - Multimarket Competition

of advertising. ... The typical retailer probably is persuaded that the leaders attract a good deal of extra business in other products. ... For the integrated food store, this practice may seem no more sinister than free delivery service, but it creates an impossible situation for non-integrated bakers.'

This is an example of one-sided entry: the chain food store enters the bread market, while non-integrated bakeries do not enter the non-bread food market. Kottke's case shows that entry deterrence is likely to fail against a combination of positive multimarket spillovers and one-sided entry. A successful entry strategy can be based upon these conditions.

Multinational enterprises (MNEs), for example Japanese firms, often engage in one-sided entry from a protected home market. This endows them with a competitive advantage:

'In the case where the U.S. market is open and a large foreign market is closed, foreign competitors would be able to achieve more efficient scale via volume in the domestic and overseas sales, while domestic competitors would be squeezed into a portion of the domestic market. ... Under these economic conditions -large scale and learning- access to foreign markets and control over the home market would become a firm's top priority' (Yoffie and Milner, 1989).

The foreign MNE benefits from a multimarket supply spillover between the entry and her (protected) home market. She recovers fixed costs of R&D and the like in her home market. This asymmetry affects pricing in the entry market as the foreign MNE prices in order to recover marginal production and transportation costs, whereas the domestic producers price in order to recover R&D and all other fixed expenses as well. Domestic suppliers perceive the MNEs pricing policy as dumping:

'Industries in Japan and other PBCs (i.e. Pacific Basin Countries) often enjoy very supportive relationships with their governments. Frequently this includes protection against imports into their domestic markets. This permits the PBCs to subsidize exports to other markets with profits from domestic sales. Zenith complained to the U.S. Trade Commission that in 1976 the least-expensive 19-inch color television set available in Japan was priced at the equivalent of $700, but the same and comparable sets were selling for less than $350 in the United States. Domestic TV set makers could not retaliate by lowering prices, since their entire domestic sales would be affected in a price war. But Pacific Basin competitors could maintain lower prices on the export portion of their sales knowing that their profitable home market was protected' (Willard and Savara, 1988).

This illustrates the importance of trade policy in enforcing one-sided or reciprocal entry. Salvatore (1990) reports the trend towards new protectionism in the form of increased incidence of antidumping cases and escape clauses. In reported cases, US firms affected seek a strategic trade policy from the US government to enforce reciprocal access to the Japanese market (Yoffie and Milner, 1989).

3.3. Global competition and reciprocal entry

Global competition shows many examples of multimarket competition and entry by existing (foreign) firms. An entry motive for US firms in Japan is to tap local resources and skills. Production by the Japanese affiliate is then exported back into the US (Encarnation, 1987). By using Japan as an export platform the US firm exploits a multimarket supply spillover from the Japanese entry market to her home market. Watson (1982) suggests another entry motive. Firms may preempt future entrants by *counter-competition*. That is, the

'pursuit of a foreign competitor's domestic markets can help protect the threatened company's own home market sales.'

Counter-competition entails actions that force the foreign competitor to tie resources to her home market, thus forcing her to forego entry. These actions include: (i) entry into her home market, (ii) introducing a product innovation in her home market to force her to match this innovation and (iii) changing the terms of competition, such as aftermarket support, in one's own advantage. Counter-competition implies a first-mover advantage for it must strike before the foreign competitor has gained a foothold in one's own home market. Watson's examples suggest the realism of this assumption. In the IO-literature (in the second section) the ability of the incumbent firm to retaliate is exogenous and constant. That is, his response lag and excess capacity are given. Watson's concept of counter-competition suggests a dynamic approach of endogenous retaliation: a pre-emptive firm tries to undermine a competitor's position before she can react.

Entry by an MNE by setting up a local subsidiary can be part of a wider strategy involving competition with another MNE in other markets (Caves, 1982). That is to say, reciprocal entry requires a local subsidiary. Or, a

'subsidiary on the invader's turf establishes both a means of retaliation and a hostage that can be staked out in any subsequent understanding between the two parents' (Caves, 1982).

Karnani and Wernerfelt (1985) show that firms do indeed use a foreign subsidiary for a reciprocal entry response. Particularly illustrative are the fights between Goodyear and Michelin in the tyre market, Maxwell House and Proctor and Gamble in the roasted coffee industry and BIC and Gillette in the markets for pens and razors. For example, in the 1970s Michelin challenged Goodyear in his US home market to exploit her own lead in radial tyre technology. By 1980 she had captured an 8% market share in the US. Goodyear reacted initially in the European market by increasing his market share from 8% to 12% in less than a year. Simultaneously,

Goodyear made an effort to catch up with Michelin's radial tyre technology, which of course would pay off only later. Michelin, therefore, did enter the American market, although the American market leader Goodyear had a foothold in Europe, and did react to Michelin's entry by reciprocal entry in her home market. This prospect failed to deter Michelin, possibly because Goodyear's imitation lag implied a long response lag. Michelin may have expected that her entry profits in the American market would exceed any losses in her European home market.

The general pattern of competition between US and EC firms may run in the opposite direction, as Graham (1978) suggests. Graham reports a study of direct investments by US firms in Europe and *vice versa*. His finding is that an increase in the number of US subsidiaries in Europe is typically followed, after a lag, by an increase of European subsidiaries in the US. The lag is four years for industries such as chemicals, refineries and instruments. Graham suggests that this fact represents rivalry: European firms install subsidiaries as a response to previous US moves. So, he suggests that reciprocal entry explains this pattern.

3.4. Multimarket collusion

As one consequence of multimarket contact, firms (in the case below Japanese semiconductor suppliers) may develop a follow-the-leader strategy:

'Japanese companies, unlike most of their American counterparts, competed in other consumer and industrial product areas as well as in semiconductors. Such diversification heightened pressures for imitative behavior at home and abroad. Sequential foreign investment was one response' (Encarnation, 1987).

A sequence of entry and reciprocal entry moves may however well induce a reduction in competition. Caves (1982) illustrates this by an example that

'at the extreme, markets can wind up less competitive after the peace treaty is signed than they were before the initial aggressive move. An example of this adverse development was the British tobacco market after the entry of American Tobacco in 1901. Induced by the British tariff structure, American purchased a leading British producer. That event caused 13 dismayed British rivals to merge into Imperial Tobacco. After a year of duopolistic rivalry, a peace treaty gave Imperial a monopoly of the British and Irish markets, and American got a guarantee that Imperial would not sell in the United States or its dependencies. British-American Tobacco was organized as a joint venture to handle business in the rest of the world.'

Market sharing agreements, such as by American and Imperial Tobacco, are an example of *multimarket collusion*. *Multimarket contact* research seeks to verify this hypothesis (Heggestad and Rhoades, 1978; Scott, 1982; Feinberg, 1985). For example, on the basis of an analysis of 1976 data from the US Federal Trade Commission's Line of Business Program Feinberg (1985) concludes that multimarket contacts tend to be positively correlated with price-cost margins for industries in the moderate range of concentration, which indicates the importance of multimarket collusion.

3.5. The case of the artificial sweetening industry

The artificial sweetening industry is an interesting illustration of multimarket competition (*Chemical Week*, August 10, 1988; *Delaware State News*, May 19, 1989; *Financial Post*, June 3, 1989; *Chemical Marketing Reporter*, June 6, 1989; *New York Times*, November 19, 1989; and *Financial Times*, November 26, 1990). In 1981 the US company Searle introduced the sweetening aspartame under the name of NutraSweet. Aspartame is about 200 times as sweet as sugar. Of the available intense sweeteners, aspartame is closest to the taste of sugar. The major quality of aspartame is that only fractions of a gram are required to produce the same degree of sweetness as much greater quantities of sugar. This implies that aspartame brings typically less than 1% of the calories of an equivalent amount of sugar.

Aspartame is sold as the tabletop sweetener Equal and under the brand name NutraSweet as an ingredient in 1700 products including soft drinks, puddings, dressings, ice creams and chewing gum. The demand from soft drinks producers (particularly Coca Cola and Pepsi Cola for their light versions) represent 75% of sales. NutraSweet's US market stands for $736 million sales in 1988. The U.S market counts for 90% of the combined North American - European sales in 1988. However, Europe has the growth potential. For example, a realistic assessment predicts a 50% growth by the early to mid-1990s.

NutraSweet is able to benefit from a secure and extremely profitable home market, since in the US NutraSweet's aspartame (carrying the companies name) is patented up until 1992. NutraSweet's 1988-profit was close to $330 million. During the period 1986-1987 the European patents expired, however. So, the US market and European market show(ed) blockaded entry in the period 1981-1992 and 1981-1986/1987, respectively: NutraSweet's point of departure is protected monopoly. In defence of this lucrative monopoly position NutraSweet started to erect strategic barriers to entry in light of the European patent expiration: the company's objective was to trigger effective entry deterrence.

Two entry-deterring strategies worth mentioning are exclusive contracting and branding the ingredient. First, NutraSweet exploited his bargaining position as a monopolist by negotiating long-term contracts with large customers (particularly Coca Cola and Pepsi Cola): for example, NutraSweet guarded 60% of the Canadian market by signing exclusive contracts with Pepsi-Cola Canada Ltd. and T.C.C. Beverages Ltd., the Canadian bottler of Coca Cola. Second, NutraSweet forced his customers to put the company's logo on soft-drink cans, which made the mere ingredient aspartame into a household name NutraSweet.

Chapter 6 - Multimarket Competition

Notwithstanding NutraSweet's entry-deterring strategies potential competitors started preparing entry into the European market after the expiration of the patents. In particular, the Irish company Angus Fine Chemicals (AFC) and the Dutch-Japanese joint venture Holland Sweetener Company (HSC) installed productive capacity upfront by making use of an innovative cost-reducing technology hoping to trigger a profitable market sharing arrangement in Europe. HSC, for example, appears to have a good hand as the joint venture could benefit from resource economizing entry and multimarket spillovers by exploiting the assets and experience of both partners (such as management skills, knowledge of European markets, R&D knowhow, financial resources and goodwill). Both parties in the joint venture - the chemical companies DSM and Tosoh - were engaged in horizontal diversification into a related market by broadening their product line.

After the expiration of his European patents NutraSweet counterattacked both entrants AFC and HSC in their European home market by an aggressive strategy which reduced price to half the American level: the price in the US market ranged from $55 to $90 a pound in 1989, whereas the European level dropped to $27. NutraSweet's retaliation strategy of intense post-entry competition in Europe was partly successful as AFC decided to exit the market: AFC appeared to be the weak player in the Chicken game. However, up until the present day HSC has been able to keep up the fight. Probably, NutraSweet's post-entry strategy implies that, *ceteris paribus*, the market only leaves room for single entry.

HSC's response to NutraSweet's aggressiveness was twofold. First, the firm attacked and attacks NutraSweet's entry-deterring practices (charge: anticompetitive contracting) and post-entry strategy (charge: below-cost dumping) in European courts. The European Commission has declared valid both charges. NutraSweet's exclusive contracts with large customers are dissolved, and stiff antidumping duties will be imposed upon NutraSweet. The combination of NutraSweet's entry-deterring and retaliation strategies and HSC's aggressive response in court induces toughness in the European market. Second, HSC attempted and attempts to undertake reciprocal entry by penetrating the North-American market so as to break down NutraSweet's one-sided entry strategy.

On the one hand, HSC has gained a 3% Canadian market share worth $875,000 in 1989 (by selling to, for example, soft-drinks producer Schweppes) since NutraSweet's Canadian patent expired in 1987. Recently, HSC won a case against NutraSweet's exclusive contracting practice in Canadian court. On the other hand, HSC brought NutraSweet to court in the latter's home state Delaware. With the purpose to provoke a trial regarding NutraSweet's patents HSC located an American subsidiary in Delaware. HSC announced the intention to bring a tabletop Sweetmatch (a perfect substitute for NutraSweet's Equal) to the US market. The expectation is that the procedure will take several years. NutraSweet has accepted HSC's challenge by, for example, announcing an intense promotion campaign and the buildup of productive capacity in Europe. Clearly, Nutrasweet's moves in

Europe and HSC's countermoves in North America are an example of a reciprocal entry game.

The outcome of the battle in the artificial sweetening market is a matter of guessing. The case clearly illustrates multimarket competition. Although NutraSweet's objective is to return to the pre-entry monopoly position by forcing HSC to exit the aspartame market, multimarket contact may well trigger (tacit) collusion. Multimarket cooperation can take the form of either multimarket sharing, both rivals signing a peace agreement in North America and Europe, or reciprocal exit, both firms creating their own spheres of influence (probably NutraSweet in North America and HSC in Europe). Anyway, HSC clearly intends to stay in the market: K. Dooley, vice president of HSC's Canadian subsidiary, communicated that "his company is committed to a long battle and is confident the preference of beverage makers for a second source of supply will eventually give them a competitive share of the market" (*Financial Post*, June 3, 1989).

4. Entry strategies and entry deterrence

4.1. Strategy choice

Multimarket competition suggests a framework for organizing experience and intuition. It suggests arguments that (should) play a role in guiding entry strategies by potential entrants as well as entry deterrence by incumbent firms. Table 2 summarizes these arguments.

By way of illustration two imperatives which determine the entry strategy are discussed: (i) protect the home market at least during the entry process and (ii) select an entry market. The next subsections discuss these imperatives and entry deterrence in turn.

Key element	Deter entry by	Select a market
1. Focus of rivalry	focusing on incumbents against entrants game	which does not suffer from predominant actual rivalry which drives profits down
2. Resource economizing entry	raising strategic entry barriers that impede economizing on entry cost	which permits to economize on entry cost
3. Multimarket spillovers	stimulating negative spillovers with potential entry market	where positive multi-market spillovers are eminent
4. Reciprocal entry	signaling a credible reciprocal entry threat	where incumbents fail to exert a credible reciprocal entry threat
5. Multimarket collusion	showing unwillingness to collude after entry	where incumbents are willing to collude

Table 2

Entry deterrence and entry strategies

4.2. The entrant's commitment to her home market

Low exit barriers are a strategic weakness, as Eaton and Lipsey (1980) have shown:

'To make an entry-deterring threat ... the sitting monopolist must threaten that in the event of entry, he will stay in the market *long enough* that the entrant's present value at time of entry will be nonpositive. "Long enough" is Δ^* periods. ... Δ^* can be interpreted as the monopolist's minimum commitment to the market or as the minimum *barrier to his exit*. It is in this sense that barriers to exit are barriers to entry.'

This proposition is translated into multimarket arguments by Judd (1985), and Hilke and Nelson (1988). The key point is that if a firm enters a second market, she may reduce her barriers to exit from the first. For example, Hilke and Nelson (1988) point out that large diversified companies are likely to face lower exit barriers than less diversified firms:

'If, instead of adopting a fight-to-the-finish strategy, firms utilize the conventional model of rational disinvestment behavior, a large diversified firm may be more likely to exit than a less diversified firm under the plausible condition that diversified firms face lower marginal costs (higher opportunity costs) in shifting resources to other markets.'

This type of argument has specific strategic implications.

Entry into another market may involve partial exit: *i.e.*, a reallocation of resources away from the home towards the entry market. Thus entry goes along with a reduction of exit barriers. This may invite entry into her own home market for two reasons. First, partial exit reduces the size of her commitment to the home market and raises expected entry profits in her home market. Second, it raises the expectation that she will react upon entry by accommodation. Since entry reduces home market profits, she may shift even more resources into her entry market, which implies that she accommodates entry by (partial) exit (Calem, 1988). Anticipating this scenario, a potential entrant may abstain from entry in the first place or she may decide to enter knowing that this implies exit from the current home market. Can a firm avoid this scenario? If available, she may select an entry market which increases the exit barrier from her home market. If an entry market induces positive spillovers to the home market, entry can raise the commitment to the home market. Suppose, for example, that a firm can only sustain her position in an entry market against competition if she benefits from joint economies of scope or any other positive multimarket spillover with her home market. Then she is credibly committed to staying in her home market.

4.3. Selection of an entry market

With multiple entry markets two criteria can be indicated which can guide selection of a specific market. The first one considers the response by the incumbent firm. The potential entrant should take into account that her entry changes the incumbent firm's opportunity cost of entry (Hilke and Nelson, 1988). The incumbent firm may respond both by reciprocal entry and by partial exit. His response is most favorable to the potential entrant if he faces an entry barrier to her home market yet low exit barriers to other markets. This rules out markets where reciprocal entry is feasible or where the incumbent is willing to fight entry (for example, as a result of insurmountable exit barriers).

The second criterion involves entry barriers and multimarket spillovers. Bain's (1956) barriers to entry can loose significance for potential entrants who are incumbent elsewhere. Economies of scale, for instance, are not a barrier if potential entrants have already realized their economies in a home market (Brunner, 1961;

Chapter 6 - Multimarket Competition

Yip, 1982). Economies of scale or scope even *invite* entry if potential entrants exceed in size the incumbent firms in a market. Similar arguments hold for other barriers: product differentiation and absolute cost advantages. To the extent that products are differentiated by the goodwill of their supplier, a potential entrant with existing goodwill has an advantage over a young and perhaps innovating incumbent firm. For example, at the time that IBM entered the market for microcomputers, she could benefit from more goodwill among potential business users than Apple, the incumbent firm. Thus multimarket spillovers can help to overcome entry barriers. Moreover, they increase the profitability of entry without undermining the commitment to the home market. The overall effect of multimarket competition on entry barriers is ambiguous:

'Often the synergies of related diversification allow entry into industries that might in their absence seem to offer insurmountable barriers. On the other hand, the process of offensive and defensive entry into related clusters of business may ultimately lead to a significant increase in overall entry barriers by forcing a newcomer to enter the whole cluster of business (be optimally diversified) or face a serious disadvantage' (Porter, 1985).

4.4. Entry deterrence

The discussion above can also be relevant for the incumbent firm. It helps to identify existing firms in related markets who could profitably enter into his market. Moreover, the multimarket competition framework allows him to assess the relevance of a reciprocal entry threat to entry deterrence. The following strategic conditions facilitate the credibility of the reciprocal entry threat: (i) entry into the potential entrant's home market is free, (ii) exit barriers to third markets are significant, (iii) the incumbent's response lag is short, (iv) the incumbent firm correctly anticipates which markets exert a credible entry threat and (v) potential entrants in these markets are aware of (i) - (iv). All kinds of signaling devices can make potential entrants recognize the reciprocal entry threat.

5. Concluding remarks

Multimarket modeling offers a framework for analyzing entry strategies and what Yip (1982) calls 'gateways to entry'. It also explores the strategic implications of transferring the battleground from the incumbent firm's home market to the potential entrant's home market. These insights gain relevance in the context of increasing global competition. The individual firm engaged in multimarket competition faces a complex process. Multimarket competition involves first and foremost the delineation of a set of *related markets*[5]. These are characterized by entry barriers to outside (new or unrelated) firms, but ease of entry for firms within the set of related markets. Related firms benefit from their tangible (for example, overcapacity, multiproduct technology and substitute products) and intangible (for instance, know how, experience and consumer goodwill) assets. In the case of reciprocal entry each firm in one of these markets can easily enter another market within the set. If the entry possibilities between markets are asymmetrical, one-sided entry can occur, where the entrant has access to a market whose incumbent firm does not have access to the entrant's home market[6]. Multimarket competition has several possible outcomes. For example, all firms may decide to enter into each other's home market. Thus they develop into multimarket firms. Or, conversely, neither firm enters for fear of provoking reciprocal entry into her home market. In an intermediate case, the 'mutual foothold equilibrium', firms maintain a foothold in each other's market[7]. Thus they have a commitment to a reciprocal entry response upon entry, without the foothold itself inviting retaliation.

Adjacent literature to the multimarket framework may indicate areas where positive analytical spillovers exist. Some examples are the literature on diversification, especially in the case of diversifying entry (Lecraw, 1984). Although this chapter focuses on markets, the conceptual framework can also be applied to market segments and strategic groups (Caves and Porter, 1977). Trade models are also related: Calem's (1988) reciprocal entry game is a further development of Brander and Krugman's (1983) reciprocal dumping model. Trade models are typically one-stage games, whereas multimarket competition models describe two-stage structures. The two-stage structure introduces a strategic dimension which we feel is typical of competition between incumbent firm and potential entrant. The distinction between trade competition and (investment in) a local foothold is also being made in literature on the entry process which considers initial trade, establishment of a local foothold, and escalating investments to be subsequent steps in an ongoing entry process (Encarnation, 1987; Willard and Savara, 1988). This suggests a dynamic framework. The internalization theory of the MNE offers points of contact with the multimarket approach (Rugman, 1982)[8].

Notes

1 Note that low entry costs can be a disadvantage if they are being associated with low exit barriers (Eaton and Lipsey, 1980; Judd, 1985). The section on strategy choice goes into this strategic weakness in more detail.

2 Compare, for example, with the internalization theory of the multinational enterprise (Rugman, 1982).

3 DeBondt and Veugelers deal with a different spillover: technology or knowledge leakages *among* rivals rather than between markets. Van Witteloostuijn (1990) presents a model with potential rivalry that is facilitated by *multimarket* R&D spillovers. Moreover, note the resemblance with SM's well-established synergy concept (Chatterjee, 1986).

4 Shakun (1965), Matutes and Regibeau (1989), Lal and Matutes (1989) and Margolis (1989), are models with multimarket demand spillovers which are worth

noting.

5 This raises the issue of market definition, which is well-known in the literature on IO (Scherer, 1980) and SM (Abell, 1980). For this chapter's purposes, the intuition in the text suffices.

6 This is the basic insight of Andrews' theory of 'potential cross-entry' (Andrews, 1964).

7 Broadly speaking, if firms are not at par, the entry threat may be asymmetric. The literature on new firm entry illustrates this point (Gilbert, 1989).

8 A further issue is the internal organization necessary to be able to exploit multimarket spillovers (Hill, 1988; Clarke and Brennan, 1990). The design of the internal organization can even be an entry-deterring device (Hendrikse).

References

Abell, D.F., 1980, Defining the Business: The Starting Point of Strategic Planning, (Englewood Cliffs, NJ, Prentice-Hall).

Andrews, P.W.S., 1949, Manufacturing Business, (London, MacMillan).

Andrews, P.W.S., 1964, On Competition in Economic Theory, (Westport, Conn., Greenwood Press).

Bain, J.S., 1956, Barriers to New Competition, (Cambridge Mass., Harvard University Press).

Bernheim, B.D., and M.D. Whinston, 1990, Multimarket Contact and Collusive Behavior, RAND Journal of Economics, 21, 1-26.

Berry, C.H., 1974, Corporate Diversification and Market Structure, Bell Journal of Economics and Management Science, 4, 196-204.

Boone, C., and A. Verbeke, 1991, Strategic Management and Vertical Desintegration: A Transaction Cost Approach, in Thépot, J. and R.A. Thiétart (Eds.), Microeconomics Contributions to Strategic Management, (Amsterdam, North-Holland).

Brander, J., and P. Krugman, 1983, A "Reciprocal Dumping" Model of International Trade, Journal of International Economics, 15, 313-321.

Brunner, E., 1961, A Note on Potential Competition, Journal of Industrial Economics, 9, 248-250.

Bulow, J.I., J.D. Geanakoplos and P.D. Klemperer, 1985, Multimarket Oligopoly: Strategic Substitutes and Complements, Journal of Political Economy, 93, 488-511.

Cairns, R.D., and D. Mahabir, 1988, Contestability: A Revisionist View, Economica, 55, 269-276.

Calem, P.S., 1988, Entry and Entry Deterrence in Penetrable Markets, Economica, 55, 171-183.

Camerer, C., 1985, Thinking Economically About Strategy, in Pennings, J.M. (Ed.), Organizational Strategy and Change, (San Francisco, Jossey-Bass Publishers).

Caves, R.E., 1982, Multinational Enterprise and Economic Analysis, (Cambridge, Mass., Cambridge University Press).

Caves, R., 1984, Economic Analysis and the Quest for Competitive Advantage, American Economic Review: Papers and Proceedings, 74, 127-132.

Caves, R.E., and R.M. Bradburd, 1988, The Empirical Determinants of Vertical Integration, Journal of Economic Behavior and Organization, 9, 265-279.

Caves, R.E., and M.E. Porter, 1977, From Entry Barriers to Mobility Barriers: Conjectural Decisions and Contrived Deterrence to New Competition, Quarterly Journal of Economics, 91, 241-261.

Chatterjee, S., 1986, Types of Synergy and Economic Value: The Impact of Acquisitions on Merging and Rival Firms, Strategic Management Journal, 7, 119-139.

Clarke, C.J., and K. Brennan, 1990, Building Synergy in the Diversified Business, Longe Range Planning, 23, 9-16.

DeBondt, R., and R. Veugelers, 1991, Strategic Investment with Spillovers, in Thépot, J. and R.A. Thiétart (Eds.), Microeconomics Contributions to Strategic Management, (Amsterdam, North-Holland).

Dei, F., 1990, A Note on Multinational Corporations in a Model of Reciprocal Dumping, Journal of International Economics, 29, 161-171.

Dranove, D., and T. Tan, 1990, Information Spillovers, Incumbency, and Conservatism, International Journal of Industrial Organization, 8, 499-604.

Dunning, J.H., 1989, The Study of International Business: A Plea for a More Interdisciplinary Approach, Journal of International Business Studies (Fall), 411-436.

Eaton, B.C., and R.G. Lipsey, 1980, Exit Barriers are Entry Barriers: The Durability of Capital as a Barrier to Entry, Bell Journal of Economics, 11, 721-729.

Edwards, C.D., 1955, Conglomerate Bigness as a Source of Power, in: National Bureau of Economic Research conference report, Business Concentration and Price Policy, (Princeton, Princeton University Press).

Encarnation, D.J., 1987, Cross-Investment: A Second Front of Economic Rivalry, California Management Review, 29, 20-48.

Feinberg, R.M., 1985, "Sales-at-Risk": A Test of the Mutual Forbearance Theory of Conglomerate Behavior, Journal of Business, 58, 225-241.

Gilbert, R.J., 1989, Mobility Barriers and the Value of Incumbency, in Schmalensee, R. and R.D. Willig (Eds.), Handbook of Industrial Organization, (Amsterdam, North-Holland).

Globerman, S., and J.W. Dean, 1990, Recent Trends in Intra-Industry Trade and Their Implications for Future Trade Liberalization, Weltwirtschaftliches Archiv, 126, 25-49.

Gorecki, P.K., 1975, The Determinants of Entry by New and Diversifying Enterprises in the UK Manufacturing Sector 1958-1963: Some Tentative Results, Applied Economics, 7, 139-147.

Green, J., and J.J. Laffont, 1990, Competition on Many Fronts: A Stackelberg Signaling Equilibrium, Games and Economic Behavior, 2, 247-272.

Harrington, J.E., 1987, Collusion in Multiproduct Ologopoly Games under a Finite Horizon, International Economic Review, 28, 1-14.

Hause, J.C., and G. Du Rietz, 1984, Entry, Industry Growth, and the Microdynamics of Industry Supply, Journal of Political Economy, 92, 733-757.

Heggestad, A.A., and S.A. Rhoades, 1978, Multi-Market Interdependence and Local Market Competition in Banking, Review of Economics and Statistics, 60, November, 523-532.

Hendrikse, G., 1991, Organizational Choice and Entry Deterrence, in Thépot, J. and R.A. Thiétart (Eds.), Microeconomics Contributions to Strategic Management, (Amsterdam, North-Holland).

Hilke, J.C., and P.B. Nelson, 1988, Diversification and Predation, Journal of Industrial Economics, 37, 107-111.

Hill, C.W.L., 1988, Internal Capital Market Controls and Financial Performance in Multidivisional Firms, Journal of Industrial Economics, 37, 67-83.

Hines, H.H., 1957, Effectiveness of 'Entry' by Already Established Firms, Quarterly Journal of Economics, 71, 132-150.

Jacquemin, A., 1989, International and Multinational Strategic Behavior, Kyklos, 42, 495-513.

Judd, K., 1985, Credible Spatial Preemption, RAND Journal of Economics, 16, 153-166.

Kantarelis, D., and E.C.H. Veendorp, 1988, Live and Let Live Type Behavior in a Multi-Market Setting with Demand Fluctuations, Journal of Economic Behavior and Organization, 10, 235-244.

Karnani, A., and B. Wernerfelt, 1985, Multiple Point Competition, Strategic Management Journal, 6, 87-96.

Kimura, Y., 1989, Firm-Specific Strategic Advantages and Foreign Direct Investment Behavior of Firms: The Case of Japanese Semiconductor Firms, Journal of International Business Studies (Summer), 296-314.

Kottke, F.J., 1962, Market Entry and the Character of Competition, Western Economic Journal, 5, 24-43.

Krickx, G.A., 1991, Transaction Cost and Resource Dependence Explanation of Vertical Integration, in Thépot, J. and R.A. Thiétart (Eds.), Microeconomics Contributions to Strategic Management, (Amsterdam, North-Holland).

Lambkin, M., 1988, Order of Entry and Performance in New Markets, Strategic Management Journal, 9, 127-140.

Lal, R., and C. Matutes, 1989, Price Competition in Multimarket Oligopolies, RAND Journal of Economics, 20, 516-537.

Lecraw, D.J., 1984, Diversification Strategy and Performance, Journal of Industrial Economics, 33, 179-198.

Margolis, E., 1989, Monopolistic Competition and Multiproduct Brand Names, Journal of Business, 62, 199-209.

Matutes, C., and P. Regibeau, 1989, Standardization across Markets and Entry, Journal of Industrial Economics, 37, 359-371.

Nti, K.O., 1989, More Potential Entrants May Lead to Less Competition, Journal of Economics, 49, 47-70.

Pinto, B., 1986, Repeated Games and the 'Reciprocal Dumping' Model of Trade, Journal of International Economics, 20, 357-366.

Porter, M.E., 1980 Competitive Strategy: Techniques for Analyzing Industries and Competitors, (New York, The Free Press).

Porter, M.E., 1981, The Contributions of Industrial Organization to Strategic Management, Academy of Management Review, 6, 609-620.

Porter, M.E., 1985, Strategic Interaction: Some Lessons from Industry Histories for Theory and Antitrust Policy, in Mansfield, E. (Ed.), Microeconomics: Selected Readings, (New York, Norton).

Ramanujam, V., and P. Varadarajan, 1989, Research on Corporate Diversification: A Synthesis, Strategic Management Journal, 10, 523-551.

Rugman, A.M.,1982, Internalization and Non-Equity Forms of International Involvement, in Rugman, A.M. (Ed.), New Theories of the Multinational Enterprise, (New York, St. Martin's Press).

Salvatore, D., 1990, A Model of Dumping and Protectionism in the United States, Weltwirtschaftliches Archiv, 126, 763-781.

Scherer, F.M., 1980, Industrial Market Structure and Economic Performance, (Chicago, Rand McNally).

Scott, J.T., 1982, Multimarket Contact and Economic Performance, Review of Economics and Statistics, 64, 368-375.

Seth, A., 1990, Sources of Value Creation in Acquisitions: An Empirical Investigation, Strategic Management Journal, 11, 431-446.

Shaked, A., and J. Sutton, 1990, Multiproduct Firms and Market Structure, RAND Journal of Economics, 21, 45-62.

Shakun, M.F., 1965, Advertising Expenditures in Coupled Markets: A Game Theory Approach, Management Science, 11, 42-47.

Shapiro, C., 1989a, The Theory of Business Strategy, RAND Journal of Economics, 20, 125-137.

Shapiro, C., 1989b, Theories of Oligopoly Behavior, in Schmalensee, R. and R.D. Willig (Eds.), Handbook of Industrial Organization, (Amsterdam, North-Holland).

Sullivan, M., 1990, Measuring Image Spillovers in Umbrella-Branded Products, Journal of Business, 63, 309-329.

Sutton, J., 1989, Endogenous Sunk Costs and the Structure of Advertising Intensive Industries, European Economic Review, 33, 335-344.

Sylos-Labini, P., 1962, Oligopoly and Technical Progress, (Cambridge, Mass., Harvard University Press).

Teece, D.J., 1980, Economies of Scope and the Scope of the Enterprise, Journal of Economic Behavior and Organization, 1, 223-247.

Teece, D.J., 1982, Towards an Economic Theory of the Multiproduct Firm, Journal of Economic Behavior and Organization, 3, 39-63.

Teece, D.J., 1984, Economic Analysis and Strategic Management, California Management Review, 26, 87-110.

Thépot, J., 1991, Dynamic Diversification and Learning Effect, in Thépot, J. and R.A. Thiétart (Eds.), Microeconomics Contributions to Strategic Management, (Amsterdam, North-Holland).

Thépot, J., and R.A. Thiétart, 1991, Introduction: Microeconomics/Strategic Management Interfaces, in Thépot, J. and R.A. Thiétart (Eds.), Microeconomics Contributions to Strategic Management, (Amsterdam, North-Holland).

Venables, A.J., 1990, The Economic Integration of Oligopolistic Markets, European Economic Review, 34, 753-773.

Watson, C.M., 1982, Counter-competition Abroad to Protect Home Markets, Harvard Business Review, January-February, 40-42.

Willard, G.E., and A.M. Savara, 1988, Patterns of Entry: Pathways to New Markets, California Management Review, 30, 57-76.

Williamson, O.E., 1989, Transaction Cost Economics, in Schmalensee, R. and R.D. Willig (Eds.), Handbook of Industrial Organization, (Amsterdam, North-Holland).

Witteloostuijn, A. van, 1990, Investment Contestability and Average Cost Reduction, European Journal of Political Economy, 6, 23-40.

Witteloostuijn, A. van, and M. van Wegberg, 1991a, Multimarket Competition: Theory and Evidence, Journal of Economic Behavior and Organization, 13 (forthcoming).

Witteloostuijn, A. van, and M. van Wegberg, 1991b, Multimarket Competition and European Integration, in Rugman, A.M. and A. Verbeke (Eds.), Research in Global Strategic Management Volume 2: Global Competition and the European Community, (Greenwich, Conn., JAI Press).

Yip, G.S., 1989, Global Strategy: In a World of Nations? Sloan Management Review (Fall), 29-41.

Yip, G.S., 1982, Gateways to Entry, Harvard Business Review, September-October, 85-92.

Yoffie, D.B., and H.V. Milner, 1989, An Alternative to Free Trade or Protectionism: Why Corporations Seek Strategic Trade Policy, California Management Review, 26, 111-131.

PART TWO

ORGANIZATIONAL ECONOMICS

KAPTER 7

CHAPTER 7

THE DYNAMICS OF POWER AND CONTROL : A CASE STUDY OF BULL

R.A.THIETART
University Paris IX-Dauphine and Essec

Abstract

Bull's history has been shaped by a series of financial restructurings during which it evolved from a tightly-held family firm to a publicly held company characterized by diverse majority-minority equity-holdings and, finally, to a publicly-held company whose capital is dominated by the French government. This paper examines the evolution of various control devices (contractual arrangements, organizational set up, competitive and financial markets forces etc.) that the successive shareholders have relied on and, in light of agency theory and transactions cost economics, explores the ramifications of these arrangements for the processes and outcomes of the dynamic interplay between power and control.

1. Introduction

The choice of agency theory and transaction cost economics--two complementary bodies of literature (Williamson, 1988)--is particularly appropriate for understanding the dynamics of the relation between power and control over time. Transactions cost economics, as it was initially formulated (Coase, 1937), is concerned with the following question: when does the firm rely on the market to carry on its economic activity and when does the firm directly "produce" what is necessary to fullfil its needs? A comparison of the costs of coordination and information, under different governance structures (market *vs* hierarchy), necessary to the functioning of the firm activities shapes the choice of the organizational structure.It is an ex-post "organizational economics" theory. It suggests the best organizational arrangement depending on the nature of the transactions necessary to the functioning of the economic activity.

I want to express my gratitude to Kathryn Gordon for her insightful help on this chapter.The chapter is based on a previous work that I co-authored with her.

Costs may be of several types: costs of obtaining information necessary for engaging in a transaction, costs of writing contracts, costs of overseeing contract compliance, costs of dispute resolution between the transacting parties, and costs of a possible maladjustment between the contractual form governing transactions and a changing economic environment. These costs are compared with other costs: costs of coordination and control of the internalized activity (Alchian and Demsetz, 1972; Williamson, 1975, 1979). Depending on the nature of the transaction, "rational" (limited rational in Simon's sense (Simon, 1946)) actors will choose the best management mode by balancing the costs of handling transactions with the market against the costs of internalizing the transactions inside the firms, while adopting an organizational design which protects against opportunistic behavior (Williamson, 1975).

In its positive presentation (Fama and Jensen, 1983a), agency theory, --a complementary body of literature, first proposed by Berle and Means (1932)--, looks at the monitoring of activities through contracts and organizations. It shows how financial and other types of contracting and organizational arrangements shape the incentive structure facing various parties to the firm. These parties include management, outside shareholders, bankers, wage earners, and parties with vertical linkages to the firm such as input suppliers and clients. Starting from the hypothesis that there is a misalignment between shareholders (principals) and managers' (agents) objectives and interests, the theory aims at determining ex-ante the best organizational, control and incentives structure to minimize the agency costs *i.e.* the costs of monitoring agents' (managers') behavior (Fama, 1980; Fama and Jensen, 1983a, 1983b; Jensen and Meckling, 1976).

Bull SA, because of the myriad financial contracting arrangements it has adopted over the years, provides an interesting case study in which the following questions can be examined:

1/ How does governance structure evolve with the nature and characteristics of ownership over time?
2/ What special contractual arrangements have the successive owners created for organizing their control of Bull? How do these compare over the 1930-1990 period?
3/ How do these arrangements alter the exercise of corporate control ?
4/ How do these arrangements affect monitoring of both corporate and executive performance at Bull?

2. Sixty years of history

The Compagnie des Machines Bull was created in 1933. Originally a Swiss company, Bull A.G., was founded in 1930 to develop, manufacture and market a new machine. A forerunner of the computer, the machine tabulated information stored on cards. It was designed in 1922 by Frederik Bull, a Norwegian engineer who patented his invention in 1922 in Oslo. The only competing product at that time was produced by IBM. However, the commercial exploitation of this new machine (by a Swiss company named HW Egli) soon ran into financial difficulties. In 1933, the Cailliès family, allied with the Michelins and an owner of paper manufacturing company, Aussedat, came to the rescue of the almost bankrupt HW Egli-Bull. They bought the company's assets and licence, thereby creating the first French firm in what was later to become the computer industry.

2.1. The entrepreneurial firm: 1933-1963

For thirty years, Bull remained the only French computer producer. Its growth and financial results were impressive. It had 50 employees and 36000 FF in capital in 1933 and 18000 employees and 140 millions FF in equity thirty years later. Shares valued at 130FF in 1958 were quoted at over 800FF in 1961. On foreign markets, Bull was also highly successful, exporting 45% of its production . The Cailliès family philosophy for running the firm was based on two tenets: 1/ absolute family control and 2/ refusal of state interference in any form. The board of directors was entirely under the control of the "family". Furthermore, family members held key executive positions.

During this period, the alignment between the interests of major shareholders and the firm objectives was nearly perfect. Also, an active stock market could have acted as a protection for the interests of Bull's small shareholders. However, unfriendly takeovers, although theoretically possible were rarely undertaken in France in this period.

By the late 1950's, Bull faced difficulties stemming from increasing competition, its inability to finance innovation (which already absorbed 13% of its sales), and lack of financial resources for the leasing of computers to its clientele (an increasingly common practice in the industry). In the early sixties, the market failure of a key product -the Gamma 60- combined with the successful introduction of the IBM 1401 undermined Bull's situation. In 1964, Bull's growing financial difficulties came under media, corporate and governmental scrutiny and soon became "l'affaire Bull".

2.2. The era of the professional managers: 1964-1975

In 1962, Jacques Cailliès, Chairman of Bull, and Georges Vieillard, his CEO started looking for financial solutions to what appeared to be an increasingly serious situation.They explored two solutions: 1/ a capital infusion from a group of European banks and 2/ a cooperative agreement in technology and marketing with General Electric (GE). None of the solutions was acceptable to the French government which had the right to veto foreign participation in Bull. A "French solution" with CGE and CSF was then attempted at the Government's request. However, since this approach did not seem promising, Jacques Cailliès and Georges Vieillard decided that the best way to counter the government project was to propose an alternative one. This new project with GE was based on a simple commercial agreement between the two firms. After active lobbying by Bull, the French government finally accepted the new agreement on April 1964. Ironically, the agreement gave GE 49% of Bull's shares, instead of the 20% initially proposed. The financial arrangement created the Companie des Machines Bull (CMB) which was a holding company, controlled by the Cailliès family. CMB had a 51% stake in the new corporation, Bull-General Electric, while GE took 49% of the new shares. Two years later, GE increased its share to 66% by means of a new equity offering in which CMB did not participate. By that time, GE had the majority of the seats at the board and took control of the company.

During the following years, GE's contribution was mainly managerial: "product planning", "product marketing", "management control and financial management". It also removed the Cailliès family members from their key executive roles and appointed professional managers to fill the positions. A new incentive system was adopted. Under this scheme, executives were to receive a yearly bonus based on Bull performance. When objectives were achieved, the bonus could account for 3 to 4 months of a manager's salary and even more if objectives were surpassed. In addition to this financial incentive, Bull executives were to be rewarded with a "super bonus" based on the parent (GE) performance.

On the strategic front, GE, which had recently entered the computer industry, rationalized its worldwide operations by sharpening the focus of its different subsidiaries. Bull concentrated on the mini and mainframe computer markets. In 1970, after several years of unsuccessfully trying to establish a foothold in the industry, Bull-GE controlled only 5% of the world market. At that point, GE decided to withdraw from the sector entirely and to sell its computer activity to Honeywell. On July 1970, the sale agreement was signed, making Honeywell the world's second largest computer manufacturer, with 9% of the world market. The new company, Honeywell-Bull (HB), also earned its first profit in 10 years. In 1972, Jean-Pierre Brulé, formerly an executive at IBM, was appointed Chairman of the Board. He was to stay at the helm of the company for almost 9 years. Prior to his appointment, Bull-GE and Honeywell Bull had always been run by American executives. Management processes similar to those used at G.E. were retained under Brulé (*i.e.* product, market, financial planning and performance based incentives). Also, the structure of the board of directors did not change. Honeywell's representatives merely took over the seats left by GE.

Chapter 7 - Dynamics of Power and Control 127

During this same period, several parallel developments were taking place. In the early sixties, President Charles de Gaulle was developing an independent "force de frappe". This policy implied a concomitant independent weapons engineering capability. As part of this weapons development program, an order was passed in 1963 with Control Data Corporation for delivery of one of its largest computers. However, the American government had a long-standing policy of preventing the export of technologies needed for nuclear weapons development. For this reason, it refused to authorize the sale. The decision infuriated de Gaulle and motivated him to reinforce French independence in the sector. Three years later, the "Plan Calcul" was launched. The CII--Compagnie Internationale pour l'Informatique -- was created.
A near-monopoly position of CII in supplying computers to the French government and an ever-increasing supply of direct and indirect subsidies did not prevent CII from losing money. In 1972, CII and the French government began to realize that they could not compete on their own in the world market. They decided to look for partnerships with European compagnies while maintaining technological leadership. As a result of opposition from several sources, no feasible solution could be found. Ambroise Roux, the Chairman and CEO of CGE, one of the major shareholders of CII, then suggested another project: a merger of CII with HB. The "Délégation à l'Informatique", a ministerial department, immediately opposed the plan and convinced the government that CII should not fall into "American hands". The "Délégation", however, was suppressed a few months later. Consequently, one of the major opponent of the merger was removed.

Meanwhile, the conflict between the two majority shareholders of CII: CGE and Thomson, which had been temporarily resolved after the so-called "Yalta of Electronics", began to heat up again. After negotiations, Thomson decided to leave the leadership of CII to CGE. As a result, CGE could again promote its project to merge CII with HB. The Delegation à l'Informatique being suppressed, the government agreed to the merger of CII and HB.

2.3. The struggle for control: 1976-1979

A new company, CII-HB, was formed in 1976, with Honeywell agreeing to reduce its stake to 47%. The remaining 53% were in the hands of Companies des Machines Bull (CMB). At that time, CMB was 60% owned by the public and the Cailliès family. The French State had 20%. The remaining 20% was in the hands of OPAGEP, which was in turn controlled 51% by CGE and 49% by several French banks. The board was composed of a more diverse set of directors: CMB had six seats of which two went to the State and two to CGE. Honeywell had four. An eleventh member was to be jointly selected by CMB and Honeywell. As one of its representatives, the government chose to name the head of DIELI (Direction des Industries de l'Electronique et de l'Informatique) of the Ministry of Industry. This gave the French government access to an important inside view of how the company was being run and allowed it to take a more detailed look at how its subsidies were being used. The appointment of this particular "fonctionnaire" to CII-HB shows that the French government was not interested in maintaining a silent partner relationship with its co-owners in Bull.

However, Honeywell retained some important control tools. It retained the power to constrain some key decisions. For instance, a majority of eight was required to make decisions regarding 1/ appointment of the chairman and CEO, 2/ allocation of resources for investments greater than 30 Million FF, 3/ capital increases, 4/ acquisitions of compagnies. This effectively gave Honeywell a controlling minority. Futhermore, several essential strategic decisions, such as product line development and technological choice, were under the supervision of a Honeywell dominated-committee. Finally, to protect its interest against a potential nationalization, a sister company was created : HN-Bull NV. This Dutch based company, in which Honeywell had a controlling interest of 53%, was made of the fourteen foreign subsidiaries of the former Honeywell-Bull. This gave a counterweight to Honeywell in any negotiation with its new partners and protected it against greater involvement of the French state in Bull (which seemed increasingly likely at that point).

In return for taking over the ailing CII, which had failed to earn a profit since its inception, Bull was promised 1.5 billion francs in subsidies (to be given until 1979) plus a preferred supplier position in the market for government orders. Under the leadership of Honeywell from 1970 to 1974, Bull earned a comfortable profit. 1975, however, saw the first losses in 5 years. CII was in poor financial health and marketing problems arose from the heterogeneity of the merged product lines. During that same year, Honeywell-Bull, had it stood alone, would have earned 96 million francs. From 1976 to 1978, the new group was profitable thanks to government subsidies (1.2 billion francs) and guaranteed orders (4 billion francs) over the period.

After the reorganization, Bull's technological dependence on Honeywell remained high. Honeywell-conceived products continued to dominate the upper and lower ends of the product line. However, several decisions were taken to free the company from the Honeywell's dominance. An agreement was reached with the French government to develop an entirely new French-designed computer, the DPS 7. Another strategic action taken by CII-HB in 1978 in order to lower its dependence of Honeywell technology, was the acquisition of R2E (forerunner of the microcomputer Micral). This acquisition was supposed to provide CII-HB with the expertise it lacked at the bottom end of its product line. JP Brulé, Chairman and CEO of CII-HB also wanted to reinforce his position in the mini-computer market. This decision ultimately became a source of conflict with CGE. In 1979, Hermès-Olympia, a subsidiary of the German company AEG, was put up for sale. Hermès-Olympia had a good European distribution network. This network was well adapted to the sale of mini-

Chapter 7 - Dynamics of Power and Control

computers. However, the move by CII-HB to acquire Hermès-Olympia was perceived as a threat to CGE's subsidiary, Transac-Alcatel, in the mini computer field. In early 1979, a Board meeting was held to decide on the interest of such an acquisition. Honeywell allied itself with CGE to reject the proposition. From then on, the conflict between JP Brulé and CGE was an open one. CGE wanted to get rid of Brulé while Brulé wanted CGE to leave CII-HB and suggested a greater dilution of its capital.

During this period, several major events took place: -the rise of a more diversified ownership, -the still important influence of Honeywell through the control of key decisions and a favorable bargaining position vis a vis other shareholders, - the tendency of the CEO to play the shareholders against each others to free Bull from their direct influence.

2.4. A new owner takes control:1979-1981

Another important parallel development in the life of CII-HB was the adoption of new industrial strategy by Saint Gobain-Pont-à-Mousson (SGPM). SGPM was one of the oldest French compagnies. It was involved in traditional and stagnating, though profitable, sectors such as glass, carton board and pipe manufacturing. SGPM decided that it needed to diversify into a growing sector. Roger Martin, Chairman of SGPM, and Roger Fauroux, second in command and the designated future Chairman, wanted to build an entirely new division devoted to the computer industry.

In 1979, CII-HB developed an ambitious five year plan for growth. This plan required new financial resources.The French state, which controlled 20% of CMB through the Ministry of Industry, was looking for a French industrial partner to finance the CII-HB plan. It turned to CGE and its Chairman, Ambroise Roux, for support. His response was lukewarm. CGE was unhappy with the CII-HB's competition with its subsidiary and also with Brulé's leadership style. The government then turned to SGPM, which was still looking for a major firm to acquire in the computer sector. Roger Fauroux welcomed the offer and in 1979, SGPM bought CGE's 20% stake in CMB. In contrast to CGE's fairly passive behavior as a minority shareholder, SGPM wanted to use CII-HB as an important staging ground for its own strategy.

In 1980, SGPM reinforced its participation in CMB. This was done through a share exchange arrangement. Under this arrangement, CII-HB issued new equity to which SGPM had the exclusive subscription rights. Payment for its new holdings was made by transfering Cadamas, a financial holding company of which SGPM was the sole owner, to CMB. Cadamas owned substantial minority interests in Olivetti, Suez (a prominent French merchant bank) and in SGPM itself. The first result of this operation was that CMB held a more diversified portfolio. After the exchange, it held

53% of CII-HB and smaller portion of Olivetti, Suez and SGPM's shares capital. The second result was that SGPM gained majority control over CMB with 53% of the stock and took immediately four seats at the CII-HB board. The public's stake was diluted to 27% from a high of 60%. The banks and the State shared equally the remaining 20%. Once again, CII-HB had a strong majority shareholder and Saint Gobain (SGPM) controlled the largest European computer company.

In order to obtain greater control of the company, SGPM appointed Alain Minc to the executive committee of CII-HB. He was nicknamed the "Fauroux submarine" and was said to be SGPM's "mole" by the executives of the very secretive and independent-minded CII-HB. At the same time, however, the incentive system was revised and the compensation package was flattened because, according to the new owner's managerial philosophy, "executives should not be spoiled".

Although Brulé and Fauroux seemed to share the same overall vision of what a French computer firm ought to be, they differed substantially in terms of how they wanted to achieve it. Roger Fauroux wanted to build St-Gobain-Informatique, a tightly-controlled division of SGPM. Jean-Pierre Brulé wanted Bull to be an independent company. Also, his decision to enter the office automation business conflicted with SGPM's interest in Olivetti, in which it controlled a 30% equity stake (10% directly and 20% through CMB). SGPM might have hoped for a cooperative relationship between CII-HB and Olivetti. However, Jean-Pierre Brulé was not open to cooperation with Olivetti's Carlo de Benedetti and even tried to develop an independent office automation strategy with the government backing. The contribution of the State to this strategy was to be 1 billion francs spread over 5 years. As a result of these differences, Saint Gobain's Roger Fauroux, wanting to cement his leadership, informed the French government of his decision to fire Brulé. He was asked to postpone his decision until the coming presidential election was over.

2.5. The French state takes power : 1981-

On May 10th, 1981, François Mitterand was elected President of France and the Socialists came to power. A few weeks later Saint Gobain was nationalized. Meanwhile, the financial situation at CII-HB deteriorated. At the July 3, 1981, board meeting, M. Brulé was fired by a nearly unanimous board decision. The two government representatives (who then represented a Socialist government) abstained. Maxime Bonnet, Bull's Marketing Vice President, was appointed as the new chairman.

With the election of Mitterand to the Elysées Palace in May 1981, negotiations with Honeywell to reduce its stake in CII-HB began almost immediately. Honeywell's

Chapter 7 - Dynamics of Power and Control

stake was reduced to 19,9% from 47% and the company was paid one billion francs as compensation. CMB took over the remaining 27.1%. The government, which by then controlled 80% of the CII-HB equity, took seven seats on the board. Honeywell lost all the privileges that it had previously enjoyed such as veto power on the appointment of the Chairman, on acquisitions and on investment projects bigger than 30 million francs. However, it did maintain two directors (down from 4) on an 11-member board. The technological accords between Honeywell and CII-HB were also renegotiated. The French government wanted to maintain Honeywell technical assistance while restoring CII-Bull's strategic autonomy.

The French government, which controlled 63% of the CMB stock, also began acquiring the CMB shares still held by the public. These shares were exchanged for convertible bonds designed so that the exchange was very attractive for the public. The conversion clauses were specified so as to discourage conversion. The convertible bond had a 500 FF face value and a yield of 12%. It could be converted against two shares and allowed the holder to subscribe retroactively to all equity issues.

In May 1982, Maxime Bonnet resigned and was replaced by Jacques Stern. Mr. Stern was chairman and founder of SESA, a French software company. He was also the chairman of CII-HB systems, a joint subsidiary of CII-HB and SESA. Four months later, Francis Lorentz, a highly-placed civil servant at the Ministry of Finance with brief management experience at Lyonnaise des Eaux, joined CII-HB as chief executive officer.

On the strategic front, CMB took control of Thomson's SEMS (91%) and CGE's Transac (100%) in deals arranged by the Socialist government as part of its nationalization of the parent compagnies in question. In 1983, the government bought SGPM's majority stake in CMB. By the end of the year, the French government controlled 97% of CMB which, in turn, controlled 80,1% of CII-HB. At that time, CII-HB changed its name to Bull. During the same year, the government provided a 1.5 billion franc capital infusion, which was the first installment of a total capital infusion of 4.5 billion extended over 3 years. The indirect effect of this capital infusion was to dilute Honeywell's participation to 9%. The government also assumed the interest payments on the convertible bonds issued during its quasi-nationalization.

This capital infusion was not extended without conditions. The chairman of the Board was now directly responsible to the French government and his appointment was made at the Council of Ministers level, chaired by the President of Republic. Also, Bull was the first "nationalized" company to sign a "contrat de plan" with the government. In this "contrat de plan", Bull committed itself to establish market leadership in computer networks, office automation, mini and mainframe computers and peripheral equipment; to reinforce its relationship with French software compagnies and to return to profitability by 1986. The "contrat de plan", which includes the company objectives and the strategy that it intends to implement, was (and still is) directly negotiated with the Ministry of Industry and the Treasury for a three year period through an iterative process. It is quite similar to the strategic plans that most large compagnies develop and leads to an allocation of financial resources from the State to the company. The major difference lies in the setting of extra market goals such as contribution to the balance of payments, regional development and employment. Once the plan has been negotiated between the firm and the Ministry of Industry and the Treasury, the Council of Ministers gives its final approval. Through this mechanism, the French state has the power to limit certain decision alternatives and impose some of its ideas.

In 1984, a new board of directors of 18 members was appointed. In this board, which was tightly controlled by the French state, six members were civil servants (one for the Ministry of Finance, one for the Treasury, two for the Ministry of Industry and two for the Ministry of Telecommunication); six members were government appointees (CEOs and experts in the computer field); and six members were elected by the employees.

Since 1981, Bull had been losing money; it experienced a catastrophic year in 1982 during which it lost about 1.3 billion francs. It lost 449 million FF in 1981, 625 million FF in 1983 and 489 million FF in 1984. In 1985, however, (one year before the planned return to profitability) Bull showed a profit of 110 million FF. This recovery was to be confirmed in 1986, when Bull earned 271 million FF on sales of 17.8 billion FF, and in 1987 and 1988, when the profits were 225 and 303 million FF respectively.

In 1986, the Socialists were defeated in the Parliamentary elections and Jacques Chirac, a neo-Gaullist and the mayor of Paris, was appointed Prime Minister. Under Chirac's sporadic free-market policy, the former Minister of Industry, Alain Madelin, lifted some of the protective barriers against foreign competitors in the computer market. Also the State said that it would cease capital infusions. However, it appeared that, because of the 1987 stock market crash, the government was once again the principal subscriber to a convertible bond offering which was originally intended for placement with the private investing public. Jacques Stern and Francis Lorentz, nevertheless, were confirmed at the head of Bull.

In 1987, Bull took control of its former ally, Honeywell Information Systems, in partnership with Nippon Electric Company (NEC). Bull took 42.5% of the equity (scheduled to increase to 65% by 1989). NEC took 15% and the remaining 42.5% was purchased by Honeywell Information Systems from its parent company.

Chapter 7 - Dynamics of Power and Control

Furthermore, Bull worked on the development of its strategic alliances by reinforcing its ties with Ridge Computer, Convergent Technologies and Trilogy, and by building a cooperative network with American, Japanese and European firms (the European network is under the aegis of the EEC's Esprit Project).

However, 1989 and 1990 proved to be difficult years for Bull, due partly to lower state intervention. In spite of the 1988 landslide reelection of François Mitterand and the return of the Socialists to power with a fragile parliamentary majority, Bull was more like other compagnies in terms of its competitive posture. In 1988 Bull lost 432 million FF and in 1990 losses amounted to a colossal 6.8 billion FF. Three new capital infusions of 2 billion FF each should take place in 1991 and during the two following years. Finally 3.7 billion FF in research funds should also be allocated to the company.

Bull, with its majority position in Bull S.A. (97.5%) and Bull HN (69.4%), and its total ownership of Bull International S.A., formerly HN Bull N.V. and in Zenith Data Systems, is now the 8th largest information systems company in the world with 34.6 billion FF in sales in 1990, down from a high 41.3 billion FF in 1989. Groupe Bull has, at least nominally, maintained its publicly traded status. However, its ownership structure is now comparable to that of a very tightly held firm which has issued a small amount of equity to outside shareholders. These outside shareholders are necessarily "silent partners" because the shares they hold, due to their small relative importance, have no potential for conferring control. In this respect, oddly enough, Bull's present organization of ownership now resembles most closely its form under the tight Cailliès-family control.

It is likely that, in the near future, the state-owner will ask Bull to revise its traditional policy of offering a full line of computers. With the recent catastrophic performance, the major shareholder will probably play a larger and more active role in Bull decision making.

3. Interpretation and conclusions: the evolution of ownership and control

Based on the insights provided by agency theory (Fama, 1980; Jensen and Meckling, 1976), the organization of ownership, along with the contractual arrangements associated with the firm's debt, are important to the extent that they define a governance structure. The governance structure defines, in particular, the nature of the relationship of the various equity-holders to the firm. The contractual relationship between shareholders and the firm gives rise to discretion-based governance structure which is frequently called corporate control. Transaction cost economics (Williamson, 1986, 1988) a complementary body of literature, views firm survival as being determined partially by a contract configuration which is transactions cost minimizing and which allows low cost adaptation to any misalignment of the configuration with a dynamically shifting environment.

Using transaction cost economics and agency theory, an interpretation of the evolution of control at Bull as a response to a change in the ownership structure can be made. Table 1 summarizes the evolution of Bull over five phases. During the first years of its existence (1933-1963), Bull was family-controlled. The family, with a 30% minority stake, was able to control the company because ownership of the remaining 70% was very disperse. In this period, although Bull was a publicly traded company, it was run like a closely-held company. Family interests were identified with company interests. Members of the family held key executive positions and exercised full control over every decision. The public acted more like a sleeping partner and never intervened in Bull management. From a theoretical perspective, capital markets could have been used as safeguard against mismanagement by the family. However, during the period under study, it is likely that transaction costs associated with a takeover aimed at sanctioning and ousting the management were higher than they are today. First, key financial instruments were missing. Second, takeover techniques were less developed than they are now. Third, reliance on such a drastic solution was perceived as an unfair practice in the French environment. Consequently, capital market mechanisms for sanctioning Bull's management through hostile takeover was practically impossible. On the other hand, because Cailliès family members were both major shareholders and top executives at Bull, price movements in capital market provided effective sanctions against perceived mismanagement. However, up to the Gamma 60 commercial failure, the capital market prices always implied a positive evaluation of Bull's management team. This probably reinforced the Cailliès family strategic position at the helm of the company. The product market played an important role in the indirect control of the managerial performance at Bull. The stiff product market competition that Bull had to face, eventually led to the departure of the family members from the key executive positions.

During the second phase (1964-1975), when GE and later Honeywell were in control, several important control mechanisms were introduced. First, GE implemented new management techniques aimed at better monitoring of marketing and financial decisions. It also reinforced management control in order to provide the different levels of management with improved means for evaluating performance. Second, an incentive system was developed. This system sought to keep managers' interests in line with those of shareholders. The implementation of such a system was necessary since professional managers took the positions formerly held by the Cailliès family members. Under GE, then Honeywell, capital market sanctions could only play a subsidiary role. The only way to change the Bull management team would had been to take over the parents. However, labor and product markets had a major influence.

Years	1933-1963 The entrepreneurial firm	1964-1975 The era of professional managers
Main event	The Cailliès family takes over	GE, then Honeywell (HN), takes over
Name of the company	Compagnie des Machines Bull	Bull-GE, then Honeywell-Bull
Shareholder structure	100% in the hands of the Cailliès family; later reduced to minority holding	66% in the hands of GE, then Honeywell 34% in the hands of CMB
External mechanisms for control		
1. Capital market	Originally, no; later, yes	Yes, as a control device. GE is listed on the NYSE. CMB is listed in Paris
2. Product market	Some (mostly from IBM)	Yes, active
3. Labor market	Family members hold key management position	Yes, active. Managers are professionals
4. Third parties	Some	Yes, active
Internal mechanisms for control		
1. Board of directors	Fully controlled by the Cailliès family	GE (then Honeywell) has the majority of the seats
2. Literal control (*)	Complete	Some (management control, product planning, financial planning, etc.)
3. Power to constrain decisions (*)	Complete	Some, by the Board
4. Incentive scheme	None. However, the majority shareholder is the manager	Bull-yearly bonus+GE performance based multi-year bonus

Table 1. The evolution of power and control at Bull

Years	1976-1978 The struggle for control	1979-1981 A new owner takes control
Main event	CII merges with Honeywell-Bull	Saint-Gobain controls CII-HB
Name of the company	CII-HB	CII-HB
Shareholder structure	53% in the hands of CMB (CMB has no dominant shareholder) 47% in the hands of HIS	53% in the hands of CMB (CMB is 53% controlled by Saint-Gobain) 47% in the hands of HIS
External mechanisms for control		
1. Capital market	Yes, through CMB, of which 60% of equity is dispersed in the public	Yes, but more as a signalling device rather than as a takeover tool
2. Product market	Some (CII-HB has a preferred order status with the French state)	Some (CII-HB has a preferred order status with the French state)
3. Labor market	Professionals run the company, but less active	Professionals run the company, but less active
4. Third parties	Yes, active. Scrutiny of different industry experts	Yes, active. Scrutiny of different industry experts
Internal mechanisms for control		
1. Board of directors	Conflicting opinions between members	Saint-Gobain and HIS share power on the Board
2. Literal control (*)	Product line and technological choices under the supervision of an HIS-dominated committee	SGPM has a representative in the executive committee. HIS controls product line and technological choice
3. Power to constrain decisions (*)	HIS has a controlling minority to make decisions regarding major issues	Yes, Saint-Gobain. But HIS has a controlling minority to make decisions
4. Incentive scheme	Performance based bonus	Reduced

Table 1 (cont.). The evolution of power and control at Bull

Chapter 7 - Dynamics of Power and Control

Years	1982- The French state as a majority shareholder
Main event	The French government takes control
Name of the company	Bull
Shareholder structure	97.5% in the hands of the French state
External mechanisms for control	
1. Capital market	None
2. Product market	Yes, active
3. Labor market	Yes, but less active
4. Third parties	Yes, but less active than in earlier periods
Internal mechanisms for control	
1. Board of directors	12 French state appointees in an 18 member board: - 6 French Ministries representatives (1 Treasury, 1 Budget, 2 Industry, 2 Telecommunication),- 6 industry "experts",- (+ 6 employee representatives)
2. Literal control (*)	Some, through the "Contrat de plan" (strategic choices and global resource allocation)
3. Power to constrain decisions (*)	Yes
4. Incentive scheme	Reduced

Table 1 (cont.). The evolution of power and control at Bull

(*) Herman's terminology is used to define "literal control" and "power to constrain". "Literal control" is the power to make key decisions; "power to constrain" is the power to limit certain decision choices (Herman, 1981).

The performance of professional managers was monitored by well informed industry experts. Inability to compete in the product market led to GE's withdrawal from the computer industry and, subsequently, induced a change in Bull management. Finally, third parties, such as industry experts, financial analysts and stokbrokers were very active during this period. Their reports and analysis were a complementary source of information that shareholders could use in their monitoring of the management performance.

The 1976-1979 period witnessed the merger between CII and Honeywell-Bull. It is a troubled period which exemplifies a breakdown of corporate control. The market for products and services was no longer a strong external force pushing Bull to perform according to the best interests of the shareholders. The "preferred supplier" status, conferred by the French government, did not allow product market sanctions to work properly. The labor market had also narrowed after the merger of the only two French computer manufacturing compagnies. The board was divided and it was easy for management to play shareholders against each other. The only owner which kept a reasonable amount of control was Honeywell. First, Honeywell dominated a committee which gave it control over technological and product development decisions. Second, Honeywell kept a minority in the board of directors which conferred veto power over decisions such as: important resource allocation, equity increases, acquisitions, appointment of the CEOs and chairman. Third, Honeywell had a well entrenched bargaining position with its majority control of Bull's foreign subsidiaries. Clearly, this situation could not last long. A new and powerful shareholder took over: St.Gobain (SGPM).

St.Gobain's rule lasted two years (1979-1981). New control devices were implemented. First, with the support of the French State representatives, St.Gobain took *de facto* control of the board of directors. Second, St.Gobain appointed one of its representatives to Bull's executive committee. Since it exercised greater direct control over strategic decisions, St.Gobain abandoned the incentive system aimed at aligning executives' interests with those of shareholders'. St.Gobain believed in more direct intervention in Bull's affairs. One consequence of this direct involvement was the open conflict between Fauroux of St.Gobain and Brulé of Bull. In a transaction economics framework, the choice of a more direct involvement also means that St.Gobain did not believe that market pressures were efficient enough to control Bull's economic activity. This favorable attitude toward hierarchy is typical of French industrialists and, in general, of the French environment. This can be contrasted with the managerial choices of the former shareholders who were both American and who were more open to the market as a means of control. In the same vein, St.Gobain strategy was to build St.Gobain Computer System which was to have become an integrated division of the company

Chapter 7 - Dynamics of Power and Control

Finally, the last phase (1982-present) witnessed the arrival "en force" of the French State in Bull capital. In principal the contractual rights and obligations, conferred by equity participation in the firm have been operative in Bull much as they would have been in any other publicly-quoted company. However, the "contrat de plan" established an extra-market contractual relationship between Bull and the Ministries of Industry and Finance which are in large part a substitute legal arrangement for the discretionary rights normally conferred on its shareholders. Here, the term "extra market contractual relationship" is defined as one in which the rights and obligations conferred by the arrangement cannot be transferred by means of a capital market transaction. The main purposes of this contract seem to be to impose extra market goals such as contributions to balance of payments surpluses and employment creation. As we have already seen in Bull's history, the exercise of this meta-control by the French state has been an important element in Bull's decision making process even before the government held any formal equity stake in the company. This is illustrated by the need for government authorization for a reorganization of Egli-Bull by the Cailliès family and for GE's sale to Honeywell. In some respects, then, the "contrat de plan" is a formalization of an implicit contractual relationship which has always existed between Bull and the State, the legal basis of which was primarily government control over foreign acquisition of French-owned assets.

What are the implications of these parallel contractual arrangments and of the total dominance of Bull equity by the French state for how corporate control is exercised in Bull? One of the most obvious results of the way the French government has chosen to structure its ownership claims on Bull is that a variety of market mechanisms for monitoring managerial performance has been suppressed. For example, Bull's management has been insulated from the threat of hostile takeover. The existence of such mechanisms establishes an incentive to monitor management's performance to all capital market participants wielding the financial resources needed to engage in such transactions. It should be pointed out that the hostile takeover mechanism, in spite of a recent surge of activity, is used only infrequently in France as well as in other continental, bank-dominated financial systems. Thus, in France, the mechanism figures less importantly as a means of monitoring management performance than it currently does in capital market dominated systems such as the the United States and the United Kingdom.

Nevertheless, the absence of an active market in Bull shares has led to the suppression of other capital market-induced monitoring mechanisms. For example, actively traded compagnies are normally subject to intense external reviews performed by securities analysts, information vendors and institutional investors. For Bull, this external scrutiny is minimal due to lack of public interest in Bull's shares. As we have seen the public holds only about 3 percent of Bull shares, a state of affairs which leads to a very illiquid market. In 1984, for example, average daily trading volume was a miniscule 1592 shares out of a total number of outstanding shares of nearly 100000000. Even though Bull nominally maintained its publicly traded status, its ownership structure is that of a tightly held company which has issued a small number of shares to various "silent partners". Thus, interest and investment in such external monitoring is small.

The government's contractual arrangements for its controlling interest in Bull have also attenuated and, in some respects, eliminated the role played by another market-induced institution: the board of directors (BD). The BD's first responsibility is to look after and coordinate the interests of the shareholders. Since the French state is by far the dominant shareholder, it is appropriate that it should suppress or alter the BD's role as it sees fit. Since the quasi-nationalization, the members of Bull's BD have consisted of roughly one third civil servants (fonctionnaires), one third Bull labor representatives and one third members appointed because of their special competence (this last category includes CEOs from other compagnies, outside computer and finance experts; of course none of these directors holds a significant stake in Bull). The State control of the BD is total (as is normal for such a tightly held company). This contrasts with the previous situation in which dominant shareholders (GE, Honeywell, and SGPM) shared the directors' table with diverse minority shareholders controlling a considerable stake in the company (Suez, CGE, at one point SGPM which, as we have seen, created an implicit alliance with Olivetti, the French state before 1981, Honeywell and so on). As we have seen, the Board contained members with important vested interests in Bull's peformance and strategic decisions. The BD, even with the fairly tightly-held control that characterized Bull in it pre-"nationalization" days, provided a forum in which conflicting views on industrial strategy could be and were aired and resolved between highly-informed, highly-motivated shareholders. Thus, a subsidiary function of the BD and, by implication, of diversifying the range of important equity holders seems to have been suppressed.

Some people will argue that the French government has created a stable environment for strategic decision making by establishing its position as the totally dominant shareholder. Indeed, disagreement and bickering between majority and minority shareholders and between the shareholders and Bull's top management (take, for example, the disagreements between Brulé and Fauroux over cooperation with Olivetti or between CGE and Brulé over the proposed Hermes-Olympia acquisition or between CGE and the French state on the development plan for CII-HB) did characterize the pre-"nationalization" period and have now been eliminated. Although conflicts of opinion concerning industrial strategy certainly occur within the Ministry of Industry, within Bull itself, and between the Ministry and Bull, the resolution of these conflicts now takes place through mechanisms which are internal to those organizations. The right to decide who has a voice in the debate and who does not is firmly in the hands of the French government. In contrast to the previous

Chapter 7 - Dynamics of Power and Control 141

situation, where persons or compagnies with sufficient funds to buy a sizeable block of shares could and occasionally did purchase the right to participate in Bull's strategic debate (as we have seen, SGPM, CGE and the French government itself all did this through the purchase of what were originally minority holdings), the debate is now a closed loop between the Ministry and Bull and between any outsiders they choose to let participate.

Capital market mechanisms for overseeing executive performance and decisions have been replaced by a "contrat de plan". This plan is a control and monitoring mechanism which is specific to French nationalized compagnies. The "contrat de plan" and Bull's state-dominated BD mean that, while goal orientation may change as circumstances change, the parties to the strategic identification do not change. This unchanging participation contrasts with recent capital market developments. The present system seems to have established a closed decision-making loop between the Ministry of Industry and Bull. The airing of conflicts of opinion between different entities with radically different relationships to Bull (majority shareholder, minority shareholder, security analyst and potential raider and so on) has been suppressed. Time will tell whether this closed loop system lives up to the expectations of the State that put it into place.

Other market mechanisms seem to operate in Bull much as they would in any other firm. Now that favorable treatment of Bull in certain parts of the domestic market has been eliminated, product market competition is as intense for Bull as for its competitors. Indeed, the French government appears to have deliberately increased product market pressure at the same time it was reducing capital-market pressure. Likewise, external labor market discipline, which subjects Bull's management to performance-based pressure coming from external assessments of management's opportunity value, appears to be present. The presence of this discipline is apparent because Bull's top executives (with the exception of Lorentz) have been hired from the executive labor market pool which is standard for this sector (internally or from competing computer firms). On the whole, Bull's top executives do not appear to be closet "fonctionnaires" (who would have the option of returning to a bureaucratic career path if things do not work out at Bull). Thus, the loss in the opportunity value of their human capital if they are perceived as being incompetent or lazy is probably the same as in other firms.

The case study of Bull over a sixty years period, highlights the shift of control with the change in the power structure. It is a further test of the agency theory in its positive presentation. It shows how control adapts over time to an evolving ownership structure. At each phase: entrepreneurial (1933-1963), professional (1964-1975), struggle for control (1976-1978), new owner control (1979-1981), state owned (1982-), new control devices had been implemented as a response to the new ownership structure. The observed evolution of control at Bull gives additional support to agency theory. Transaction costs economics, also, proved to be an effective theoretical complement to explain the dynamic interplay between power and control.

References

Alchian A., and H. Demsetz, 1972, Production, Information Costs and Economic Organization, American Economic Review, 62, 777-795.

Berle A.A. and G.C. Means, 1932, The Modern Corporation and Private Property, (New York, Mac Millan).

Coase R.H., 1937, The Nature of the Firm, Economica, 4, 386-405.

Fama E.F., 1980, Agency Problems and the Theory of the Firm, Journal of Political Economy, 88: 2, 288-307.

Fama E.F., and M.C. Jensen, 1983a, Separation of Ownership and Control, Journal of Law and Economics, XXVI, 301-325.

Fama E.F., and M.C. Jensen, 1983b, Agency Problems and Residual Claims, Journal of Law and Economics, XXVI, 327-349.

Herman E.S., 1981, Corporate Control, Corporate Power, (Cambridge, Cambridge University Press).

Jensen M.C. and W.H. Meckling, 1976, Theory of the Firm: Managerial Behavior, Agency Costs and Ownership Structure, Journal of Financial Economics, 3:4, 305-360.

Simon H.A., 1946, Administrative Behavior, (New York, Free Press).

Williamson O.E., 1975, Markets and Hierarchies: Analysis and Antitrust Implications, (New York, Free Press).

Williamson O.E., 1979, Transaction-Cost Economics: the Governance of Contractual Relations, Journal of Law and Economics, XXII, 233-261.

Williamson O.E., 1986, Economic Organizations, (Sussex, Wheat Teaf Book Ltd.).

Williamson O.E., 1988, Corporate Finance and Corporate Governance, Journal of Finance, XLIII:3, 567-591.

MICROECONOMIC CONTRIBUTIONS TO STRATEGIC MANAGEMENT
J. Thépot and R.-A. Thiétart
© 1991 Elsevier Science Publishers B.V. All rights reserved.

CHAPTER 8

VERTICAL INTEGRATION:
Why transaction cost and resource dependence explanations can't be easily separated

G. A. KRICKX
University of Pennsylvania

Abstract

Transaction cost and resource dependence theory both are useful to explain vertical integration. However, these theories may be related. The goal of this chapter is to analyze how these theories are related. Possible factors that affect the relation between transaction cost theory and resource dependence are: the reliance by both theories on uncertainty, the contemporaneous theoretical linkage between the concepts resource dependence and asset specificity, the stage of maturity of the industry, and finally, the possible competitive and intertemporal linkages between asset specificity and resource dependence.

1. Introduction

One key research question for strategy is to identify the factors that cause firms to vertically integrate. In strategy and organization theory, two competing explanations

---

The comments of Ned Bowman, Jean-François Hennart, Gordon Walker and an anonymous reviewer are greatly acknowledged as are the contributions by the participants of the Workshop on Economics/Strategy Interfaces, held at EIASM, Brussels, November 1989 and the participants of the Strategy Seminar at the Wharton School, January 1991. The research on which this paper was based was sponsored by the Andrew Mellon Foundation and the Office of Naval Research (Bill Ouchi, Principal Investigator; Jay Barney Investigator), while the author was sponsored by a grant from the "Interuniversitair College voor Managementwetenschappen" in Brussels, Belgium.

exist. Both are based on paradigms from economics. Resource dependence theory (RDT) draws on the insights from the Structure-Conduct-Performance (SCP) paradigm. Formulated by organization theorists (Pfeffer and Salancik, 1978; Pfeffer, 1978) it has developed along different lines and currently is distinct from the SCP paradigm. Resource procurement (supply relations) is one of three key research areas. The second paradigm, transaction cost theory (TCT), is based on the contribution of economists (Williamson, 1989, 1985, 1975) and organizational theorists (Barney and Ouchi, 1986).

Little evidence exists that tests the relative predictive abilities of asset specificity, resource dependence and uncertainty to explain vertical integration. Marketing researchers have long been concerned with the problem of dependence for channels of distribution. Recently, following Anderson's (1982) example, transaction cost propositions have also been considered. Some recent articles investigate TCT and RDT propositions.

Spekman and Strauss (1986), for a sample of recurrent transactions tested the impact of uncertainty, asset specificity and resource dependence (importance of purchase) on perceived strategic vulnerability. This last variable influenced anticipated transaction costs, which in turn affected concern with long term planning and coordination. With "strategic vulnerability" and "concern with long term planning" as dependent variables, asset specificity, uncertainty and one of two measures of resource dependence were consistently significant in regression equations. Explained variance in each case was moderate. No further evidence on the relation between asset specificity and resource dependence was presented. Implicit in the design and empirical test of this study, resource dependence and asset specificity were considered independent and not correlated. Since the ordinary least square regression results did not discuss or correct for multicollinearity or correlation, resource dependence and asset specificity were considered independent variables.

This result differs from my own findings. My research was based on a detailed examination of the vertical governance patterns used by major computer mainframe makers from 1950 to 1970. Vertical integration patterns were examined for computer logic and memory components. A total of 47 vertical governance events were identified (Krickx, 1990a, 1990b). For these events I found a significant overlap between the ability of TCT and RDT to explain the observed patterns of exchange. In fact, 25 of the 47 events (53%) were consistent with both theories. Only eight events fit one theory but not the other (three events favored TCT, five favored RDT). Fourteen patterns fit neither theory. This result suggested a significant overlap between RDT and TCT.

A third finding suggests that the linkage between TCT and RDT may be more complex. Heide and John (1988) found that when vertical integration is precluded, firms try to reduce their dependence by developing better relations with *customers*, to offset the effect of troublesome specific assets in the relation with *suppliers*. This means that asset specificity in some vertical relations can affect resource dependence and governance of other vertical relations.

How can these different research findings be reconciled? To answer this question, the nature of the relationship between RDT and TCT, and their ability to explain vertical integration should be investigated. Three plausible explanations for the relation between TCT and RDT are: 1) these theories are different and explain a different set of vertical governance events (TCT and RDT explain different events). Their relation reported by some researchers (Krickx, 1990a, 1990b) is spurious; 2) both theories provide partial explanations of complicated events, which are undertaken to fulfill multiple objectives (TCT and RDT explain different aspects of the same events). These theories are related and detailed examinations of the context surrounding specific governance problems allow to derive insight about the nature of their relation (for example, Heide and John, 1988); 3) TCT and RDT explanations may not be all that different. At present, empirical findings do not conclusively support one of these explanations.

The goal of this paper is to analyze if and how TCT and RDT are related. I briefly describe the current formulations of TCT and RDT. Next, I discuss the theoretical overlap between these theories. It is caused by the fact that TCT and RDT both share uncertainty as one key variable and that asset specificity and resource dependence are theoretically and empirically related. Next, the role of uncertainty, asset specificity and resource dependence are investigated in a dynamic perspective to demonstrate further ways in which TCT and RDT can be related. Finally, I review how TCT and RDT are related and suggest some directions for further research.

2. Transaction cost and resource dependence theory: basics

Vertical integration is the paradigm problem for TCT and is one of the three important research areas of RDT. Vertical integration is defined as ownership of all the assets required for the manufacturing of a component. Vertical integration is the governance pattern at one end of the continuum, while market exchange at the other extreme, involves supply relations between independent suppliers and buyers[1]. The theoretical overlap between the key concepts of transaction cost theory and resource dependence will be investigated.

2.1. Transaction Cost Analysis

Williamson's "Markets and Hierarchies" (1975) introduced the first modern and comprehensive formulation of the transaction cost framework. According to Williamson, contractual governance is difficult when the following pairs of conditions prevail: 1) Uncertainty/Complexity and Bounded Rationality; and 2) Opportunism and Small Numbers Bargaining (Williamson, 1975). Small Numbers of traders and uncertainty are environmental conditions, while opportunism and bounded rationality involve assumptions about decision makers (human factors).

Klein, Crawford and Alchian (1978) introduced the notion of asset specificity, defined as the difference between the value of an asset in its present use and the value of that asset in its second best use (Klein et al., 1978). Williamson adopted asset specificity and made it the key variable that explains the choice of governance patterns. In terms of Williamson's earlier work, high levels of specific assets transform large numbers of traders before contracts are executed (competitive markets) into post-contractual

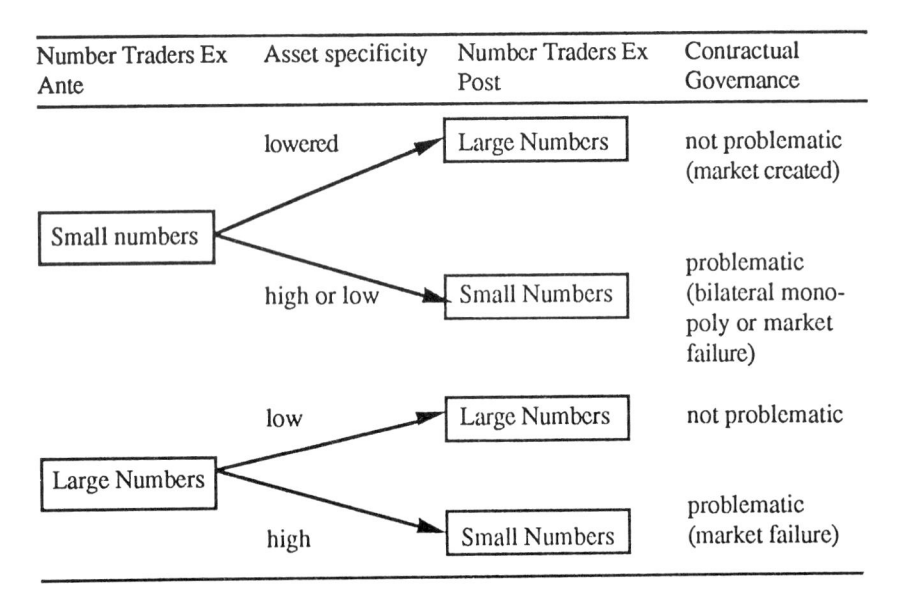

Number Traders Ex Ante	Asset specificity	Number Traders Ex Post	Contractual Governance
Small numbers	lowered	Large Numbers	not problematic (market created)
Small numbers	high or low	Small Numbers	problematic (bilateral monopoly or market failure)
Large Numbers	low	Large Numbers	not problematic
Large Numbers	high	Small Numbers	problematic (market failure)

Figure 1
Asset specificity and number of traders

Chapter 8 - Vertical Integration

small numbers conditions. Asset specificity changes competitive contractual relations into relations that resemble bilateral monopoly. Figure 1 shows how asset specificity affects contractual relations.

Williamson (1989,1985,1983,1981,1979) has proposed that governance patterns depend on: 1) asset specificity, 2) frequency and 3) uncertainty. The simplified prediction is that increased integration is expected for recurrent transactions when increased asset specificity occurs along with increased uncertainty. This hypothesis only expects an increase in the occurrence of vertical integration. As Williamson (1979) points out, firms have choices even when high levels of uncertainty and asset specificity are present. Firms can use market contracting and settle for goods with less specific requirements (more standardized) or they can surround the transaction with more elaborate governance apparatus (Williamson, 1979), which in the extreme can lead to internal organization.

Resource dependence and transaction cost theory both rely on uncertainty. The treatment of uncertainty is different for these two theories. The current formulation of TCT does not acknowledge that uncertainty may have a separate effect on the degree of vertical integration, independent of asset specificity. Elsewhere I have argued that this position is inconsistent with the available evidence (Krickx, 1990c). Resource dependence theory does acknowledge this independent effect of uncertainty (Galaskiewicz, 1985). However, uncertainty is defined in a similar way by both theories. For recurrent transactions, only asset specificity separates TCT from RDT.

Over time, the concept of asset specificity was expanded. Early on, human and physical capital were identified as possible sources of transaction-specific assets (Williamson,1979). Next, site specificity (Williamson, 1981), specificity due to dedicated assets (Williamson, 1985), and brand name capital were recognized (Williamson 1988, 1989). These five types of specific assets will be discussed.

Human asset specificity arises from learning by doing (Williamson, 1981, 1989). This learning by doing can be for an individual or for a team. If it is substantive, employment contracts are favored over autonomous contracting (Williamson, 1985). If firms are unique as strategy researchers hold, then human asset specificity is always present to some extent.

Physical asset specificity occurs when the production of the goods to be exchanged requires customized assets. A typical example is specialized dies (Williamson, 1989, 1985). As Williamson explains (1985), when the customer owns the dies, market contracting may be preserved. Lock-in is avoided because the owner can reclaim the specialized asset and reopen market bidding. In one example, IBM paid for a specialized die to make custom sizes of ferrite cores (a memory component). IBM allowed General Ceramics to keep the die and to sell the cores in question to other companies. General Ceramics had been unwilling to make these cores expressly for IBM (Krickx, 1988). This example shows that additional payments or incentives may be required to preserve market contracting in the presence of specific physical assets.

Site specificity has been defined on different occasions. In Williamson (1989), the source of site specificity was the cheek-by-jowl location of successive stations in a chain of production. Williamson (1989, 1981) emphasized the transportation and inventory expenses. This argument is related to Thompson's concept of core technology (Thompson, 1967; Williamson, 1981). However, elsewhere (Williamson, 1985) the asset immobility aspects of site specificity (setup and relocation costs) were emphasized.

One example is drawn from the computer industry. All major mainframe makers assembled their own computers in-house from 1955 to 1970. There was a distinction in the degree to which subassemblies were done internally. Buying complete computers for resale to customers by major mainframe makers only happened on two occasions (both involving National Cash Register). This company obtained one computer model each from General Electric and from Control Data Corp. This pervasive pattern of internal assembly for mainframes was not replicated for terminals and peripherals. For these, vertical integration and a variety of contractual relations coexisted for much of the period until 1970. Peripherals and terminals were self-contained devices, frequently able to directly plug into the controllers that manage input and output by the computer. Assembly of peripherals could take place almost independently of mainframes, especially when interfaces became standardized. The assembly of computers required many parts that had to be physically connected to other parts and other subassemblies. Poor connections, poor assembly or faulty components in any subassembly could affect performance of the entire system. In order to assemble components into subassemblies or subassemblies into computers, external suppliers would virtually have to work side-by-side with employees of the computer company. Each stage separately (subassembly and final assembly) could be performed by different firms. Although most firms relied on market supplied subassemblies to some extent, all computer firms chose to perform final assembly in-house.

"Dedicated assets refer to discrete additions to existing plant that would not be made but for the prospects of selling significant product to a particular buyer on a long term basis" (Williamson, 1988). The assets in question are general-purpose. Williamson points out that despite trading hazards, common ownership (vertical integration) is rarely adopted (Williamson, 1985). Firms occasionally expand the contractual relation to effect symmetrical exposure (Williamson, 1985). This is equivalent to firms putting up a bond or creating conditions under which both firms are mutually dependent. Agreements to make one firm a dominant supplier for a specific component may facilitate supply by companies which are asked to invest in dedicated assets. In December 1957, for example, IBM agreed to buy the majority of its transistors from Texas Instruments, and later devised numerous incentives to lower production and governance costs for Texas Instruments.

Brand name capital consists of an investment in reputation. If it is easily dissipated, additional safeguards are required (Williamson, 1988). This latest type of asset specificity is not as fully developed. Brand name capital has low salvage value and can be viewed as a bond put up by firms to signal value to customers (Klein and Leffler, 1981). Brand name capital sends a signal ex ante of the willingness by the supplier to engage in fair trade.

These extensions have given the concept of asset specificity more empirical salience. Williamson (1988) acknowledges that other types of asset specificity may still be discovered. No empirical work has extensively tested the incidence and significance of these different types of asset specificity.

2.2. Resource Dependence Perspective

The resource dependence perspective provides a general theory of interorganizational relations, which can take place in three relevant areas: resource procurement and allocation, political advocacy, and organizational legitimation (Galaskiewicz, 1985). This paper limits itself to the area of resource procurement and allocation. To survive firms compete for resources (Hannan and Freeman, 1977; Pfeffer, 1978). Resources are broadly defined as generalized means or facilities that are potentially controllable by social organizations and that are potentially usable in relationships between the organization and its environment (Yuchtman and Seashore, 1967). Changes in vertical governance are changes in how resources are managed.

The role of uncertainty in RDT is somewhat ambiguous. Important antecedents (Simon, 1957; March and Simon, 1958; Thompson, 1967) all acknowledge the important role of uncertainty for organizations. The formal treatment of uncertainty in the classical statements of RDT (Pfeffer, 1978; Pfeffer and Salancik, 1978) is not consistent. Pfeffer (1978) does not consider uncertainty to be a problem for organizations without the presence of interdependence. This implies a significant interaction effect between uncertainty and resource dependence. Likewise, Pfeffer and Salancik (1978) view uncertainty as problematic only when it involves interactions with other environmental elements. However, they also consider that interdependence (resource dependence) positively influences uncertainty, both directly and indirectly, via the effect of interdependence on conflict, which itself positively affects uncertainty (Pfeffer and Salancik, 1978). On the other hand, Galaskiewicz (1985) argued that the relation between uncertainty and interorganizational relations was characterized by an independent effect as well as an interactive effect.

No conclusive evidence exists about the relation between uncertainty, resource dependence and vertical integration. Uncertainty in conjunction with resource dependence may be significant in explaining interorganizational relations. Uncertainty may be caused by resource dependence. On the other hand, as Galaskiewicz (1985) argues, uncertainty by itself may explain some interorganizational relations. Empirical studies have investigated few aspects of uncertainty. Turbulence and complexity are the aspects of uncertainty measured most (Galaskiewicz, 1985). Uncertainty is typically not separated into different types. Subjective and objective measures of uncertainty have been used (Galaskiewicz, 1985).

By definition, resource dependence is problematic or high: 1) because firms rely on others for components which are important. These components are important, either because they are critical for the customer in question (1a) or because the goods make up a large share of inputs or outputs (1b); 2) because other firms have discretion over needed resources; or 3) because few sources of supply exist for required inputs or outputs.

Resource importance may be caused by the relative magnitude of resource exchange and by the criticality of the input or output for the organization (Pfeffer and Salancik, 1978). Critical resources affect the governance choices which firms make. For example, in the computer industry, Sperry Rand and Control Data Corp. both manufactured transistors. Meeting promised performance specifications for state of the art computers was critically dependent on high speed transistors. When internal development efforts failed, both firms turned to market contracting to obtain devices that allowed the promised performance improvements and delivery times (Krickx, 1988).

An example of the impact of magnitude on governance is IBM's vertical integration in basic components in 1961, although other considerations played a role too (Krickx, 1988). IBM started to manufacture basic components for integrated circuits. These integrated circuits were critical for the success of IBM's third generation computers. The sheer size of IBM's requirements was staggering. From 1964 to 1966, IBM made almost twice as many integrated circuits as all other manufacturers in the world combined. During the same period IBM's learning curve had been 71% (IBM Journal of Research and Development, 9/1981). Under those conditions

Chapter 8 - Vertical Integration

contractual relations would have been very difficult. Economies would have been lost if IBM's requirements were split among many suppliers (to reduce IBM's dependence and to keep dependence of suppliers on IBM limited). On the other hand, supply from a few concentrated suppliers would have required these firms to invest in a significant expansion of plant to accommodate IBM's volume. They would have been strategically vulnerable to IBM's ability to shift its requirements.

Discretion over allocation and use of a resource is one possible cause of resource dependence (Pfeffer and Salancik, 1978). Firms may own the resource, may control access to it or may be able to regulate its use. Ownership is not necessary to exert discretion. During the 1960s, IBM's peripheral business was attacked by independent peripheral suppliers which offered cheaper equipment that represented a plug-compatible replacement for IBM's devices. IBM set the standard for mainframe systems (the computer and how the computer interfaces with terminals and peripherals). IBM responded to the competitive advances of peripheral makers by changing computer-peripheral interfaces and by moving critical circuitry to the computer where competition was less intense and less based on price. IBM's standard setting ability in mainframe systems allowed it to significantly affect the rules of competition for some of the peripheral segments in which it operated.

Dependence caused by few available suppliers implies that supply markets are concentrated. The degree of dependence for a downstream firm also depends on a firm's position in its own market, on the concentration of that market and on the importance of the downstream firm for a given supplier. Concentrated suppliers may face customers with significant countervailing power.

Consistent with recent treatments of RDT (Galaskiewicz, 1985; Koberg and Ungson, 1987), interorganizational relations which firms undertake depend on uncertainty, resource dependence and the interaction effect between these two variables. When dependence is high, firms can reduce their dependence on others or make other firms more dependent on them (Hannan and Freeman, 1977; Thompson, 1967), essentially by managing their vertical exchange relations differently.

The simplified central hypothesis based on RDT is: Vertical integration is expected to a greater extent when uncertainty and resource dependence both are high. Increased integration allows firms to better control critical resources (Pfeffer and Salancik, 1978). Hence, vertical integration can reduce dependence, because it increases discretion over resources and avoids hold-up problems when few suppliers exist. Market exchange is more likely when both uncertainty and resource dependence are low.

3. Asset specificity and resource dependence: theoretical overlap

In order to establish the relation between asset specificity and resource dependence, I investigate to what extent these concepts overlap. The elements of asset specificity are mapped onto resource dependence (and vice versa). The goal is to investigate whether one of these concepts is a subset of the other. The discussion is framed for a company which buys goods and services from an upstream supplier. The argument is symmetrical for forward integration, except when noted. The degree to which asset specificity and resource dependence overlap is summarized by the matrix in Figure 2. The discussion on which this matrix is based, follows.

Resource Dependence Asset specificity	1a. Critical component	1b. Large % of input	2. Discretion over ressources	3. Fewness of sources
a. Human asset specificity	Some / Yes	Yes	Some / Yes	Yes
b. Physical asset specificity	Yes		Yes	Yes
c. Site specificity		Yes	Yes	Some
d. Dedicated assets		Some / Yes		Yes
e. Brand name capital			Some / Some	

Figure 2

Relationship between asset specificity and resource dependence

Notes: Entries above the diagonal describe how resource dependence affects asset specificity. Entries below the diagonal describe how asset specificity affects resource dependence. "Yes" implies that the overlap is essentially complete for the relation described. "Some" implies that there is some overlap which may not be complete. For unshaded cells or relations in shaded cells that are not labeled, the overlap is minimal or not existant.

Human asset specificity (learning by doing for an individual or for a team) implies resource dependence. When employees have company-specific knowledge or have achieved economies in the operation of their jobs, they are a less costly input compared to a work force that consists of independent short term contractors. These advantages are more important when the company-specific (or job-specific) learning is significant, and when learning benefits are more long term. Human specific assets can create a dependence because labor represents a critical component (which it does in most companies) (1a), because it represents a large portion of inputs (for example, for service organizations) (1b) and/or it entails a fewness of sources condition (3) (for example, independent contractors are a poor substitute for a trained labor force). These arguments hold strongly for the work force as a whole, but are less robust for the single individual[2]. For a group or individual, significant human asset specificity implies discretion over resources (2) as well.

The presence of physical asset specificity (b) always implies the existence of resource dependence. When suppliers own specialized dies and other assets, it means that the required inputs are somewhat unique or critical (1a), that suppliers have discretion over resources (2) and/or that few acceptable sources of supply may exist (3). Once IBM paid for a die to make ferrite cores and gave the die to General Ceramics, IBM was locked into a supply relation with this company, unless IBM purchased a new die.

Site specificity (c) raises resource dependence as well. The cheek-by-jowl production implied by Thompson's concept of core technology means that transportation and storage costs would be higher with increased distance. The logistics of assuring steady supply, the prevention of breakdowns (eg. by stockpiling), the costs of reestablishing product characteristics (if specific product characteristics as temperature, elasticity and the like are important for the manufacturing process) all entail costs. Under those conditions resource dependence is higher mainly because these inputs make up a large percentage of costs (condition 1b) and because of the associated discretion over resources (condition 2). Because of the interdependence in production, the cost of breakdown of supply is likely to be substantial. Site specificity may also imply a fewness condition. Firms cannot entice many suppliers simultaneously to locate assets in close proximity, because these firms would be in a very poor bargaining position. Sunk cost aspects of assets located in close proximity create the ex-post contractual dependence (and asset specificity). If contractual solutions are used in the presence of site specificity, significant restrictions on the freedom of trading partners may be imposed. These function as safeguards for buyer and supplier.

Dedicated assets (d) also affect resource dependence. When firms add capacity to accommodate the large demand of specific customers their sales will be relatively concentrated (large proportion of output - 1b) and a few customers will buy a large percentage of output (3). These inputs may not be substantial for the downstream customer.

Brand name capital (e) can affect discretion over resources in some cases. Firms with considerable brand name capital (reputation) that are not integrated, may nevertheless have discretion over independent downstream suppliers. Firms can sensitize final consumers about the required quality via advertising. Customers can buy from independent downstream suppliers that offer products with the required quality (for example refrigeration of beer that is not pasteurized). Quality conscious customers without strong brand preference will buy other brands, while brand loyal customers will buy from suppliers that offer products with the added quality.

To summarize, when asset specificity is high, it implies that resource dependence is high as well. The only exception is brand name capital, which does not map as strongly onto resource dependence. Hence, asset specificity overlaps with resource dependence to a great extent. I investigate whether the reverse is the case as well. This will establish that resource dependence is broader than asset specificity.

Criticality of a component (condition 1a) does not match asset specificity very well. Presumably all inputs are critical at some level or for some functions or they would not be required. If multiple suppliers exist (ex post contract) and if existing suppliers do not have a decisive advantage over those that are not currently supplying the firm, than criticality does not affect asset specificity.

If critical supplies are unique, the upstream supplier is a monopolist. This does not mean that asset specificity is high. Uniqueness (lack of substitutes) describes a small numbers condition ex ante. For transaction cost theory, the relevant small number condition is ex post contractual. For unique goods, transaction cost still considers the choice of whether to buy or to make as a real choice, unless legal restrictions (for example, patents or government restrictions) make vertical integration impossible. In other words, if a firm has or can get all required resources to make a unique input internally, without significant cost penalties, then the fact that at present it is monopolistically supplied, is trivial from a transaction cost standpoint[3]. TCT is concerned with uniqueness ex post facto caused by the presence of asset specificity. The only exception concerns human asset specificity related to individuals. When suppliers have unique individual or team talent and these are a critical resource, then asset specificity may be high as well. It may be very hard to duplicate these talented human resources.

Chapter 8 - Vertical Integration

If dependence is high because a company needs inputs that make up a large portion of total requirements (condition 1b), no specific governance problems are presented in general. The characteristics of these goods may make market exchange problematic, not their total volume. Asset specificity is not affected, except under those unusual circumstances when the size of requirements of a specific customer (or supplier) requires added plant (dedicated assets).

Discretion over resources (condition 2), rarely raises asset specificity: only brand name capital and human asset specificity are affected. All firms control the production factors which they own. In general, when firms supply goods, they have discretion over resources and assets needed to make those goods. Withholding supplies (non-performance) is not without costs: it can negatively affect brand name capital. Even when a firm has complete discretion over a resource, it only implies small numbers conditions or monopoly market structure, and not necessarily asset specificity. The argument for the relation between discretion and human asset specificity is similar. Discretion is not complete: labor is not owned and controlled completely. Non-performance affects the reputation (and the value) of the individual or team. Termination of the contract for the individual or team (for example, divestiture) to redress nonperformance may also result in a loss of human asset specificity.

Resource dependence can be caused by the existence of a small number of suppliers (condition 3). The small numbers condition in RDT is broader than in TCT. In RDT, the small numbers condition can be ex ante or ex post. For TCT, the relevant small number condition always is ex post. Ex ante small numbers are related to uncompetitive supplier (or customer) markets and to market power. Fewness of sources does not imply high asset specificity.

This discussion suggests there is a significant overlap between TCT and RDT. Both rely on uncertainty, while the remaining concepts, asset specificity and resource dependence, are theoretically linked. Resource dependence is broader than asset specificity. Almost all types of asset specificity are subsumed by resource dependence. The reverse relation does not hold: many causes of resource dependence do not raise asset specificity. Furthermore, if TCT and RDT are in effect different theories, then TCT is more narrow and limited in the specific predictions it makes about the conditions and variables that affect vertical integration. How does this affect the ability of TCT and RDT to explain vertical integration? Preliminary evidence suggests that observed patterns of vertical exchange are not described significantly better by resource dependence theory (Krickx, 1990a). The more narrow focus of transaction cost theory does not result in significantly weaker explanatory power. These conclusions are tentative and subject to further investigation.

4. Uncertainty and dynamics: further indeterminacies

When uncertainty is conceptualized as a multidimensional concept, expected governance patterns are harder to predict based on TCT or RDT. A dynamic view of vertical integration and competition also affects the ability of these theories to explain observed governance patterns, given that resource dependence and asset specificity may be dynamically linked.

4.1. Uncertainty

Uncertainty is multidimensional. Multiple dimensions of the environment create problems for the prognostics of TCT and RDT. This problem is more severe when different types of uncertainty are related with vertical integration in opposite directions. This problem is rooted in the fact that the nature of the relation between vertical integration, and the variables uncertainty, resource dependence and asset specificity is not completely specified.

Assume there are two relevant dimensions of uncertainty (called technological and market uncertainty), and that both are positively related to vertical integration. When a summary measure of uncertainty can be constructed without significant loss of information, the number of interactions between uncertainty, asset specificity and resource dependence is limited. Assuming three values (high, medium or low) for each variable, nine possible combinations result. However, the inability to create a summary measure for uncertainty results in 27 combinations (Krickx, 1990a). For many of these interactions, neither RDT nor TCT suggest appropriate governance patterns. Should firms become integrated when asset specificity (or resource dependence) increases, while market uncertainty does not change and while technological uncertainty decreases? Current theory provides no guidance and in fact may lead to inappropriate choices: some types of uncertainty have been found to be negatively related to vertical integration in empirical studies, contrary to predictions by TCT.

Unresolved issues exist about the functional form, critical levels for any variable, and the sign of the relation between key variables and vertical integration, while data limitations pose their own problems. I will discuss each in turn. First, current theory is not sufficiently rich to specify the relation between vertical integration, asset specificity (or resource dependence) and uncertainty, especially if multiple dimensions of these variables are considered. Those aspects of uncertainty that are positively related with vertical integration should not be combined with those that are negatively related. At present theory does not predict which dimensions of uncertainty are positively or negatively related to vertical integration or whether they may be

Chapter 8 - Vertical Integration

aggregated. Second, changes in a single variable may change governance patterns. Asset specificity, resource dependence and uncertainty are always present to some extent. If one variable reaches a critical level and other variables are sufficiently high, governance will change. Hence, tests of TCT and RDT hypotheses should test interaction terms, as well as "main effects". Third, TCT and RDT treat uncertainty differently. TCT limits the relation between interactions of uncertainty and asset specificity with vertical integration to positive relations. RDT does not impose this constraint on resource dependence.

Fourth and finally, some data problems are mentioned. The first concerns sample sizes. The refinements proposed here rapidly increase minimally required sample sizes. On the other hand, to obtain robust and precise measures of asset specificity, resource dependence or uncertainty, detailed knowledge is required at the level of the individual transaction. Appropriate data gathering approaches are labor intensive, which limits feasible sample sizes. The troublesome result is that conclusive findings are hampered by small sample sizes (and robust measures). Other data collection strategies using secondary data can yield larger sample sizes, but have difficulty obtaining valid measures of the key concepts at the level of the transaction. A second data problem concerns the choice of industry. In a review of the relation between uncertainty and vertical integration, I found that this relation was affected by measures, type of uncertainty, and industry-specific variables (Krickx, 1990c). Conclusive tests of these theories may require testing the same hypotheses for different industries. The ability of RDT and TCT to predict vertical integration is not complete. None of the hypothesized relations have been conclusively tested or should be considered universally valid.

To conclude, it cannot be excluded that uncertainty has an independent effect on vertical integration. Without uncertainty, neither asset specificity nor resource dependence may be particularly troublesome. Different types of uncertainty are related to vertical integration in opposite directions (Krickx, 1990c). Based on our current understanding, we cannot exclude that the ability of TCT and RDT to explain vertical integration is caused by the independent effect of uncertainty on vertical integration. Any relation between TCT and RDT may be an artifact of their reliance on uncertainty. Resolution of this important issue will have to be settled by empirical findings.

4.2. Dynamic aspects

Industries change over time along many dimensions. In many industries, mature stages are characterized by different competitive forces. The relation between asset specificity and resource dependence may be influenced by the stage of the life cycle and may be related dynamically. Each is investigated in turn.

4.2.1. *Static comparison*

First, I investigate the relation between vertical integration, asset specificity and resource dependence in mature and emerging industries. The decision to change governance in a mature market is relatively straightforward, given that the key success factors and the costs of alternative governance structures are typically well understood. One exception occurs when revolutionary changes in technology uproot the established rules of competition. Existing governance patterns in a mature market often are the outcome of choices made during earlier periods. Some governance patterns are caused in part by historical accident, strategic considerations, and imitation of successful competitors. These factors are not captured by asset specificity or resource dependence[4].

During early periods of an industry's existence, the key success factors are often unclear. Considerable uncertainty exists with respect to dominant technology and emerging standards for products and service. Change is often dramatic and revolutionary. Poor strategic choices with respect to technology may be costly to undo. In general, offering products that incorporate the strategically important technology (effectiveness) often dominate concerns with governance and efficiency. In their pursuit of significant competitive advantages, firms experiment with different technologies and governance forms. The strategies of firms that appear successful are copied. Over time, governance patterns may be widely adopted that have little to do with careful consideration of TCT and RDT considerations. Hence the relation between vertical integration, asset specificity and resource dependence may be weaker for emerging industries.

An added complication is that governance patterns adopted experimentally during early industry stages, could be preserved during later stages, even if significant changes occur for the key variables considered here. This is especially likely when significant economies of scale or scope are available to early innovators that adopt vertical integration. Production cost savings may be much larger than any governance or dependence cost disadvantage of being inappropriately integrated. Three examples illustrate this point. First, with IBM's adoption of and integration in the production of integrated circuits, significant experience curve effects were realized (see earlier discussion). Second, IBM's vertical integration in ferrite cores was associated with volume requirements that increased 2000-fold and costs that decreased by a factor 200 from 1955 to 1970. Even in the period 1958 to 1960, IBM's cost of ferrite cores was $.008 per core, about half the price IBM paid for commercially sourced cores. Finally, IBM was integrated in disk drives. For IBM's drives, recording density

Chapter 8 - Vertical Integration

increased dramatically, along with faster access times and lower cost of storage. IBM was integrated in these three areas, which all were associated with fast growth and decreasing production costs. IBM's size and scale may have put it in a position to more easily take advantage of vertical integration.

In emerging industries, production cost considerations may significantly influence vertical integration choices and may greatly exceed in importance governance and dependence costs. Imitation and copying of early adopters may result in widespread use of vertical integration. Vertical integration patterns considered as part of the technological core in mature stages of an industry, may be based on incremental vertical integration decisions influenced by production cost considerations and made during early stages. These governance patterns may also be consistent with TCT or RDT explanations, even though production cost considerations drive this process. TCT and RDT may explain such vertical integration, because firms may invest in highly specific assets or in assets that require greater interdependence *after vertical integration has been chosen*. Retrospectively, it may be impossible to separate these different explanations. One interesting question is what happens when production cost considerations lead to different vertical integration choices than TCT or RDT would predict: it would be useful to know whether TCT or RDT explanations dominate and under what conditions. Based on this discussion, it cannot be excluded that the observed patterns of vertical integration are caused by factors other than those based on TCT or RDT (for example production cost savings).

4.2.2. A dynamic example

I present two examples that demonstrate how governance choices by some firms affect the governance choices of other firms. The first example is limited to a vertical chain of production. The second example includes competitive effects of vertical integration. This demonstrates that a competitive effect, which unfolds over time, may affect the ability of TCT and RDT to explain vertical integration.

Heide and John (1988) for a sample of small firms (insurance agencies), investigated what firms do when asset specificity is high, but vertical integration is not possible. Under those conditions, firms try to link themselves more closely with clients, when highly specific assets are present in the relation between the firms and the upstream supplier. In this manner the insurance agency can more easily replace the supplier. Vertical governance is thus influenced at the same time by transaction cost and resource dependence concerns. Moreover, the response to high asset specificity for the relation with upstream suppliers, is to change governance (at the margin) for the relation with the downstream customer. The strategic objective is to reduce dependence. Thus high asset specificity with limited freedom to choose vertical governance leads to strategic dependence. Firms change the nature of vertical governance relations with others to provide some countervailing power.

A second example is more complex and unfolds over a thirteen year period in the computer industry. The impact of dynamic change on the relation between asset specificity and resource dependence is demonstrated for disk drives for mainframe computers, which became highly popular as memory devices during this period.

IBM originally invented disk drives in 1956 and was vertically integrated for these devices (Fisher et al., 1983 discuss the disk drive industry in some length). IBM's disk drives were a success. IBM supplied disk drives to its mainframe competitors, which rented these devices. In 1964, IBM announced its 360-family of mainframes which became the new standard for third-generation computers. Advanced disk drives were instrumental for the performance improvements of these mainframes. Hence, access to high-speed disk drives was an important strategic factor.

On October 1 1965, IBM announced a change in its prices and terms for equipment rental: IBM decided to only sell peripherals and to no longer allow competitors to rent these devices. But IBM was able to set standards for computers and peripherals. Its decision to only sell disk drives shifted the risk of obsolescence to its competitors. This risk was amplified because IBM also could affect standards. In response, IBM's mainframe competitors started to look for other sources of disk drives. Independent peripheral makers offered disk drives compatible with IBM's, with similar performance, and lower in price. The existence of viable suppliers of disk drives, reduced the reliance of mainframe makers on IBM's disk drives.

Over time, most major mainframe companies became integrated in disk drive manufacturing. Burroughs became integrated in 1960, followed by Control Data, Digital Equipment, General Electric, Radio Corp. of America and Scientific Data Systems between 1965 and 1967, and by Honeywell and National Cash Register between 1968 and 1970. Of the 10 major mainframe companies only Sperry Rand did not make its own disk drives by 1970.

Some disk drive makers were acquired, for example by computer mainframe companies. Other disk drive companies sought new profitable sales opportunities: some targeted IBM's customers directly. The disk drives of these independent companies matched the performance of IBM's devices, but had a lower price. Moreover, these disk drives could directly replace the disk drives supplied by IBM, without any other changes in equipment or without any change in performance. IBM's innovation and early integration had sheltered it from price-based competition. In fact, IBM had maintained 100% market share of the disk drives installed on its

Chapter 8 - Vertical Integration 161

own computers until 1966. Now this profitable rental base ($14 million in monthly rental revenues by December 1967) was attacked.

Around May 1969, IBM decided to place controllers for its disk drives in the mainframe for its future product family of 370 computers. IBM thereby managed the bundle of goods (a mainframe system including computer, controllers and peripherals) to limit the competitive inroads of specialized peripheral makers. The relocation of the disk drive controller helped to shelter some of its disk drive business from price-based competition.

This example presented a dynamic analysis of competition in the disk drive segment. Vertical integration and standard setting abilities played an important role. Here, governance choices by some competitors affected the asset specificity and resource dependence of other competitors in later periods. This suggests that incremental changes in governance may affect competitive dynamics, which in turn may affect asset specificity and resource dependence in later time periods for suppliers, customers, or competitors. Thus, the link between TCT and RDT may be intertemporal and competitive.

A static analysis of vertical integration would be severely limited in this case. Computer firms made their respective governance choices (for example to become integrated) in different periods and were motivated by different time-dependent considerations. Mainframe makers generated demand for independent disk drive makers, while attempting to reduce their dependence on IBM. When mainframe firms integrated, disk drive makers sought to reduce their dependence by targeting IBM's customers. IBM in turn changed its integrated strategy to reduce the substitution of its own disk drives and controllers by lower priced ones from independent peripheral makers.

This example shows that asset specificity and resource dependence may be related over time. A contemporaneous correlation between these concepts may be an artifact of sample and method. Firms make successive incremental governance choices in response to firm-specific problematic resource dependence or asset specificity, or driven by other considerations as production costs. These choices in turn generate dependence or affect levels of specific assets for other firms (competitors, buyers, suppliers). These exchange partners in turn may adapt to reduce resource dependence or asset specificity. Vertical integration at a given point in time may be explained by either theory, because significant levels of asset specificity and resource dependence are present. However, these levels of asset specificity and resource dependence may be the outcome of successive and incremental changes in governance. Each incremental change in governance, adopted in response to competitive pressures, may indeed only be explained correctly by a single theory (TCT or RDT). Retrospective measures of asset specificity, resource dependence and vertical integration may not be sufficiently precise to separate TCT and RDT. A dynamic study of incremental change in governance allows more conclusive findings on the relative explanatory power of each theory.

The dynamic scenario I have proposed suggests useful directions for future research. A dynamic theory of vertical integration that encompasses transaction cost, resource dependence and production cost considerations is needed. Such a theory at present does not exist. Theoretical development can be spurred on by empirical findings. The example of the disk drive industry suggests that appropriate research designs should consider and control for the possible contemporaneous and intertemporal linkage between asset specificity and resource dependence.

The central research question of this paper concerns the relation between transaction cost and resource dependence theory. I suggested before that this relation may be caused by the significant overlap between the concepts of asset specificity and resource dependence (contemporaneous effect), and the reliance on uncertainty by both theories. Earlier, I suggested that the stage of industrial development may play a role. In this last section, I have demonstrated that a dynamic relation between asset specificity and resource dependence over time may be responsible for the relation between TCT and RDT. Static approaches using aggregate and retrospective measures cannot explain this dynamic and incremental process of change in governance or identify whether TCT or RDT is more powerful.

5. Conclusion

Transaction cost and resource dependence explanations of vertical integration may be hard to separate. In this chapter, I have tried to identify the possible reasons. Reliance on a common variable (uncertainty), a theoretical relationship between asset specificity and resource dependence, the stage of industry development, and static approaches and retrospective measures may all be partially responsible.

First, both theories rely on a common variable, uncertainty, which has an independent effect on vertical integration. In fact, at present it cannot be ruled out that the similar explanation of vertical integration by TCT and RDT, is entirely due to the independent effect of uncertainty. The relation between uncertainty and vertical integration complicates any effort to determine whether observed governance patterns are consistent with TCT or RDT explanations.

Second, there is a theoretical relation between the concepts of asset specificity and

Chapter 8 - Vertical Integration 163

resource dependence. Asset specificity is a more narrow concept. Significant asset specificity typically implies problematic resource dependence. The reverse is not the case. Although resource dependence is a broader concept, preliminary evidence (Krickx, 1990a) does not indicate that this results in a significant reduction in the predictive power of TCT in comparison to RDT. The linkage between the key concepts of each theory does suggest that they are related explanations.

Third, a static comparison of the forces that shape competition in emerging and mature markets suggested other factors that affect vertical integration. Production cost consideration may dominate many governance decisions during early stages of an industry, when neither technological nor product or service standards have been set. When TCT and RDT explanations coincide with explanations based on production cost considerations, their similar explanatory power is an artifact of the production costs, which drive the process. Imitation of governance patterns adopted by industry leaders may quickly diffuse and become dominant and, during later stages, may be seen as part of the technological core. This explanation cannot be discounted at present. It suggests that the relation between TCT, RDT and vertical integration may be caused by other explanations.

In fact, the link between asset specificity and resource dependence may depend on the stage of development of an industry. The main forces that shape competition in an emerging industry may be very different from those in mature industries. The connection in emerging industries between asset specificity, resource dependence, uncertainty and vertical integration may be much weaker than in mature industries. In emerging industries, trial and error, misguided choices (accidents), and an incomplete understanding of the economics of emerging technologies may lead to vertical governance choices that do not fit with or are poorly explained by TCT and RDT.

Finally, I have demonstrated that TCT and RDT may provide separate and different explanations for observed patterns of vertical integration. When analysis is detailed and focuses on change in governance patterns by different firms over time, I have shown that the governance choices of some firms can affect suppliers, customers and competitors. Choices made for one reason (production costs, dependence, transaction costs) by one firm, may change the nature of the buyer-supplier relation or the nature of competition. Other firms may change their governance patterns in response, possibly based on a different rationale. In our example, a dominant firm chose to minimize production costs for emerging technologies, but created troublesome dependencies for other firms. These firms in turn tried to eliminate dependencies by changing their governance. This suggests that each fine-grained governance choice by a specific firm may be based on a single explanation (TCT, RDT or other explanations as production costs). Choice of vertical governance was described as a dynamic and incremental process whereby firms act in response to changes imposed on them by the governance and competitive choices of others. As Heide and John (1988) and my work suggests, TCT or RDT alone may explain many changes in governance.

Evidence that supports each of the three explanations of the relation between TCT and RDT has been found. Given that both theories rely on uncertainty and that uncertainty may have an independent effect on vertical integration, we cannot exclude that any relation between TCT and RDT is an artifact of the effect of uncertainty. Second, given that these theories are not completely identical, that empirical findings found cases that fit one but not the other theory, and that the basic objective of each theory is different, we cannot exclude that TCT and RDT describe different aspects of the same events. Finally, when dynamic and competitive dimensions are considered and when incremental changes in vertical integration patterns are investigated, we found that successive changes in integration resulted in contemporaneous effects in asset specificity or resource dependence for the firm that adopted the change, but followed later by changes in asset specificity or resource dependence for other firms. Hence, each change in vertical integration may be explained by TCT or RDT alone. If this process is evaluated with retrospective and aggregate measures, a connection between TCT and RDT could be observed, which would be an artifact of not controlling for dynamic and competitive dimensions.

This chapter has identified some directions for future research. Our knowledge of the relation between vertical integration, asset specificity, resource dependence and uncertainty is less complete than is commonly assumed. Other possible explanations should be controlled for. Any empirical work that clarifies these relations is helpful. The most successful approach will require multiple fine-grained measures of the key variables, studied for a homogeneous set of transactions over time. This approach will at least yield robust findings. As more settings are investigated, it will become clear, which contingencies (for example, maturity of industry, technology and strategy) affect the ability of TCT and RDT to explain vertical integration.

Notes

1 Many intermediate governance patterns are possible. These can entail partial ownership or not. Intermediate patterns essentially consist of market governance with added relations, that change the incentives for all parties involved (Klein, Crawford and Alchian, 1978; Williamson, 1985).

2 Human asset specificity can affect dependence in other domains. Borden's managers

adopted a "people pill" to ward off unwanted takeovers. Borden's top and middle management agreed to resign massively if an unwanted takeover took place (Business Week, 1/16/1989). In Borden's case such action would be effective, since upper and middle managers responsible for all key operations would resign and because a lot of detailed and key operating knowledge is held by the middle level managers who have long average tenure at Borden. The key reason why this people pill works is the significant human capital held by Borden's managers.

3 This is represented by the case in Figure 1 where small numbers ex ante are (or can be) transformed to large numbers ex post. Under those conditions monopoly is innocuous because it is not necessarily permanent (because markets can be created). Many product innovations, when first introduced, resemble a monopoly, but they are not permanent monopolies.

4 One cannot assume that the governance patterns that prevail, are also ones that entail the lowest specificity or lowest dependence. This would make RDT and TCT tautological.

References

Anderson, E.M., 1982, Contracting the Selling Function: the Sales Person as Outside Agent or Employee, UCLA unpublished PhD dissertation.

Barney, J.B., and W.G. Ouchi (Eds.), 1986, Organizational Economics, (San Francisco, Jossey Bass).

Business Week, 1/16/1989, First it was Poison Pills - Now It's 'People Pills'.

Fisher F.M., J.W. McKie and R.B. Mancke, 1983, IBM and the US Data Processing Industry: an Economic History (New York, Praeger).

Galaskiewicz J., 1985, Interorganizational Relations, American Review of Sociology, 281-304.

Hannan, M.T., and J.H. Freeman, 1977, The Population Ecology of Organizations, American Journal of Sociology, reprinted in Meyer and Associates, Environments and Organizations, (San Francisco, Jossey Bass), 1978, 131-171.

Heide, J.B., and G. John, 1988, The Role of Dependence Balancing in Safeguarding Transaction-Specific Assets in Conventional Channels, Journal of Marketing, 52, 20-35.

IBM Journal of Research and Development 9/81, Anniversary Issue, 25: 9, 361-832.

Klein, B., Crawford and A. Alchian, 1978, Vertical Integration, Appropriable Rents and the Competitive Contracting Process, Journal of Law and Economics, 21: 2, 297-326.

Klein, B., and K.B. Leffler, 1981, The Role of Market Forces in Assuring Contractual Performance, Journal of Political Economy, 89: 4, 615-641.

Koberg, C.S., and G.R. Ungson, 1987, The Effects of Environmental Uncertainty and Dependence on Organizational Structure and Performance: A Comparative Study, Journal of Management, 13: 4, 725-737.

Krickx, G.A., 1990a, Transaction Cost and Resource Dependence Explanations of Vertical Integration: Strategic and Technological Considerations, The Wharton School Wharton Working Paper: 8.

Krickx, G.A., 1990b, Transaction Cost and Resource Dependence Explanations of Vertical Integration: Towards an Integration, The Wharton School, Wharton Working Paper: 9.

Krickx, G.A., 1990c, Uncertainty, Transaction Costs and Vertical Integration: Theory and Evidence, The Wharton School Wharton, Working Paper: 13.01.

Krickx, G.A., 1990d, Vertical Governance in the Computer Mainframe Industry: A Transaction Cost Interpretation, The Wharton School, Wharton Working Paper: 12.

Krickx, G.A., 1988, Historical Evidence on the Evolution of Vertical Exchange Mechanisms: Examples from the Computer Systems Industry, unpublished PhD dissertation, UCLA.

March, J.G., and H.A. Simon, 1958, Organizations, (New-York, John Wiley).

Pfeffer J., 1978, Organizational Design, (Arlington Heights IL, AHM Publishing Co).

Pfeffer J., and G.R. Salancik, 1978, The External Control of Organizations - A Resource Dependence Perspective, (New-York, Harper & Row).

Simon, H.A., 1957, Administrative Behavior, (New York, The Free Press).

Spekman, R.E., and D. Strauss, 1986, An Exploratory Investigation of a Buyer's Concern for Factors Affecting more Co-operative Buyer-Seller Relationships, Industrial Marketing & Purchasing, 1: 3, 26-43.

Thompson, J.D., 1967, Organizations in Action, (New-York, McGraw Hill).

Williamson, O.E., 1989, Transaction Cost Economics, in R. Schmalensee and R.D. Willig (Eds.), Handbook of Industrial Organization (Amsterdam, North-Holland).

Williamson, O.E., 1988, Technology and Transaction Cost Economics: A Reply, Journal of Economic Behaviour and Organization: 10, 355-363.

Williamson, O.E., 1985, The Economic Institutions of Capitalism, (New-York, The Free Press).

Williamson, O.E., 1981, The Economics of Organization: the Transaction Cost Approach, American Journal of Sociology, 87: 3, 548-577.

Williamson, O.E., 1979, Transaction Cost Economics: the Governance of Contractual Relations, Journal of Law and Economics, 23-261.

Williamson, O.E., 1975, Markets and Hierarchies, (New-York, Free Press).

Yuchtman, E., and S.E, Seashore, 1967, A System Resource Approach to Organizational Effectiveness, American Sociological Review, 32, 891-903.

MICROECONOMIC CONTRIBUTIONS TO STRATEGIC MANAGEMENT
J. Thépot and R.-A. Thiétart
© 1991 Elsevier Science Publishers B.V. All rights reserved.

CHAPTER 9

INTER-FIRM ALLIANCES: THE ROLE OF TRUST

C. KOENIG and G. van WIJK
ESSEC ESSEC

Abstract

Considering an inter-firm alliance as an organizational practice in itself, this chapter argues that its emergence and stability depend on the development and maintenance of trust between partners, where trust is an informal mode of control defined as a set of mutual anticipations and obligations. Examining the role of trust in the creation and performance of alliances helps understand phenomena not covered by usual paradigms.

1. Introduction

This paper argues that the emergence and stability of inter-firm cooperations depend on the development and maintenance of trust.

Regardless of the degree of formality in a cooperation, the existence of separate loci of control creates a strong need for integration. This integration is achieved only to a limited extent by contracts and other formal means (Williamson, 1975). Yet, minority participations, joint-ventures, research and marketing consortia, partnerships in subsidiaries or special projects, and cross-licensing have all become common instruments to increase a firm's activity in the face of changing markets and managerial practices, and increasingly complex technology. Notably alliances, as opposed to mergers and acquisitions, accelerate the access to new markets and new technologies in financially advantageous conditions, and with limited risk when appropriate checks and controls are used by partners (Ghemawat, Porter and Rawlinson, 1986; Hamel, Doz and Prahalad 1989; Reich and Mankin, 1986). Alliances are also sometimes considered a means of controlling or preempting competition. Unexpected circumstances can arise even in predictable situations and they lead to firms' opportunistic behavior in the cooperation. A form of flexible control like trust is necessary.

Trust is an informal mode of control governing mutually identified actors (van Wijk 1985). It reduces uncertainty regarding mutual behavior through a process of self-control. The trusting party develops mostly implicit anticipations regarding the trusted party's behavior. Aware of the anticipations regarding its general conduct, the trusted party becomes "trust-worthy" if it feels the obligation to fulfill these anticipations. The combination of anticipation and obligation yields an effective informal mode of coordination. In addition, the existence of trust in a relationship gives the cooperation a flexibility not available in formal transactions: initiatives are possible outside the agenda. This entails one firm drawing upon a form of credit while the other forbears, with the expectation that ultimately both will be better off (Buckley and Casson, 1988).

Economic analysis supports the existence of alliances as a strategic and economic improvement over other forms of internal coordination and free market forces. But it does not explain how cooperation in alliances can actually be succesful from an (inter) organizational point of view, when the mother firms are entirely distinct entities with diverging priorities. At the inter-organizational level, transaction cost analysis and game theory emphasize the cooperation/competition dilemma. The attempts to resolve this dilemma lead to the introduction of *ad hoc* exchange structures (e.g. exchange of hostages), of extensive formal contracts, and to an overemphasis of the benefits of increasing interdependence among the firms. Still, this is not sufficient to completely discourage opportunistic behavior. Strictly rational behavior, informed by transaction cost analysis and game theory, will lead markets or hierarchies to prevail, whereas alliances are seen as unstable, costly and risky governance structures (Kogut, 1988b). Yet alliances are not only viable in practice but they strive and proliferate. In this process, trust is crucial in reducing the uncertainty about a partner's behavior, including opportunism (Lynch, 1989). Trust is therefore necessary in order for firms to make strategic commitments, for instance in capital and technology, and in order for the alliance to be creatively productive through the unprogrammed initiatives of allies.

2. A working definition of alliances

The term "alliance" has been used at one time or another in strategic literature to describe: (1) informal inter-firm arrangements (for example, mutual understanding about "normal" market share, competitive pricing etc.); (2) formal inter-firm deals (e.g., contract defining the supply of essential components); (3) joint-ventures whereby collaborating firms have a formal stake in an independent operation; (4) partnerships such as collaborative research projects or manufacturer-distributor relationships. Some common threads seem to run through these definitions:

1 - Firms keep their formal identity, even if they sacrifice varying degrees of autonomy.
2 - The collaboration entails the transfer or the sharing of tangible or intangible goods or assets.
3 - There is incomplete information on the value of what is transferred.
4 - Some amount of control over the object of the cooperation is delegated.

Chapter 9 - Inter-firm Alliances

In view of these observations, an alliance is defined as a cooperative agreement between independent firms designed to achieve mutually relevant outcomes through the transfer or by the sharing of tangible or intangible goods, with little or no mutual "hard" control. Hard control describes situations of ownership, and in a weaker sense, of binding formal commitments. In contrast, soft control describes situations in which the enforcement of agreements can only proceed through informal channels: persuasion, threats, whistle-blowing or outright conflict. No formal sanctions or litigation procedures are available. An alliance is hence more of a willful cooperation than just another formal arrangement. With this definition, cross-licensing is not considered as an alliance; neither is a formal inter-firm deal, such as a type of joint-venture in which one party only contributes in cash, so that the above conditions are not met.

The section below briefly reviews the contributions and the limitations of resource dependence, transaction cost analysis and game theory. This review helps explain how the concept of trust may overcome some of these limitations. Then the nature of trust, its emergence and its development will be examined in relation to the existence of an alliance. Finally, the need for trust will be related to the characteristics of the cooperation, and of the partner firms in the alliance.

3. Inter-firm relations: current paradigms

Two theoretical frameworks provide insights into the main reasons for firms to develop more than anonymous market relations. Introducing different but not exclusive rationales, the resource dependency and transaction cost models proceed from organization and economic theory respectively.

The resource dependency model is firm-centered and suggests that organizations actively seek to reduce environmental uncertainty. Critical dependencies are identified, and control over the relevant actors is sought by means of contracting, acquiring, lobbying, etc. (Aldrich, 1976, Pfeffer and Salancik, 1978). The theory does not predict the prevalence of any particular inter-organizational form. However, the emphasis on control, with the firm at the logical center, implies a preference for formal control through ownership, binding contracts, etc., whenever possible.

Empirical results concerning, in particular, the pattern of acquisitions within and among industries have provided good evidence in support of the theory (Pfeffer and Salancik, 1978: Ch. VI). Basically, however, any form of control including for instance soft forms like cooptation (Selznick, 1949) and interlocking directorates (Burt, 1980 ; Pennings, 1980) can be analyzed in a resource dependence perspective. However, there never occurs a shift in the locus of control corresponding to the implementation of an actual cooperation between firms. The focal firm always seeks to realize its own objectives through control over its environment. Therefore, the resource dependency model never raises the issue of changing the unit of analysis and moving to a supra-organizational logic, as it is argued to be necessary, and problematic, in alliances.

The transaction cost model posits that coordination should minimize total production and transaction costs. With this perspective, a change in the unit of analysis, from firm to alliance is perfectly possible. The question is whether or not the model provides insights as to the appropriate organizational form.

The transaction cost approach emphasizes the relative efficiency of various forms of organizing economic activities since it focuses on the "comparative costs of planning, adapting and monitoring task completion under alternative governance structures" (Williamson, 1985, p. 2). Three factors are responsible for differences among transactions and are thus to be used in a predictive theory of economic organization.

The first and foremost factor is the asset specificity of the transaction, (i.e. the degree to which each party invests in assets that are specific to the transaction). This factor, as well as the second one, the frequency of the transaction, explains why the parties to the transaction depart from a short-term market relationship or standard contracting practices. The third factor, uncertainty, also explains why short-term relationships are to be avoided and why integration (i.e. unified governance structure) may be preferable.

The transaction cost framework has been used extensively to explain various strategic choices (e.g. forms of international development such as direct foreign investment as opposed to exporting or licensing (Buckley and Casson, 1988; Rugman, 1981; Caves, 1982), or modes of exploiting technological innovation (Teece, 1986; Walker, 1988)). Moreover, it has been widely used to explain the emergence of joint-ventures and alliances as organizational forms that are intermediate between markets and hierarchies (Beamish and Banks, 1987; Hennart, 1988; Koenig and Thiétart, 1988; Kogut, 1988a). However, Williamson (1985, p. 83) recognized that his original work on transaction costs had neglected these intermediary forms on the basis that they were unstable, costly and difficult to organize.

Under what conditions, or for what reasons, then, would firms deem it advantageous to give up some of their "hard" control to enter an alliance or prefer this form to a standard contract? First of all, an alliance must bring what might be termed "asset synergy" (i.e. it will be chosen if internal development is deemed more costly than an alliance for at least one of the partners). Thus, alliances should fare better than integrated hierarchies in terms of production cost. However, if two firms with potentially conflicting objectives get together, the risks of ex-post shirking and haggling arise. Comparing alliances with contracts, the former may be deemed more efficient than the latter when the return to each party is based on a share of the collective output, in which case, alliances provide a better incentive alignment than incomplete contracts (Koenig and Thiétart, 1988 ; Buckley and Casson, 1988).

Chapter 9 - Inter-firm Alliances

Moreover, alliances may be more "efficient" than contracts because of the use of reciprocal hostages in support of bilateral trade (Williamson, 1985, ch. 7; Kogut, 1988a): by developing mutual asset specificity, partners increase the opportunity cost of abandoning the alliance. This commitment thus makes the alliance more sustainable. Alliances will therefore be preferred if material outcomes and "sunk" commitments can replace formal contracts.

In summary, it appears that the transaction cost approach makes an important contribution in terms of strategic positioning and the efficiency of various governance structures. However, the model does not provide an explanation neither for the displacement of one configuration towards another, nor for the sustainability of potentially unstable structures as this entails more than economic arguments.

Another branch of economic theory is of interest to students of alliances, namely, game theory. Repeated games with incomplete information have highlighted the process of reputation building and the incentive to cooperate, (Kreps, Milgrom, Roberts and Wilson, 1982) and the role of the time horizon of the relationship (Axelrod, 1984). Weigelt and Camerer, (1988) applied some of these concepts in the context of corporate strategy to show how reputation building behavior affects strategic choice by generating future profits.

In the context of an alliance, reputation building behavior helps explain why member firms may want to forbear or behave cooperatively up to a point. The basic result of the reputation model is straightforward: each firm in the alliance, when it behaves cooperatively, exposes itself to the risk that the partner firm is actually dishonest and renegues. It thus runs the risk that if it is cooperative during the first period, its performance will be negatively affected by the other firm's unfriendly and unpredictable behavior. It would then not cooperate in subsequent periods. However, if the same firm cheats in the first period, it shows its unwillingness to cooperate and therefore foregoes opportunities for future profits from cooperation if the other firm is cooperative. The model shows that if the time horizon is long enough and when there is a small probability that the other firm may be cooperative, the loss of future cooperation exceeds for a period of time that of being misled by the partner. A dishonest or uncooperative partner thus has no incentive to reveal its true nature and would, therefore, act against its short-term interest. For instance it would rather invest in building a reputation on which it would cash in at a later time, near the end of the game's time horizon, when the loss of future cooperation equals the loss of being cheated on.

The main feature of the model is that, with a sufficiently long time horizon, low uncertainty about the other firm's cooperativeness acts as an incentive to build one's reputation and therefore makes cooperation sustainable. In other words, cooperation between two firms at any time increases with the time horizon of the alliance. Sobel, (1985) has extended the Kreps et al. model to include stakes in the relationship. If higher stakes are available in the future, an uncooperative firm has an incentive to cooperate early because it will have an opportunity to gain more by behaving aggressively in the future. In any case, an uncooperative firm is always likely to cheat if its current reputation has no future value. It is interesting to notice that Williamson's argument (1975) that long-term relationships help foster the accumulation of transaction-specific assets leads to a similar conclusion.

There are several problems with the game theory approach, however. First of all, as Fudenberg and Maskin (1986) have shown, repeated games of the kind described above have multiple equilibrium outcomes. Therefore, even if the intuition in the model makes sense, the outcome is indeterminate. But more importantly, repeated games with reputation building omit some important features of alliances. First of all, if one firm is cooperative and notices uncooperative behavior from its partner, it can either forbear, hoping its partner made a mistake, or it can terminate the relationship, which then will never be resumed. Secondly, reputation must play a role in the choice of whether or not to play the game. Cashing in on a false cooperative reputation must affect the dishonest partner's ability to attract candidates for future games to be played with him. Reputation has a value outside the framework of the game currently played.

Transaction cost analysis has become the usual paradigm for studying alliances. Its insights and concepts, as well as those of game theory, shed light on specific issues regarding the economics of the relationship between partner firms. But the transaction cost paradigm is also of limited use when the ongoing and evolving relationship between firms is considered. By focusing on transaction and governance structures, this paradigm treats transactions as static, where informal processes play no role. For instance, the motivation to enter a transaction or to play a game is taken for granted in institutional economics as well as in game theory, and obstacles to interpersonal relationships are not considered, even in repeated games. Moreover, the stand that each party has an intrinsic "right", and actually will pursue its best interest at the expense of others (Killing, 1988 ; Hamel, Doz and Prahalad, 1989) has been challenged by authors like Granovetter who emphasize that long-lasting personal relations may lead actors to refrain from behaving opportunistically (Granovetter, 1985). The analysis of trust and of its role in alliances will suggest how to overcome some of these limitations.

4. The nature of trust

Trust is a process involving expectations and obligations between two parties. The trusting party develops expectations regarding its partner's behavior in mutually relevant matters. If the party is trustworthy, it will feel obliged to fulfill these expectations. The process can obviously only develop if there is a mutual awareness of each other's capacity to contribute value to the common purpose: only if specific expectations can be formed on one hand, and fulfilled on the other, is a trust relationship established. A breach of trust occurs when there is awareness of the

Chapter 9 - Inter-firm Alliances

expectations with concomitant perception of obligations, but no fulfillment.

Similar to psychological contracts, prerogatives and obligations remain mostly implicit. In fact, the parties to such contracts have a very intuitive notion of the nature and the extent of their mutual expectations, except when they are challenged. This combination of fuzziness of the actors' actual expectations during their interaction and the sharpness of the feelings in case of breach indicates that trust is at once a strong and flexible mode of control. Flexibility allows creative cooperation to evolve, whereas formally expressed control, through rules or authority, is necessarily rigid and narrow. If it were not, it would depend on implicit understandings,(i.e. on trust). The strength of the control exerted by trust, despite its informality, can be ascribed to the individual and social need to act responsibly. Moreover, a breach of trust disrupts the relationship in a radical way.

Proposition 1:The creative potential of an alliance is associated positively with trust among the parties, and negatively with the emphasis on rules and procedures.

Proposition 2: The parties to an alliance consider breaching trust relatively more serious than breaking rules stated in a contract.

The same tradeoff between rigidity and loss of formal control is made in negotiation settings. The constituent and his representative must trust each other if the representative is to be effective as a negotiator (Wall, 1975 ; Walton and McKersie, 1965). In alliances, the situation has the same structure: sufficient discretion should be granted to the alliance manager for him to be able to make the necessary commitments, in the firm's best interest.

Proposition 3: A firm's contribution to an alliance is determined by the degree of trust between the manager of the alliance and his constituency.

All forms of cooperation generate problems that are unknown to independent or centralized actors: ambiguity in communication, opportunism of the parties involved, and uncertainty linked to the ultimate autonomy of the actors. Among the means available to solve these problems in a dyadic relationship, trust is the most immediate, while power, rules, norms and values all require an authority and a history. Trust generates a sense of predictability of others' behavior thus reducing that source of uncertainty (Luhmann, 1973, 1988). It hence makes incomplete contracts workable (Macaulay, 1964) and economizes on transaction costs: "Trust is one resource that, by diminishing contract uncertainty, lowers the cost of exchanges in the economy" (Brenner, 1983: 95). This point is also made in some marketing literature on manufacturer-distributor alliances (Anderson and Weitz, 1989; Anderson and Narus, 1990). The process of anticipation, in effect, leads to the implicit recognition of the parties' actual characteristics, (e.g. technical capacity, punctuality, way of doing things, and relative power). Trust therefore resolves the ambiguities arising from two loci of control. Heide and John (1988) have suggested that when partners are not equal in power or relative dependence, the more dependent firm seeks to protect its transaction-specific assets by taking various dependence-balancing actions. Trust between parties may reduce this need to offset dependence.

Proposition 4: The presence of trust among the parties to an alliance leads to the recognition of a single executive authority inside the alliance.

With respect to their allies, the managers of an alliance have to accept a social order: one dominating the other, or a third party to which authority is delegated. A third, unstable solution would be shared control, where close cooperation is mandatory. This last approach is often preferred for reasons of equity, but it depends equally on the existence of mutual trust: if it exists, dual control is superfluous, if it does not, the necessary give and take process cannot develop, and the alliance will probably fail to be productive due to numerous decision iterations and continuous haggling, as Koenig and Thiétart show in the case of cooperation in the aircraft industry (1988).

Because of the investments and the commitments that an alliance entails, an informal mode of control may appear insufficient and, at the very least, unstable. Yet, in practice, another instance of delegation of authority exists: the separation between ownership and control. The dispersion of equity ownership has endowed management with the executive power inclusive of the capacity to make strategic commitments (Berle and Means, 1932). This arrangement has proved effective, despite the risks and problems brought to light by the principal-agent theory.

The comparison suggests that the alliance between two firms can be implemented by a delegation of authority based on trust and not necessarily supported by ownership or stringent contracts.

5. Alliances in light of trust

5.1. Emergence of alliances

In its strictest sense, an alliance can be seen as a cooperative agreement among independent firms, designed to serve a strategic purpose. The process of cooperation often brings about substantial commitments in capital, technology, and other assets. For alliances in which process and outcome cannot be precisely defined in advance, the allies face an important uncertainty regarding a partner's behavior, because it cannot be controlled. Yet, paradoxically, alliances are formed just because there is no precise program of cooperation, and because the outcomes are unknown. The cooperation cannot be completely contracted formally and it requires creative inputs.

Proposition 5: firms are more likely to develop a formal relationship when their cooperation entails processes and outcomes that are narrowly identifiable at the outset.

Uncertainty is increased when, to be fruitful, cooperation requires one party to communicate proprietary information to the other (know-how, trade-secrets, etc.). Finally, uncertainty is related to the size and the value of the commitment of each party.

If, nevertheless, alliances emerge, this suggests that uncertainty has been reduced. At first sight, the logic seems circular: firms will ally if there is trust among them (Lynch, 1989) and trust will develop through experience when firms cooperate (Hirschman, 1984; Anderson and Narus, 1990). In the same vein, Geringer (1988) underlines the need to assess the trustworthiness of potential partners and emphasizes the role of trust in the perennity of an alliance.

Manifestly, these statements are valid but insufficient to account for the emergence of alliances. In order to refine the analysis, the anticipation and obligation process provides some guidance. The decision to expose oneself in a strategic cooperation is based on:

- first hand knowledge (i. e. experience),
- second hand knowledge (i. e. reputation), or
- no knowledge (i. e. gamble).

The first case leads back to the circularity problem; however, it suggests that experience can progressively grow, leading to increased stakes in a cooperation, and implying higher levels of trust. Indeed, initially small scope cooperations are seen to grow over time into major alliances, such as Pernod Ricard and Marnier Lapostolle, initially strictly competitors in the alcoholic beverages industry, finally joining forces to jointly develop their U.S. distribution network. Similarly, Killing (1988) and O'Toole and O'Toole (1981) assert that firms should try something simple first if they ultimately want to set up an alliance for moderately or highly complex tasks. As a case in point, Orsan of France and Ajinomoto of Japan formed a joint-venture to develop their biotechnology business in the US after having cooperated for over ten years in the same activity in Europe within another joint-venture. The latter, Eurolysine, started as a small entity betting on the development of a new market, and steadily became the world leader. Airbus Industrie gradually developing a full line of aircraft is another example. The difficulty is that it takes time to see the process through, in contrast with widespread short-term competitive pressures.

The second case presumably covers a substantial part of current alliances. Reputation is a reliable and simple way of identifying good allies. The reliability of a reputation is unlikely to be problematic: the cost associated in building a reputation is best recouped by the benefits reaped in developing a variety of productive business relationships. It would hardly be justifiable to waste it on a single "sting". Aside from ethical considerations, an adverse public image would develop (Williamson, 1985). Reputation helps overcome the initial asymmetry in information, and it breeds trust (Dasgupta, 1988 ; Anderson and Weitz, 1989).

The third and last case is less unusual than it may appear. Many alliances have been initiated under very fortuitous circumstances, like executives meeting in a hotel lobby or during a flight. Sheer need for a specific competence has also triggered cold calls, that fairly promptly evolved into full fledged alliances. Anticipation under these circumstances should be mostly normative. Actually, normal business practice is likely to inform and support the process, but anticipations develop beyond this point, without being backed by experience or reputation. Under these conditions, the solicited firms will either respond in kind, or signal their lack of interest in the alliance. Opportunistic behavior is very unlikely *a priori*: typically, people that meet each other for the first time always begin by trusting each other (Deutsch, 1962).

Proposition 6: The emergence of alliances is related to mutual experience, reputation, or opportunity, more than to environmental scanning and rational choice.

In summary, trust is a key component for the emergence of an alliance as it reduces the perceived uncertainty about the ally's behavior. In this way, trust supplements formal control systems such as contracts. Trust is derived from first and second hand knowledge of a firm, or from a gamble about its disposition. But trust is not only a means of reducing uncertainty, it also provides a flexible means of mutual adjustment by fostering stable and creative relations.

5. 2. Performance of alliances

The alliance is considered to be an extension of the concept of organizational structure. It relates to structure and process rather than to strategy. Therefore, the notion of performance of the alliance is to be distinguished from the success of a strategy. The alliance can be successful even if the objective which it was intended to achieve is not realized, just as an organizational structure can be efficient without adequately serving the intended purpose.

An alliance, however, is an important element of strategy inasmuch as it is part of the means to realize the strategic objectives of the partner firms. In the process of implementing strategy, a succesful alliance develops a sense of purpose of its own and its own set of rules, conducive (or not) to the ultimate strategic objectives defined by the partners at the outset. This *ad hoc* organization has the capacity to flexibly integrate each firm's creative contribution, and to ensure a smooth coordination of joint initiatives.

Chapter 9 - Inter-firm Alliances

This sense of purpose is, in itself, a characteristic of an alliance's performance, since the alliance will be in a position to achieve more than a standardized formal inter-firm contractual arrangement with more than one locus of control. Koenig and Thiétart (1988) provide illustrations, drawn from cooperations in the aerospace industry, of how the autonomy of the alliance improves its performance.

Proposition 7: Trust among the parties is associated positively with the sense of purpose shared by the members of the alliance.

What consequences does good performance have on the alliance ? Linear reasoning would lead one to expect trust to be steadily reinforced as expectations are fulfilled in the coordination process. This is, however, not expected to be the case. Indeed, the administrative process requires rules, which in turn confer legitimacy to the process. Formal agreements reinforce the control provided by trust whenever possible. Trust and formal control tend to build on each other, rather than to displace each other.

Proposition 8: The stability of an alliance is achieved by the combination of formal agreements and trust among the managers of the alliance.

Trust without formalization leads to a highly unstable situation, likely to be concluded by a rupture, with an epilogue of conflict and liquidation. It is neither legitimate with respect to the various parties involved nor economical to raise the stakes in an informal relationship like one based solely on trust. In fact, skepticism and cynicism on one hand and gullibility on the other, will make opportunism an acceptable behavior: if someone is so daring or so naive, he should be ready to accept the consequences of his behavior.

In the step-by-step process alternating trust and formalization, an alliance achieves, instead, a high level of transaction efficiency and stability combining firmness and flexibility.

6. Conclusion

An alliance is an organizational practice in its own right, breaking out of the traditional analyses of the firm. While becoming a common form in practice, it is in need of analytical frameworks dealing with the intermediate level between the organization and the market. One of the concepts necessary to make sense of the underlying processes is trust. Indeed, by introducing trust in the analysis of alliances, it was shown that their emergence, stability and performance could be explained. Trust helps overcome some of the limitations of the transaction costs approach and makes alliances workable governance structures. As already suggested, it reduces the need of the more dependent firm to offset this dependence by taking "balancing actions" to protect transaction-specific assets. The "small number" situation in which trust develops is viewed by transaction cost theory as a source of opportunism not conducive to long-term relationships. Trust makes this relationship workable because it reduces the likelihood of defection and opportunistic behavior. It is believed that useful elements were introduced towards the operationalization of critical concepts, and testable propositions were formulated. Finally, it is interesting to note that the problem of trust is transposable inside the organization, and has thus highlighted the important role of a hitherto fairly secondary concept.

References

Aldrich, H., 1976, Resource Dependence and Interorganizational Relations, Administration and Society, 7: 4, 419-455.

Aldrich, H., 1979, Organizations and Environnements, (Englewood Cliffs, N.J., Prentice Hall).

Anderson, E., and B. Weitz, 1989, Determinants of Continuity in Conventional Industrial Channel Dyads, Marketing Science, 8: 4, 310 - 323.

Anderson, J., and J. Narus, 1990, A Model of Distributor Firm and Manufacturing Firm Working Partnerships, Journal of Marketing, 54, 42-58.

Axelrod, R., 1984, The Evolution of Cooperation, (New-York, Basic Books).

Beamish, P., 1988, Multinational Joint-Ventures in Developing Countries, (London, Routledge).

Beamish P.W., and J.C. Banks, 1987, Equity Joint-Ventures and the Theory of the Multinational Enterprise, Journal of International Business Studies, Summer 1987.

Berle A.A., and G.C. Means, 1932, The Modern Corporation and Private Property, (New-York, Harcourt, Brace and World).

Brenner, R., 1983, History - the Human Gamble, (Chicago, University of Chicago Press).

Buckley P.J., and M.Casson, 1988, A Theory of Cooperation in International Business, in Contractor F. and P. Lorange (Eds), Cooperative Strategies in International Business, (Lexington, Mass., Lexington Books), 31-54.

Burt, R.S., 1980, Cooptative Corporate Actor Networks: a Reconsideration, Administrative Science Quarterly, 25 : 3.

Caves, R.E., 1982, Multinational Entreprise and Economic Analysis, (Cambridge MA, Cambridge University Press).

Deutsch, K., 1962, Cooperation and Trust: Some Theoretical Notes, Nebraska Symposium on Motivation, 275-319.

Fudenberg, D., and E. Maskin, 1986, A Folk Theorem in Repeated Games with Imperfect Information, Econometrica, 54, 533-54.

Ghemawat, P., Porter, M.E. and R.A.Rawlinson, 1986, Patterns of International Coalition Activity, in M. Porter, (Ed.), Competition in Global Industries, (Boston, Harvard Business School Press), 345-365.

Geringer, J.M., 1988, Joint Venture Partner Selection, (New York, Quorum Books).

Granovetter M., 1985, Economic Action and Social Structure: The Problem of Embeddedness, American Journal of Sociology, 91, 481-510.

Hamel, G., Doz, Y., and C.K. Prahalad, 1989, Collaborate with your Competitors and Win, Harvard Business Review, January.

Heide J.B., and G. John, 1988, The Role of Dependence Balancing in Safeguarding Transaction-Specific Assets in Conventional Channels, Journal of Marketing, 52, 20-35.

Hennart, J.F., 1988, A Transaction Costs Theory of Equity Joint Ventures, Strategic Management Journal, 9:4, 361-374.

Hirschmann, A.O., 1984, Against Parsimony: Three Easy Ways of Complicating Some Categories of Economic Discourse, American Economic Review, 74, 88-96.

Killing, J.P., 1988, Understanding Alliances: the Role of Task and Organizational Complexity, in F.J. Contractor and P. Lorange (Eds.), Cooperative Strategies in International Business, (Lexington, Mass., Lexington Books), 55-68.

Koenig C., and R.A. Thiétart, 1988, Managers, Engineers and Government: The Emergence of the Mutual Organization in the European Aerospace Industry, Technology in Society, 10: 1, 45-70.

Kogut, B., 1988a, Joint Ventures: Theoretical and Empirical Perspectives, Strategic Management Journal, 9: 4, 319-332.

Kogut, B., 1988b, A Study of the Life Cycle of Joint-Ventures, in F.J. Contractor and P. Lorange (Eds.) Cooperative Strategies in International Business, (Lexington, Mass., Lexington Books), 169-186.

Kogut, B., and H. Singh, 1988, Entering the United States by Joint-Venture: Competitive Rivalry and Industry Structure, in F.J. Contractor and P. Lorange (Eds.) Cooperative Strategies in International Business, 251-251.

Kreps, D.M., Milgrom, P., Roberts, J., and R. Wilson, 1982, Rational Cooperation in the Finitely-Repeated Prisoner's Dilemma, Journal of Economic Theory, 27, 245-252.

Luhmann, N., 1973, Vertrauen, (Stutgart, Ferdinand Enke Verlag).

Luhmann, N., 1988, Familiarity, Confidence, Trust: Problems and Alternatives, in D. Gambetta, (Ed.), Trust, (Oxford, Basil Blackwell), 94-107.

Lynch, G., 1989, The Pratical Guide to Joint-Ventures and Corporate Alliances, (London, John Wiley).

Macaulay, S., 1963, Non Contractual Relations in Business: A Preliminary Study, American Sociological Review, 28, 55-67.

O'Toole, R., and A.W. O'Toole, 1981, Negotiating Interorganizational Orders, The Sociological Quarterly, 22, 29-41.

Ouchi, W.G., 1980, Markets, Bureaucracies and Clans, Administrative Science Quarterly, 25, 120-142.

Pennings, J.M., 1980, Interlocking Directorates, (San-Fransisco, Jossey Bass).

Pfeffer, J., and G. Salancik, 1978, The External Control of Organizations: a Resource Dependence Perspective, (New-Yor,: Harper and Row).

Polanyi, M., 1964, Personal Knowledge, (New York, Harper and Row).

Reich, R.B., and E.D. Mankin, 1986, Joint-Venture with Japan: Give Away your Future, Harvard Business Review, March 1986.

Rugman, A.M., 1981, Inside the Multinationals: the Economics of Internal Markets, (New York, Columbia University Press).

Selznick, P., 1949, TVA and the Grass Roots, (Berkeley, Cal., University of California Press).

Sobel, J., 1985, A Theory of Credibility, Review of Economic Studies, LII, 557-573.

Teece, D., 1986, Profiting from Technological Innovation: Implications for Integration, Collaboration, Licencing and Public Policy, Cambridge, Mass., Ballinger, 185-219.

Van Wijk, G., 1985, The Role of Shared Understanding and Trust in Loan Decisions, (Unpublished Doctoral Dissertation, Columbia University).

Vickers, G., 1967, Towards a Sociology of Management, (New York, Basic Books).

Walker, J.W., and T.G. Gutteridge, 1979, Career Planning, Amacor Practices, An AMA Survey Report.

Walker, G., 1988, Strategic Sourcing, Vertical Integration and Transaction Costs, Interfaces, 18: 3, 62-73.

Wall, J.A., 1975, The Effects of Constituent Trust and Representative Barganining Visibility on Intergroup Bargaining, Organizational Behavior and Human Performance, 14: 2, 244-256.

Walton, R.E., and McKersie R.B., 1965, Behavioral Theory of Labor Negotiation, (New York, Mc Graw Hill).

Weigelt, K., and C. Camerer, 1988, Reputation and Corporate Strategy: A Review of Recent Theory and Applications, Strategic Management Journal, 9: 5, 443-454.

Williamson, O.E., 1975, Markets and Hierarchies, (New-York, Free Press).

Williamson, O.E., 1985, The Economic Institutions of Capitalism, (New-York, Free Press).

MICROECONOMIC CONTRIBUTIONS TO STRATEGIC MANAGEMENT
J. Thépot and R.-A. Thiétart
© 1991 Elsevier Science Publishers B.V. All rights reserved.

CHAPTER 10

STRATEGIC MANAGEMENT AND VERTICAL DISINTEGRATION: A TRANSACTION COST APPROACH

C. BOONE and A. VERBEKE
State University of Antwerp   Free University of Brussels
and Belgian National Foundation
of Scientific Research

Abstract

In this chapter a new conceptual framework is developed to explain the present tendency toward vertical disintegration in several manufacturing industries. It appears that existing transaction cost theory, which emphasizes the benefits of vertical integration, cannot fully explain this trend. Hence, the transaction cost paradigm is extended through the introduction of conceptual elements from organization theory and strategic management theory. The new framework allows to explain the tendency toward vertical disintegration taking into account both the benefits and costs of vertical integration as compared to other governance structures.

1. Introduction

Several authors have recently observed a tendency toward vertical disintegration of large corporations.

Child (1987) discusses this phenomenon based upon an analysis of U.K. firms, in sectors such as electronics, foodstuff, distribution, textiles, etc. A similar evolution was reported by Jarillo (1988) for the United States. Furthermore, several case studies on vertical disintegration in companies such as Benetton, Rank-Xerox, British Steel Corporation, McKesson Corporation, Chrysler and British Leyland have been reported (Child, 1987; Johnston and Lawrence, 1988; Shutt and Whittington, 1987).

The authors thank Prof. Dr. B. De Brabander for his helpful comments on an earlier draft.

When assessing this large body of empirical material, Child (1987, p. 37) concludes that "... greater recourse to market and quasi-market transactions is likely to be a continuing feature - and not merely a passing fashion reflecting inter alia the Japanese use of subcontracting - because it offers identifiable advantages in modern economy".
In this context, Ford and Farmer (1986) have coined the term "shrinking organization", especially in high technology sectors. This implies the substitution of internal production within the firm by contractual arrangements with suppliers, in spite of the obvious costs entailed by such an organizational change (Freeman and Hannan, 1975). Thompson and Wright (1988) have argued that this shift from internalization toward other institutional arrangements to regulate transactions needs more systematic analysis.

The purpose of this chapter is to develop a conceptual framework aimed at explaining vertical disintegration. This framework incorporates both elements of Williamson's (1975, 1985) transaction cost based framework and insights obtained from traditional organization theory, agency theory and the recent model of Jones and Hill (1988).
The main proposition of this chapter is that firms engaged in a competitive strategy emphasizing innovation and flexibility on the downstream side (as a result of particular characteristics of the final producer-consumer transactions) may reduce transaction costs by externalizing a number of production activities on the upstream side (thus influencing the buyer-supplier interface).

The first section of this chapter argues that the present tendency toward vertical disintegration is not entirely consistent with the predictions of the traditional transaction cost model (Williamson 1975, 1985). Although Williamson has written an article on the "incentive limits" of firms (Williamson, 1984), he does not really emphasize the internal costs of operating a hierarchy i.e., the bureaucratic costs of internalization.
For example, Grossman and Hart (1986) and Evans and Grossman (1983) have clearly demonstrated that common ownership does not eliminate opportunistic behavior. In addition, the problem of bounded rationality is not solved automatically either in a hierarchy, a point which has not yet been discussed by Williamson in the context of vertical integration.

In the second section, we develop the argument that the bureaucratic costs associated with the internalization of transactions may increase substantially as a result of strategic responses to rapid environmental changes. This increase in bureaucratic costs then partly explains the observed phenomenon of vertical disintegration. In this context, the present chapter builds upon Jones and Hill's (1988) insights, as to the impact of bureaucratic costs on firm behavior.

However, there are three important differences between our framework and Jones and Hill's (1988) model. First, in our view the optimal level of vertical integration can

Chapter 10 - Strategic Management 187

only be determined if the firm is explicitly regarded as a network of different types of transactions, in the spirit of Kogut (1988). Hence, corporate strategic behavior at the final producer-consumer interface (downstream) may substantially influence the optimal institutional arrangement for the supplier-buyer interface (upstream). Second, Jones and Hill's (1988) model only deals with multidivisional companies, whereas our framework is also applicable to determine the limits of functionally organized firms. Third, Jones and Hill's (1988) model does not explicitly deal with the issue of vertical disintegration. The applicability of their model to the issue of vertical disintegration is only dealt with in a footnote.

The third section of the chapter extends Williamson's transaction cost theory by simultaneously taking into account the relative benefits of vertical integration resulting from asset specificity and the bureaucratic costs of vertical integration resulting from specific strategic choices of firms.

The fourth section provides an analysis of intermediate forms of organization located between the extremes of vertical integration and short term contracts. It is demonstrated that these intermediate forms of organization defined as quasi-integration by Blois (1972, 1980), may lead to a minimization of transaction costs. In addition, the preference of firms for quasi-integration can also be partly explained by problems of transfer of organizational knowledge and learning, as demonstrated by Kogut (1988) in the realm of joint ventures.

The last section provides suggestions as to the empirical testing of the main proposition put forward in the chapter.

2. Limits of the Williamsonian transaction cost paradigm

The transaction cost framework developed by Williamson (1975, 1985) does not allow to perform adequate predictions of the present tendency toward vertical disintegration.

Williamson's (1975, 1985) main contribution in this area has been the identification of vertical integration and outside sourcing as alternative institutional arrangements. He has argued that outside sourcing will be associated with comparatively higher transaction costs in cases where only a limited number of suppliers can provide the required inputs ("small numbers bargaining") and both the firm and the selected supplier(s) need to engage in specific investments and develop proprietary know-how to make transactions possible ("asset specificity"). For example, this occurs when a supplier needs to invest in highly specialized equipment in order to ensure quality for a unique buyer. Small numbers bargaining and asset specificity imply that "switching costs" become very high for both the supplier and the buyer. In other words, cancelling the contractual arrangement could lead to severe losses for both parties. If the contract were cancelled, the supplier would be faced with substantial

difficulties when attempting to use his specific assets for other purposes.
In a similar vein, it could be extremely difficult for the buyer to secure a similar contract with another supplier in the short run, if specific know how, both machine- and people embodied, would be required from this supplier. From the point of view of the buying firm, the problem of opportunism could then arise. Opportunism refers to cheating behavior, e.g., when a supplier knowingly does not respect required quality standards expected by the buyer. Such opportunism cannot be prevented, as it is never possible to develop contractual arrangements that would take into account all possible contingencies (Williamson, 1979). In such circumstances, vertical integration becomes the most efficient institutional structure (Hennart, 1987). Vertical integration thus creates "integration economies". These may result from three elements. First, the danger of opportunistic behavior by outside suppliers is eliminated. Second, vertical integration leads to a more efficient allocation of recources within the integrated firm. Third, the costs of developing and managing complex contractual arrangements with outside suppliers are eliminated.

In reality, however, the present tendency toward vertical disintegration is sometimes observed in industries characterized by small numbers bargaining and at least some degree of asset specificity such as the automobile industry and consumer electronics. The existence of asset specificity in consumer electronics is described in Kumpe and Bolwijn (1988). Nevertheless, Jarillo (1988, p. 33) has identified vertical disintegration in the consumer electronics industry : "... more and more American firms are subcontracting part of their products - or even the whole manufacturing function - to Japanese or Korean competitors."

In addition, several companies, e.g., in the automobile industry actively search for component suppliers located near their main operations (Fabrimetal, 1987). Shonberger and Gilbert (1983) have described the case of Tricon, which supplies seats to Kawasaki in the U.S. Tricon is located very near Kawasaki as geographical proximity is very important for the efficient operation of the supply function. This is an example of "site specificity", as described by Williamson (1985, p. 95). This author argues, however, that site specificity will lead to vertical integration, as a result of the fact that once such assets are located, the parties are thereafter operating in a bilateral exchange relation for the useful life of the assets. This prediction is in contradiction with the present tendency toward vertical disintegration.

The main reason for this faulty prediction is the neglect of bureaucratic costs, associated with vertical integration (Jones and Hill, 1988 ; Perrow, 1981), although it must be recognized that the declining relative benefits of vertical integration as a result of lower asset specificity may be equally important (see next section). The issue of agency costs is especially important in this respect. Agency costs refer to the results of sub-goal pursuit and opportunism by (lower-level) employees and subunits in complex organizations, in the spirit of Jensen and Mecklin (1976) and Fama and Jensen (1983). In other words, vertical integration may increase coordination and control costs in the organization and thus facilitates the pursuit of local goals which conflict with organizational goals. In addition, the problem of "bounded rationality" arises, i.e., the limited capacity of the human mind for formulating and solving complex problems, as compared with the size of problems whose solution is required for objectively rational behavior in the real world (Simon, 1957). If vertical integration implies a larger size of the firm, this will lead to a higher complexity of the organization. Thus, new (and costly) coordination and control systems will be required to cope with the problem of bounded rationality.

Hence, a careful analysis is required of both the benefits and costs of vertical integration, before predictions can be made as to the optimal level of internalization.

In the next section, it will be argued that the competitive strategy chosen by the firm largely determines the level of bureaucratic costs and may thus influence the optimal level of vertical integration.

3. Competitive strategy and bureaucratic costs

In order to explain vertical disintegration, the organization needs to be viewed as a network of different types of transactions, each of which is associated with specific participants, e.g., suppliers, buyers and employees, see also March and Simon (1958). Kogut (1988) has clearly demonstrated in an important article on the conceptual foundations of joint ventures that transaction cost based theories and strategic management theories are largely complements, not substitutes. The former emphasize the joint minimization of production and transaction costs, whereas the latter focus on profit maximizing behavior through the improvement of a firm's competitive position vis-a-vis rivals (Kogut, 1988, p. 322). In our view, both approaches are strongly interrelated. For example, a competitive strategy aimed at improving the firm's competitiveness through innovation and flexibility may lead to changes in the bureaucratic costs associated with vertical integration. Transaction cost considerations may then lead firms to externalize certain transactions. The general conceptual framework is represented in Figure 1.

Figure 1 suggests that upstream vertical disintegration partly results from an increase in bureaucratic costs. These bureaucratic costs are largely determined by strategies of vertically integrated firms aimed at achieving innovation and flexibility on the down-stream side. Such strategic behavior reflects a dynamic environment, which includes elements such as a short product life cycle, rapid changes of customer needs or product specifications, the globalisation of competition etc... Other determinants of innovation which are not dealt with in this article are discussed in Miller, Kets De Vries and Toulouse (1982), Miller and Friesen (1982) and Miller (1983).

The relationship between environmental dynamism and strategic management is reciprocal, as the pursuit of strategies of innovation and flexibility in an industry increases environmental dynamism (Miller, 1988).

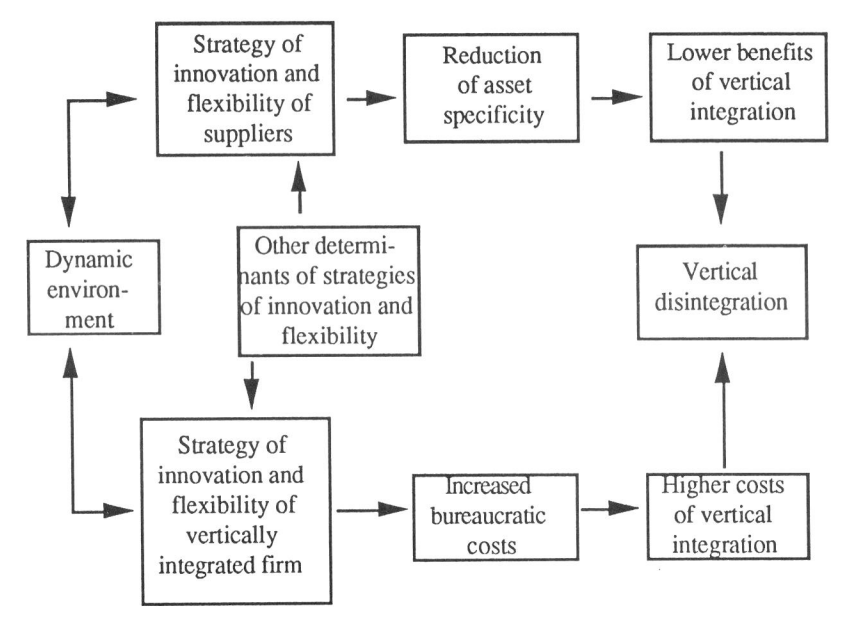

Figure 1:

Competitive strategy, transaction costs and vertical disintegration

Such strategies strongly influence bureaucratic costs. The reasons for an increase of these costs, however, are different for functionally organized firms (U-form) as compared to multidivisional companies (M-form). The increase of bureaucratic costs in a U-form is related to a rise in organizational complexity and the associated problems of bounded rationality. In contrast, higher bureaucratic costs in an M-form primarily result from agency problems (information impactedness) and the incentive limits in the M-form. Therefore, both types of firms will be discussed below although the process described in Figure 1 is valid in both cases.

Apart from this increase of bureaucratic coordination and control costs, it should of course be recognized that the relative benefits of vertical integration may simultaneously decline, because of similar strategies of innovation and flexibility being pursued by suppliers. In many industries, such as metal processing for instance, suppliers attempt to increase flexibility (Fabrimetal, 1984, 1985, 1986) through investments in advanced manufacturing technology (AMT). The final result of such increased supplier flexibility is a reduction of "asset specificity", which is one of the major determining factors of vertical integration, and thus allows increased competition at the supplier side. This reduces the risk of opportunism and makes contractual arrangements with suppliers more attractive.

3.1. The limits of the U-form

Bureaucratic costs may rise substantially for firms that implement competitive strategies aimed at achieving innovation and flexibility. Therefore, vertical disintegration may become comparatively more efficient than a hierarchical form of organization.

First, many firms engage in strategies of flexibility so as to adapt themselves to an increase of "demand risks", in the spirit of Child (1987, p. 34). Demand risks reflect rapid changes in consumer needs and product specifications. Examples include the introduction of flexible manufacturing systems (FMS), computer aided manufacturing (CAM), Just In Time (JIT), Kanban, etc... (Herroelen and Lambrecht, 1984). These techniques are used to bring production possibilities closer in line with customer needs and to reduce inventories. Especially competitive firms in the electronics sector, metal processing and the automobile industry presently attempt to introduce such systems. In practice, this often implies an evolution from mass production to "batch" production (small production runs). Reeves and Turner (1972) suggest that the required organizational complexity for such firms is very high, as compared to mass producers. The main organizational problem resulting from batch production systems is the occurrence of reciprocal dependence among the different production units in the vertical chain. This is in contrast with the sequential dependence characterizing mass production (Thompson, 1967 ; Galbraith, 1970). Sequential dependence can easily be coped with through the introduction of buffer stocks. However, reciprocal dependence requires complex organizational structures, since coordination through mutual adjustment (e.g. coordination committees) becomes necessary (Reeves and Turner, 1972). For example, organizational complexity sharply increases when JIT-systems are introduced.
In other words, higher environmental dynamism stimulates the development of strategies of flexibility. The implementation of such strategies then requires the introduction of more complex (and costly) organizational arrangements (March and Simon, 1958). As a result, coordination and control problems occur, which reflect a problem of bounded rationality.

Second, many firms recognize the increasing importance of innovation as a source of competitive advantage. Strong innovation activities in specific industries mostly reflect a dynamic and heterogenous environment (Miller, Kets De Vries and Toulouse, 1982). Lawrence and Lorsch (1967) have demonstrated that the effective functioning of a firm in an unstable environment requires again specific (and costly) organizational arrangements. In such a case, each functional department needs a differentiated organizational approach, in terms of coordination and control systems used. Organizational differentiation of the different subunits then requires integration, however, so as to allow the achievement of the firm's goals. Lawrence and Lorsch (1967) concluded that highly performing companies in unstable environments were characterized by strong organizational differentiation and integration. In the context of vertical integration, it can be expected that highly innovative firms will incur high internal costs to set up differentiated coordination and control systems in all their different subunits. For example, Miller (1988) has shown that innovative organizations require a large number of staff people, high decentralisation, many "liason" functions etc... This is consistent with an "organic" structure (as opposed to a "mechanistic" structure) described by Burns and Stalker (1961). Williamson (1975) has recognized that the number of hierarchical levels strongly increases when functionally organized corporations become larger. This results from bounded rationality of the managers and the related limits on the "span of control". The consequence of a larger hierarchy, however, is a mechanistic, formalized structure, which hinders innovation. Thus, it can be predicted that the bureaucratic costs will strongly increase for large firms which build upon innovations as a source of competitive advantage. As a result, vertical disintegration can be expected.

Furthermore, the need for strategies of flexibility and the importance of innovation as a source of competitive advantage, both upstream and downstream, require the use of high-powered incentives. As Williamson (1984, p. 746) argues : only "... markets elicit high-powered incentives which are degraded upon organizing the same transactions within firms. And internal organization has access to control apparatus which markets are denied". Thus, high-powered incentives are not equally important to all transactions, but could, according to Williamson (1984), be extremely important in situations in which opportunities for innovation exist. This could be an important reason why new organizational forms (hybrid forms) can be observed in the semi-conductor industry (Williamson, 1984).

3.2. The limits of the M-Form

It could be argued that the problem of control loss in large integrated and functionally organized firms (U-form) could be solved by the introduction of a multidivisional structure (M-form) in which headquarters would intervene selectively (Williamson, 1975). However, an M-form structure does not allow unlimited vertical integration.

Several authors have argued that the M-form is not necessarily optimal for backward vertically related production processes (Caves, 1980 ; Cable, 1988). This is because interdependencies between activities create particularly important problems (Wright, 1988). For example, Otley (1988, p. 104) has suggested that : "... accounting measures of performance become less appropriate when the degree of interdependence between operating units increases". Hence, it is necessary to use subjective evaluations which may become extremely difficult in highly dynamic environments

Chapter 10 - Strategic Management

as will be explained below.

Furthermore, Eccles (1985) has observed that many firms are of the "collaborative" type, i.e., both highly diversified and highly vertically integrated. Such firms require very complex multidivisional structures. In such firms subunit managers must cooperate and compete simultaneously. Unfortunately, optimal M-form implementation requires the separation of strategic and operational decisions (Williamson, 1975), which is not possible when interdependencies among subunits occur. Strong diversification and vertical integration may also result in the use of varying management styles within the same firm (Wright, 1988), which may be incompatible. In this context, Hill (1988) argued that a trade-off must be performed between realizing benefits from an internal capital market with a pure M-form, or reaping benefits from exploiting interrelationships among subunits. To realize both seems to be incompatible.

In our view, the conditions and reasons why the M-form may fail in the case of vertically related business units are approximately the same as the ones proposed in the discussion of figure 1. That is, under high environmental dynamism - which requires strategies of flexibility and innovation - common ownership may be suboptimal. This argument draws heavily on the analysis of Evans and Grossman (1983) ; suppose that an integrated firm has two divisions : an upstream and a downstream division. If the consumer market of the downstream division is highly dynamic, i.e., characterized by technological changes, frequent shifts in customer needs, short product life cycles and volatility of demand, it is likely that costly midstream modifications in transactions may arise. To fully reap the benefits of integrated activities, headquarters then have to intervene selectively when taking decisions on midstream modifications. However, due to environmental dynamism, information is decentralized which results in an information asymmetry between headquarters and divisions (Wright, 1988). This agency problem (information impactedness) (Chenhall and Morris, 1986) makes it impossible to use the fundamental benefit of bureaucratic organization i.e., selective intervention by fiat. That is why, according to Evans and Grossman (1983, p. 118), conglomerates try to "mimic" markets by using profit centers. Indeed, a survey of Vancil (1978) demonstrates that most of the companies studied used transfer pricing to exchange resources across divisions. This study also reveals that, due to information asymmetry, headquarters used managerial incentives almost solely based on the financial performance of their profit centers in the majority of firms. The use of subjective judgement, although required in dynamic environments (Hirst, 1981 ; Govindarajan, 1984) and in cases of interdependent activities between business units (Otley, 1988) seems to be impossible in complex decentralized companies. Thus, it appears that in such circumstances high-powered (market like) incentives are used. Williamson (1984) however has argued convincingly that the use of high-powered incentives in integrated firms invariably breaks down. For example, in the case of innovation in the supplying stage the "uncorrupted" use of high-powered incentives would allow the supplying division to reap the benefits of this innovation.

However, in practice it can be expected that the purchasing division will demand a "fair share" of the gains if it contributed to the innovation. Unfortunately, in most cases the contribution of both divisions cannot be assessed objectively ex-post. Thus, selective intervention of headquarters is required to determine transfer prices. Therefore, integrated firms in a dynamic environment face a serious dilemma. On the one hand, efficient bureaucratic control (selective intervention and the use of subjective appraisal systems) is not possible due to information asymmetry. On the other hand, if firms use high-powered incentives, these will not work or lead to costly haggling. The study of Vancil (1978) clearly demonstrates these conflicts. For example, in one particular case the author found (Vancil, 1978, p. 48-49) : "The managers of the product profit centers are not required to purchase components from the manufacturing profit centers, but when they do, the price is negotiated between the two profit center managers just as it would be negotiated between an independent buyer and seller. Nevertheless, interdivisional squabbles over transfer prices are frequent and sometimes bitter". A system of market contracts would obviously face the same coordination problems in those circumstances. However, high-powered incentives, which are extremely important in turbulent environments, could be used without incentive distortion. Competitive bids are always possible if two or more possible component suppliers can be found (Evans and Grossman, 1983), risks can be spread (Harrigan, 1983) and firms focus on the activities in the vertical chain for which they have the strongest firm specific advantages (Jarillo, 1988) ; as a result they can economize on bounded rationality.

Furthermore, a frequently neglected element which curbes opportunistic behavior in markets is reputation (Richardson, 1972 ; Evans and Grossman, 1983). Every firm that wants to survive in the long run has to build a reputation for fair dealing.

In an environment characteristized by low dynamism and less complex transactions, bureaucratic control becomes possible. First, there is no information asymmetry. Corporate headquarters have the expertise to judge the benefits and costs of midstream modifications and to engage in selective interventions. The use of hierarchical, low-powered incentives becomes possible for the same reason. Headquarters can evaluate division managers in a more subjective, flexible manner, which is necessary when low-powered incentives are used. Under these conditions there is no incompatibility between incentives and selective intervention. Thus, low environmental dynamism diminishes the agency problem and therefore the bureaucratic costs of internal organization. However, because there is less need for midstream modification (i.e., low uncertainty) it could be argued that two arms-length companies can operate as efficiently as under common ownership (Evans and Grossman, 1983), except in the case of a substantial level of asset specificity.

There is some corroborating empirical evidence concerning the analysis made above. For instance, Harrigan (1983, 1985a) found that the percentage of internal purchases between business units decreases as industry volatility increases. In an extended study, Harrigan (1985b) found similar results. Strategic business units produced less in-house, and firms were engaged in fewer stages of processing, in cases where demand was highly uncertain.

4. An extension of transaction cost theory

In this section, the conceptual elements developed above are integrated into transaction cost theory. In our view two core variables need to be taken into account, when determining the optimal degree of vertical integration, namely asset specificity (which can be high, intermediate or low) and the importance of innovation and flexibility in competitive strategies (high or low). The first variable is very important as transaction cost theory developed by Williamson, which explains the benefits of vertical integration, predicts that these benefits will increase when asset specificity increases.
The importance of innovation and flexibility in competitive strategies also needs to be considered, however. It has been argued in earlier sections that the choice of a strategy aimed at achieving innovation and flexibility increases the bureaucratic costs of hierarchical organization. In other words, the level of innovation and flexibility in competitive strategies determines the implementation costs associated with the internalization of transactions.

The optimal level of vertical integration is then determined by both its benefits, as measured by the degree of asset specificity and its costs, represented by the importance of innovation and flexibility in competitive strategies.

Our suggestion is that many industries are partly characterized by both intermediate asset specificity at the buyer-supplier interface (otherwise vertical integration would not have been observed in the first place) and innovation and flexibility as important components of competitive strategy. This latter element increases the bureaucratic costs associated with vertical integration. In cases of high asset specificity, vertical integration would always remain the most efficient mode of organizing the buyer-supplier interface, irrespective of competitive strategy choices. High asset specificity is related to the concept of "firm specific advantages" (FSA) in internalization theory (Rugman, 1981). Core FSAs of a company need to be exploited within the framework of a hierarchy so as to overcome natural market imperfections.
In contrast, in cases of low asset specificity, conventional market contracts will be the most efficient governance structure for the regulation of transactions, again irrespective of the importance of innovation and flexibility in competitive strategy.

However, if intermediate asset specificity prevails and firms try to implement strategies of innovation and flexibility, the implementation costs of internalization could become so large that a shift from internal organization to market coordination can be expected.

In the next section it is argued that sole reliance on market transactions is not

sufficient to realize effective coordination and control. Therefore, the development of hybrid forms (i.e., the strategic management of market transactions) becomes necessary. In these circumstances, transaction costs associated with simple market contracts may sharply rise as a result of ineffective coordination and control and the danger of opportunism.
An alternative, but related theoretical explanation for the occurrence of such hybrid forms has been suggested by Kogut (1988) albeit in the context of joint ventures. He argues that short term market contracts may be rejected by firms, not only for transaction cost reasons but also because the very knowledge which needs to be transferred between the parties involved is organizationally embedded, see Kogut (1988, p. 323).

Both theories differ as to the motives for quasi-integration. Transaction cost theory argues that hybrid forms of organization are an efficient solution to solve the hasards of market contracts while the theory of organizational learning as discussed by Kogut views hybrid forms as an instrument to transfer organizational knowledge. Irrespective of the motives involved, in both cases hybrid forms are generated because of market failure.

5. The strategic management of contractual relations.

In the analysis made above a conceptual distinction was drawn between simple (short term) market contracts and internalization. In reality, a large number of intermediate institutional arrangements can be designed to secure the supply of components. Richardson (1972, p. 887) has described this complete set of institutional arrangements as "... a continuum passing from transactions, such as those on organized commodity markets, where the co-operative element is minimal, through intermediate areas in which there are linkages of traditional connection and goodwill, and finally to those complex and inter-locking clusters, groups and alliances which represent co-operation fully and formally developed.". In this context, Blois (1980) has coined the term "quasi-integration" or "vertical quasi-integration", while Thorelli (1986) has used the concept of "networks".

In other words, there are more alternatives for vertical integration than just the introduction of short term market contracts. Such contracts would indeed limit coordination and control possibilities of manufacturing firms that use outside suppliers. Such contracts would certainly not be suitable for manufacturers that develop strategies of innovation and flexibility. In any case, large manufacturing firms could engage in opportunistic behaviour vis-à-vis their component suppliers faced with a situation of competitive bidding for short term contracts (Lamming, 1986). Such opportunism would only lead to short run gains, as suppliers themselves would not be willing to engage in long term commitments (e.g., investments in specific assets) and could also become opportunistic (e.g. neglecting quality controls). Thus, the main challenge for manufacturers of end products is to develop strategic networks of contractual arrangements, so as to build reciprocal commitments with suppliers. A "clan atmosphere" needs to be created, whereby the different parties involved pursue common goals. In contrast, such common goals would not exist in the case of short run contracts, where contractual negotiations would always be considered as a "zero-sum game". The creation of reciprocal commitment and trust requires substantial efforts of the different parties involved. The willingness must exist to develop long term contracts and close working relationships, e.g., as concerns the exchange of information (Schonberger and Gilbert, 1983). It is also important to generate balanced contracts, e.g., in terms of the distribution of risks between the supplying firm and the manufacturer of end products. In this context, Kawasaki and McMillan (1986) have observed the willingness of large Japanese manufacturers to absorb part of the risks involved by component suppliers. For example, in most supply contracts, prices are determined based upon "cost-plus" principles as opposed to "fixed-price" principles. In the latter case, the supplier would bear the full risk of the transaction.

Only through the careful strategic management of contractual relations, can the benefits normally associated with a hierarchical organization (coordination and control) be obtained, but without incurring the bureaucratic costs of such a hierarchy (since long term contracts also benefit from the "high powered incentives" of the market system). MacMillan and Farmer (1979) have argued that such cooperative arrangements are very efficient, because market elements still exist. For example, if the manufacturer of end products is really unsatisfied with a supplier, contractual arrangements can still be cancelled in the medium run. Jarillo (1988) has extensively described the main advantages associated with the development of strategic networks of suppliers. First, risks are distributed among different legally independent corporations. Second, each firm in the network is specialized in the production of specific components. As a result, each can develop firm specific advantages or distinctive competences in particular segments of the value chain of the end product. Thus, it can be concluded, following Jarillo (1988, p. 38): "The flexibility and focus that result from disintegration, made possible by the existence of a network that takes care of the other functions, can be extremely powerful competitive weapons, especially in environments that experience rapid change, due to increasingly rapid technological pace, globalization of competition, or the apparition of new, flexible, focused, desintegrated competitors.".

A well-known example of effective strategic management of contractual relations is the case of the Japanese automobile industry. An excellent analysis of the network structure in this industry has been carried out by Nishiguchi (1987). This author has demonstrated that unstability of demand, "batch" production systems and strategies of flexible manufacturing have lead to the creation of a sophisticated system of contractual relations. For example, all large manufacturers except Honda have grouped their suppliers in so-called "Kyoryokukai" (cooperation groups). These are different from the widely documented "Keiretsu". Keiretsu refer to institutional arrangements whereby large automobile manufactures secure commitment of component suppliers through equity participation and "interlocking directorates". Such an institutional form is obviously closer to vertical integration than to a contractual arrangement. Such groups organize information exchange meetings at all levels of personnel, from low-level blue collar workers to topmanagement, especially to improve production methods and to integrate component supply and the assembly of end products. The most important suppliers which are grouped in "primary" Kyoryokukai in turn control "secondary" Kyoryokukai grouping their own suppliers. In other words, the control of secondary suppliers is in fact delegated to a small number of primary suppliers. This results in reduced comparative benefits of internalization since a substantial portion of the costs required to coordinate and control outside component supply is borne by suppliers. For example, the central purchasing department of Toyota is very small (337 buyers in 1985) as compared with that of General Motors (6000 buyers in 1987). This is remarkable, especially since outside component supply represents 70% of Toyota's production costs, whereas it constitutes only 25% in the case of General Motors.

We should emphasize that component suppliers in Japan are continuously involved in the development of new automobile designs. They are also entrusted with a high level of autonomy when designing the components and parts in which they have specialized. Hence, coordination and control costs associated with outside supply are again reduced. It could be argued that such strong involvement of primary suppliers creates risks for the automobile manufacturers. The system of Kyoryokukai can only function if the manufacturer of end products transmits proprietary information (a public good) on product and process designs to its suppliers. Since these outsiders also supply components to rival manufacturers of end products, the access to proprietary information of these manufacturers could lead to opportunistic behavior. In other words, a supplier could transmit information about a manufacturer's distinctive competences to rivals, thus generating a dissipation of the manufacturer's actual FSAs. In reality, neither the components or parts provided by outside suppliers nor the information they receive from the manufacturer, constitute an important firm specific advantage of this manufacturer. In fact, a manufacturer's actual FSA precisely consists of the core technology which remains internalized and the firm's ability to integrate all the components into an end product.

Finally, it should be recognized that the risks of opportunistic behaviour by component suppliers are very small ; it is often mistakenly asserted that small component suppliers in Japan are being exploited by large manufacturers of automobiles. The example mostly given to substantiate this claim is the fact that employees of component suppliers earn much lower wages than the employees of the automobile manufacturers. In reality, the entrepreneurs (managers - owners) in these small companies earn on average twice as much as executives of the same age and with similar professional qualifications, employed by the manufacturers of end products. Furthermore, opportunistic behaviour is prevented precisely because suppliers are allowed to sell components to different manufacturers, thus protecting them against unfavourable demand conditions faced by individual manufacturers of end products.

6. Empirical implications

Empirical research on vertical disintegration is certainly required. Unfortunately, existing studies on this subject are relatively scarce. Direct verification of the theoretical explanations for vertical disintegration as suggested in this article is difficult for two reasons.

First, many authors feel that concepts developed in transaction cost theory are too vague and lack precision (Pfeffer, 1982). Williamson (1979, p. 233) has admitted himself that there are too many degrees of freedom and several concepts need clearer definitions. The development of instruments to measure transaction costs remains a difficult task.
Second, the phenomenon of vertical disintegration and the increase of hybrid forms of organisation is relatively new. Only in the long run it will become clear unambiguously in which circumstances hybrid forms are the most efficient form of organization (Hannan and Freeman, 1977).

Nevertheless, the framework developed in this article is sufficiently general to perform empirical tests on the failure of the initially integrated firm with a U-form structure. However, these tests need to be performed in an indirect manner and without direct measurement of bureaucratic costs. Our framework predicts a clear relationship between competitive strategy choices and the optimal degree of vertical integration. More specifically, given an intermediate level of asset specificity, a negative relationship can be anticipated between vertical integration and financial results in firms pursuing strategies aimed at achieving innovation or flexibility. In practice it is important that research would be conducted in relatively homogeneous sectors in terms of product scope, because the most common measure of vertical integration, i.e. the ratio of value added to sales (MacMillan, Hambrick and Pennings, 1986), depends upon the position of the firm in the vertical chain. Hence, firms located closer to the raw materials stage will normally have a high value for the vertical integration measure, which could create an important bias in cross sectional research. In addition, the type of market contracts must be identified as the effect of disintegration on financial results of firms engaged in strategies of innovation and flexibility will largely depend upon the "strategic" character of these contracts.

In the case of an M-form, the negative impact of vertical integration on financial results cannot be empirically investigated using the procedure above, as the financial results of downstream SBUs are partly determined by transfer prices set by the corporate headquarters. In addition, overall efficiency of the firm as a whole needs to be taken into account. Therefore, it is preferable to perform direct tests of agency problems in firms with an M-form, where downstream SBUs pursue competitive strategies geared toward innovation and flexibility. Nevertheless, an indirect test is also possible. Harrigan (1983, 1985a) observed a lower level of internal sourcing among SBUs in cases of high industry volatility. Similarly, we expect a lower level of internal sourcing in SBUs that pursue strategies of innovation as a result of the agency problems described above.

7. Conclusion

In many industries a tendency toward vertical disintegration can be observed. In our view, transaction cost thinking as developed by Williamson cannot fully explain this phenomenon. The main reason is that in Williamson's framework insufficient emphasis is put on the internal coordination and control costs associated with vertical integration. In this article it has been argued, based upon an analysis of both the benefits and costs of vertical integration, that many companies presently engage in vertical disintegration for two reasons. First, both endogenous and exogenous changes in environmental variables (e.g. rapid changes in demand, development of new information technologies). Second, the emphasis on innovation and flexibility in corporate strategies, partly as a reaction to environmental dynamism. However, contractual arrangements (and vertical disintegration) only constitute an efficient alternative to internalization if managed strategically. This implies the pursuit of long term relationships characterized by mutual trust and the development of networks. Only then can the benefits of a market system be obtained and the costs of a hierarchical system avoided.

Hannan and Freeman (1977) have argued that in the long run the most efficient institutional arrangements will survive, given particular environmental characteristics. In this context, we predict that vertical disintegration will probably increase in the near future in the industries characterized by a highly dynamic environment and corporate strategies aimed at achieving flexibility and innovation.

References

Blois, K.J., 1972, Vertical Quasi-Integration, Journal of Industrial Economics, 20, 253-272.

Blois, K.J., 1980, Quasi-Integration as a Mechanism for Controlling External Dependencies, Management Decision, 18, 55-63.

Burns, T., and G.M. Stalker, 1961, The Management of Innovation. (London, Tavistock).

Cable, J.R., 1988, Organisational Form and Economic Performance, in S. Thompson and M. Wright (Eds.), Internal Organisation, Efficiency and Profit, (Oxford, UK : Philip Allan), 12-36.

Chapter 10 - Strategic Management

Caves, R.E., 1980, Corporate Strategy and Structure, Journal of Economic Literature, 18, 64-92.

Chenhall, R.H., and D. Morris, 1986, The Impact of Structure, Environment and Interdependence on the Perceived Usefulness of Management Accounting Systems, Accounting Review, 61, 16-35.

Child, J., 1987, Infomation Technology, Organization, and the Response to Strategic Challenges, California Management Review, Fall, 33-50.

Eccles, R.G., 1985, The Transfer Pricing Problem: a Theory of Practice. (Cambridge, Mass., Lexington).

Evans, D.S., and S.J. Grossman, 1983, Integration. In D.S. Evans (Ed.), Breaking up Bell: Essays on Industrial Organization and Regulation, (New York, North Holland), 95-126.

Fabrimetal, 1984, Report Subcontracting, 10, 26-39.

Fabrimetal, 1985, Report Subcontracting, 10, 30-49.

Fabrimetal, 1986, Report Subcontracting, 10, 94-101.

Fabrimetal, 1987, Philips Belgium in Search of Local Subcontractors, 1, 28-31.

Fama, E.F., and M.C. Jensen, 1983, Agency Problems and Residual Claims, Journal of Law and Economics, 26, 327-349.

Ford, D., and D. Farmer, 1986, Make or Buy - a Key Strategic Issue, Long Range Planning, 19: 5, 54-62.

Freeman, J., and M.T. Hannan, 1975, Growth and Decline Processes in Organizations, American Sociological Review, 40, 215-228.

Galbraith, J., 1970, Environmental and Technological Determinants of Organizational Design, in J.W. Lorsch and P.R. Lawrence (Eds.), Organization Design, (Homewood Illinois, Irwin-Dorsey), 113-139.

Govindarajan, V., 1984, Appropriateness of Accounting Data in Performance Evaluation: an Empirical Examination of Environmental Uncertainty as an Intervening Variable, Accounting, Organization and Society, 9, 125-135.

Grossman, S.J., and O.D. Hart, O.D., 1986, The Costs and Benefits of Ownership: a Theory of Vertical and Lateral Integration, Journal of Political Economy, 94, 691-719.

Hannan, M.T., and J. Freeman, 1977, The Population Ecology of Organizations, American Journal of Sociology, 83, 929-964.

Harrigan, K.R., 1983, Strategies for Vertical Integration, (Mass., Lexington.)

Harrigan, K.R., 1985a, Strategies for Intrafirm Transfers and Outside Sourcing, Academy of Management Journal, 28, 914-925.

Harrigan, K.R., 1985b, Vertical Integration and Corporate Strategy, Academy of Management Journal, 28, 397-425.

Hennart, J.F., 1987, Upstream Vertical Integration in the Aluminium and Tin Industries. A Comparative Study of the Choice Between Market and Intrafirm Coordination, (Working Paper, University of Pennsylvania, Wharton School, Pennsylvania).

Herroelen, W., and M. Lambrecht, 1985, Innovatie in Produktie: de Strategische Doorbraak, (Antwerpen/Deventer, Kluwer).

Hill, C.W., 1988, Internal Capital Market Controls and Financial Performance in Multidivisional Firms, The Journal of Industrial Economics, 37, 67-84.

Hirst, M., 1981, Accounting Information and the Evaluation of Subordinate Performance : a Situational Approach, Accounting Review, 56, 771-781.

Jarillo, J.C., 1988, On Strategic Networks, Strategic Management Journal, 9, 31-41.

Jensen, M.C., and W.H. Meckling, 1976, Theory of the Firm: Managerial Behaviour, Agency Costs and Ownership Structure, Journal of Financial Economics, 3, 305-360.

Johnston, R., and P.R. Lawrence, 1988, Beyond Vertical Integration - The Rise of the Value Added Partnership, Harvard Business Review, July-August, 94-101.

Jones, G.R., and C.W. Hill, 1988, Transaction Cost Analysis of Strategy-Structure Choice, Strategic Management Journal, 9, 159-172.

Kawasaki, S., and J. McMillan, 1986, The design of Contracts: Evidence from Japanese Subcontracting, Mimeo, (University of Western Ontario, Ontario).

Kogut B., 1988, Joint Ventures: Theoretical and Empirical Perspectives, Strategic Management Journal, 9, 319-332.

Kumpe, T., and P.T. Bolwijn, 1988, Manufacturing: The New Case of Vertical Integration, Harvard Business Review, March-April, 75-81.

Lamming, R., 1986, For Better or for Worse: Technical Change and Buyer-Supplier Relationships, International Journal of Operations and Production Management, 6, 20-29.

Lawrence, P.R, and J.W. Lorsch, 1967, Differentiation and Integration in Complex Organizations, Administrative Science Quarterly, 12, 1-47.

MacMillan, K., and D. Farmer, 1979, Redefining the Boundaries of the Firm, Journal of Industrial Economics, 27, 277-285.

MacMillan, I.C., Hambrick, D.C. and J.M. Pennings, 1986, Uncertainty Reduction and the Threat of Supplier Retaliation: Two Views of the Backward Integration Decision, Organization Studies, 7, 263-278.

March, J.G., and H.A. Simon, 1958, Organizations, (New York, John Wiley).

Miller, D., Kets De Vries, M.F.R. and J.M. Toulouse, 1982, Top Executive Locus of Control and its Relationship to Strategy-Making, Structure and Environment, Academy of Management Journal, 25, 237-253.

Miller, D., and H. Friesen, 1982, Innovation in Conservative and Entrepreneurial Firms: Two Models of Strategic Momentum, Strategic Management Journal, 3, 1-25.

Miller, D., 1983, The Correlates of Entrepreneurship in Three Types of Firms, Management Science, 29, 770-791.

Miller, D., 1988, Relating Porter's Business Strategies to Environment and Structure: Analysis and Performance Implications, Academy of Management Journal, 31, 280-308.

Nishigushi T., 1987, Competing Systems of Automotive Components Supply: An Examination of the Japanese 'Clustered Control' Model and the "ALP's structure", mimeo (First Policy Forum of the International Vehicles Program).

Otley, D., 1988, The contingency Theory of Organisational Control, in S. Thompson and M. Wright (Eds.), Internal Organisation, Efficiency and Profit, (Oxford, UK, Philip Allan), 86-106.

Perrow, C., 1981, Markets, Hierarchies and Hegemony, in A.H. Van De Ven and W.F. Joyce, (Eds.), Perspectives on Organization Design and Behavior, (New York, John Wiley), 375-386.

Pfeffer, J., 1982, Organizations and Organization Theory. (Cambridge, Mass., Ballinger Publishing Company).

Reeves, K.T., and B.A. Turner, 1972, A Theory of Organization and Behavior in Batch Production Factories, Administrative Science Quarterly, 17, 81-98.

Richardson, G.B., The Organization of Industry, The Economic Journal, 82, 883-896.

Rugman, A.M., 1981, Inside the Multinationals: the Economics of Internal Markets, (London, Croom Helm).

Schonberger, R.J., and J.P. Gilbert, 1983, JIT Purchasing: a Challenge for US Industry, California Management Review, 26, 54.

Shutt, J., and R. Whittington, 1987, Fragmentation Strategies and the Rise of Small Units: Cases from the North West, Regional Studies, 21, 13-24.

Simon, H.A., 1957, Models of Man, (New York, Wiley).

Thompson, J.D., 1967, Organizations in Action, (New York, Mac Graw-Hill).

Thompson, S., and M. Wright, 1988, Concluding Comments: Internal Organisation and Organisational Evolution, in S. Thompson and M. Wright (Eds.), Internal Organisation, Efficiency and Profit, (Oxford, UK, Philip Allan), 228-234.

Thorelli, H.B., 1986, Networks: Between Markets and Hierarchies, Strategic Management Journal, 7, 37-51.

Vancil, R.F., 1978, Decentralization: Managerial Ambiguity by Design. A Research Study Prepared for the Financial Excutives Research Foundation, (Homewood, Il, Dow Jones-Irwin).

Williamson, O.E., 1975, Markets and Hierarchies: Analysis and Antitrust Implications, (New York, Free Press).

Williamson, O.E., 1979, Transaction Cost Economics, the Governance of Contractual Relations, Journal of Law and Economics, 22, 233-261.

Williamson, O.E., 1984, The Incentive Limits of Firms: a Comparative Institutional Assessement of Bureaucracy, Weltwirtschafliches Archiv, 120, 736-763.

Williamson, O.E., 1985, The Economic Institutions of Capitalism, (New York, Free Press).

Wright, M., 1988, Redrawing the Boundaries of the Firm, in S. Thompson and M. Wright (Eds.), Internal Organization, Efficiency and Profit, (Oxford, U.K, Philip Allan), 183-210.

CHAPTER 11

ORGANIZATIONAL CHOICE AND ENTRY DETERRENCE

G. HENDRIKSE
Tilburg University

Abstract

A centralized structure will set prices higher and locate products closer together than a decentralized structure. A decentralized organizational structure is chosen because the entry-deterring effect of such an organizational structure outweighs the monopoly effects of a centralized structure for sufficiently low levels of the entry fee.

1. Introduction

Industrial Organization has traditionally been concerned with the competition between firms at the market level of analysis. Economists do have a "theory of the firm", but this theory is rather silent about the internal functioning of firms. This is a rather unsatisfactory state of affairs because a significant part of the allocation of resources of a society occurs within firms. This chapter analyzes the relationship between the choice of organization structure and the location and pricing decisions of products of these organizations.

An organizational structure formulates some broad rules with respect to the division of labor into distinct tasks. We will consider only two well known organization structures. A functional structure has departments organized around functions like finance, sales and manufacturing, whereas a divisional structure is organized around products. A feature of a divisional structure is that the departments are usually inde-

---

This research was supported by funds from the Department of Business Economics at Tilburg University. I like to thank Joseph Stiglitz for a helpful conversation and the participants at the 1989 meetings of EARIE in Budapest and EEA in Augsburg. The helpful comments of two anonymous referees are appreciated. The usual disclaimer applies.

pendent profit centers, whereas this is not possible in a functional structure due to the interdependency of departments regarding the final product(s). The departments of a divisional structure act independently of each other, which implies that they are competitors on the market. The decisions of a functional structure regarding the market are taken centrally. We will focus on this issue.

The entry-deterring effect of organizational choice is modelled as a four stage game. A decision in an early stage reflects a choice which is costly to change and has therefore a long term effect. The cost involved can not be completely recovered and are called sunk cost. Such a decision is therefore made only once in many years and provides a commitment to certain competitive strategies in subsequent periods. Examples are choices regarding capacity, research and development, product line and organizational structure. Decisions in later stages of the game reflect choices which are made on a monthly or weekly basis and are not expensive to change, e.g. prices. Such decisions serve in general not a strategic role in the market because they lack the credibility of being executed when faced with actual competition. The ex ante optimality of a strategy of low prices may not be ex post optimal when entry has actually occured because profits will be higher when there is not a price war. Smiley (1988) offers empirical evidence on the contents of these ideas and supports the claim that certain irreversible aspects of an investment are required in order to be able to serve a strategic role in markets.

An organizational structure can not be sold to a third party and casual empiricism suggests that there are considerable costs involved in changing it. The costs associated with an organization structure change are therefore sunk and the subsequent choices regarding the market are commitments. These features are captured in this chapter's model. The first stage consists of a choice between a functional or divisional structure. The second stage considers the positioning of products. The third stage analyzes entry and the fourth stage the choice of the prices. It is found that a functional structure will set prices higher and locate products closer together than a divisional structure. A divisional structure is chosen from merely an industrial organization point of view because the entry deterring effect of such an organization structure outweighs the monopoly effects of a functional structure for sufficiently low levels of the entry fee. It pays therefore to adopt a divisional organization structure from a strategic point of view when internal organization considerations favor a functional structure not too much.

There have been a few other papers linking the internal and industrial organization of firms. We mention Willig (1986), who analyzes management performance as a function of exogenously given market conditions, Fershtman and Judd (1987) and Vickers (1985), who study the effects of delegation on market rivalry, Nalebuff and Stiglitz (1983) and Hart (1983), who focus on the use of market competition as a mechanism for assessing management performance and mitigating moral hazard problems, and Bull and Ordover (1987), who investigate the relationship between the decision rule for rejecting projects, the degree of competition and the size of the organization. Brander and Lewis (1986) and Maksimovic (1988) look at oligopoly and financial structure, Bonanno and Vickers (1988) and Coughlan and Wernerfelt (1989) analyse oligopoly and vertical separation. The last two authors show also the importance of the observability of decisions in the first stage for the results. Schwarz and Thompson (1986) consider the use of divisions in order to preempt entry in a homogeneous product world. Our analysis deals with centralization and decentralization in a product differentiation model. We don't assume that managerial diseconomies rule out a centralized structure and it will be shown that such a structure might actually be chosen in equilibrium. We will explicitly analyze the claim made by Caves (1980, p. 77) that "... strategies facilitated by the multidivisional corporation may have their drawbacks in that they raise entry barriers to new competitors - an issue not dealt with in this chapter - ..." and a similar claim by Vickers (1985, p. 139) that "... the horizontal organization of a firm (e.g. into separate divisions) can be seen as a form of delegation that may have strategic advantages in relation to other firms".

The chapter is organized as follows. Section two formulates the model and the following section presents the results. The final section offers some conclusions.

2. Locations and prices

A divisionalized structure allocates the decision power regarding products and prices to the divisional departments, whereas these decisions are executed at a more centralized level in a functional structure. The implication is that an organization adopting a functional structure will act as one entity on the market, whereas the departments of a divisional structure will compete with each other. This is in a spirit similar to Stiglitz: "If the monopolist could delegate the responsibility for the management of each store to a different individual, and could pre-commit himself not to intervene to coordinate their actions, then it would pay for him to do so" (1986, p. 64). We will analyse the outcome of the organizational structure choice for the market and consider the entry decision of other firms in a standard location model.

These considerations are modelled by a multistage game. The commitment effect of various decisions is reflected in the sequencing of the stages. A decison in a particular stage will structure (or channel) all subsequent decisions, i.e. firms anticipate that decisions in early stages affect decisions in subsequent stages. We assume that firms maximize profits. The first stage consists of a choice between a divisional or functional structure. The subsequent decisions regarding product specifications and prices are taken independently by each department of a divisional structure, i.e. the organization has decentralized all its product and pricing decisions. A functional structure has centralized these decisions. The incumbent decides which product to produce in the second stage, given the organization structure choice of the first stage. The positioning of products will be analyzed in a location model of product differentiation. The decisions regarding the introduction of new products by potential entrants are dealt with in the third stage, given the decisions in the first and second stages. Finally, firms compete in prices in the fourth stage while taking the prices of the other firms as given, i.e. the firms behave as Bertrand competitors.

This four stage game is solved for its subgame perfect Nash equilibrium by using the method of backward induction. First, the profit maximizing prices of the fourth stage are calculated, given the choices of the three previous stages. Second, the profit maximizing entry decisions of the third stage are analyzed, given the choices of the previous two stages and taking into account the subsequent profit maximizing prices in the fourth stage. Third, the profit maximizing positioning of products by the incumbent is considered, given the choice of the first stage and taking into account the profit maximizing responses in the third and fourth stage. Finally, the profit maximizing organizational structure is calculated, taking into account the profit maximizing choices in the next three stages.

One way of modelling product differentiation is the so-called location or spatial differentiation model, in which different consumers are located at different places. This model can also be interpreted as consumers having heterogeneous tastes; each location represents a different taste. The distance that consumers have to travel to the location of a firm is interpreted as a utility loss from not consuming their preferred commodity. We adopt a circular city model of product differentiation in order to circumvent problem regarding the existence of equilibrium and the boundary issues of the linear city model (Tirole, 1988). However, the results are not sensitive to this specification.

Consumers are uniformly distributed along a circle with unit circumference. Each consumer buys either zero or one unit of the product. A consumer buying one unit of a product produced at x has a surplus of

$C - d_x - p_x$,

where C is the reservation price common to all consumers, d_x is the distance between the consumer and the location where x is sold and p_x is the price of product x. Each consumer buys one unit, provided that this leaves her with a non-negative surplus.

The incumbent firm is assumed to produce two products, whereas (potential) entrants produce only one. This simplifying assumption is not influencing the results. The marginal costs are set equal to zero.

Figure 1 shows the incumbent two-product firm and one entrant. The incumbent offers products at a and b and the entrant at c. The prices are p_a, p_b and p_c, respectively. We assume that the whole market is served by taking C high enough. We will take a = 0.

Chapter 11 - Organizational Choice

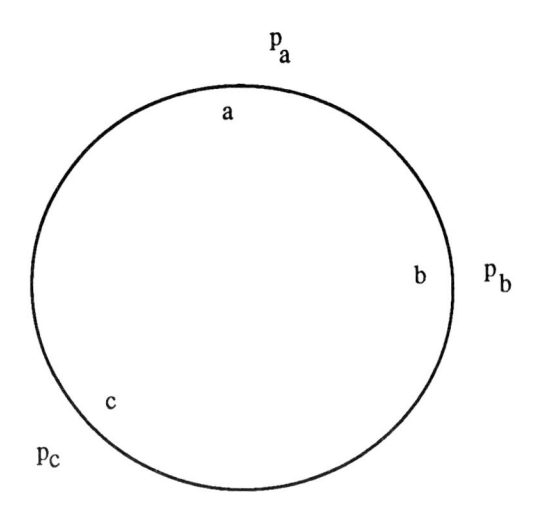

Figure 1:

Location of firms and consumers on a circle.

A firm with a functional organization structure will maximize the joint profits of his products sold at a and b, whereas a firm with a divisional organizational structure will maximize the profits of the two producs independently. The results with respect to the pricing decision are shown in Table 1. The fourth location is labelled d and profits associated with location i by p_i. The case of functional organizational structure with two entrants, one on [0,b] and one on [b,1] is identical to a divisional organizational structure with two entrants. The appendix derives these results for the case of one entrant on the segment [b,1].

The results presented in Table 1 show the solution to the fourth stage of the game, i.e. the profit maximizing prices, given any entry pattern, location and organizational choice in the three previous stages. Notice that the first three stages are indeed treated as paramaters in table 1. They are repremsented in the horizontal and vertical entries of this table and the location parameters a, b, c and d. It is now easy to determine the profit maximizing choices in the third, second and first stage of the game. This is done in the next section.

Organizational choice number of entrants	F-structure	D-structure
no entrants	$p^*_a = p^*_b = C - 1/4$ $\pi_a + \pi_b = C - 1/4$	$p^*_a = p^*_b = 1/2$ $\pi_a + \pi_b = 1/2$
one entrant on $[b,1]$	$p^*_a = \dfrac{7+3b-2c}{12}$ $p^*_b = \dfrac{5+b+2c}{12}$ $p^*_c = \dfrac{3-b}{6}$ $\pi_a + \pi_b = \dfrac{30b+12c+39+7b^2-6bc+12c^2}{144}$ $\pi_c = \dfrac{(3-b)^2}{(6)}$	$p^*_a = \dfrac{2+b-c}{5}$ $p^*_b = \dfrac{1+c}{5}$ $p^*_c = \dfrac{2-b}{5}$ $\pi_i = (p^*_i)^2$
two entrants on $[b,1]$	$p^*_a = \dfrac{44(b-d)+14c+73}{145}$ $p^*_b = \dfrac{14(b-d)+44c+43}{145}$ $p^*_c = \dfrac{3c-32(b-d)=26}{145}$ $p^*_d = \dfrac{3(b-d)-32c+61}{145}$ $\pi_a + \pi_b = \dfrac{1516(b-d)^2+332c(b-d)+1516c^2+2014c+4714(b-d)+4039}{145 \cdot 145}$ $\pi_c = (p^*_c)^2$ $\pi_d = (p^*_d)^2$	$p^*_a = \dfrac{1+2(1-d+b)}{8}$ $p^*_b = \dfrac{1+2c}{8}$ $p^*_c = \dfrac{1+2(d-b)}{8}$ $p^*_d = \dfrac{1+2(1-c)}{8}$ $\pi_i = (p_i)^2$

Table 1:

The optimal prices and profits, given locations and organizational structure.

Chapter 11 - Organizational Choice

3. Results

This section will establish results regarding the relationship between the choice of organizational structure and the industrial organization of firms. Choices regarding organizational structure, locations, entry and prices are made by firms in order to maximize profits of the whole game.

Table one enables us to calculate the entry fee E for which entry of the first or second potential entrant is deterred for each organization structure. We will now present a specific example to illustrate our main results. Suppose that $E = 1/8$. The profits of the incumbent with a functional structure are 7/12.7/12 and the profits of the entrant are (5/12.5/12-1/8). A second entrant will not make positive profits. The profits of the incumbent with a divisional organizational structure are 1/2 and there is no entry because the profits of the first entrant would be negative (1/3.1/3-1/8).

This example illustrates several results. First, if a functional organizational structure is adopted instead of a divisional one, then at least as much product variety will be offered and prices will be higher, given a certain level of the entry fee E. This is the effect described by Stiglitz (1986, p. 37). He writes: "A monopolist, controlling all stores, simply chooses the price at each store optimally. He knows that lowering the price at one location lowers profits at adjacent locations and takes this into account. This induces him not to lower his prices as much in response to entry; thus to make entry less attractive, he must place his stores closer together".

Second, the above model shows that a divisional organizational structure will be adopted from merely an industrial organization point of view when the entry fee is below a certain level (i.e. $E \leq 25/144$). The reason for the higher profits of a divisional structure is that the entry- deterring effect of the commitment to a more competitive profile by the divisional structure outweighs the monopoly effects of a functional structure. A functional structure is chosen when $E > 25/144$.

Third, it is clear that internal organizational considerations might result in adopting a different organizational structure than from a merely industrial organization point of a view would be expected. The scale disadvantages of a divisional structure might be more important then the profit- decreasing effect of entry and therefore result in a functional organizational structure. If the entry fee is sufficiently low then there will be entry and mill price dispersion. The mill price dispersion is due to two forces. A higher price charged by the incumbent increases his profits in the area between his two stores, but decreases them in the areas where he is facing a rival. The profit-maximizing price choices result in higher mill prices of the incumbent than the entrant.

On the other hand, it might also be that industrial organization considerations may change the internal organization choice. If the entry deterring effect of a divisional structure dominates the monopoly effect of a functional structure, then this implies that strategic considerations will to some extent influence the choice of organizational structure. So a divisional organization structure might be adopted even when on merely internal organization grounds a F-structure would be preferred. This establishes the entry deterring effect of organizational choice.

Finally, the strategic adoption of a divisional organizational structure improves welfare from merely an industrial organization point of view. We have assumed that the market is covered and consumers are characterized by inelastic demand. The sum of consumer and producer is therefore insensitive to changes in organizational structure. It is therefore sufficient to compare the decrease in transportation costs of consumers due to the adoption of a functional organization structure with the cost of entry. If $E = 1/8$, then the transportation costs of consumers are equal to $1/8$ when a divisional organizational structure is chosen by the incumbent. A welfare loss is therefore associated with a functional organization structure because the transportation costs have still to be added to the entry fee.

A classic example of entry deterrence by choosing an appropriate organizational structure is the General Motors company (Chandler, 1962). General Motors offers many different types and sizes of cars. It could have decided to organize the productions around wheels, bodies and engines and to allow each salesperson to sell every product. However, it was decided to organize the activities around products in separate divisions. These divisions compete independently and no attempts were made by the general office to limit the operating authority of each division.

4. Conclusions and further research

We have analyzed the relationship between the internal and industrial organization of firms in a model focussing on the effect of the choice of internal (de)centralization on market behavior and have established a link between the internal and industrial organization of firms. It was shown that a centralized organization structure (i.e. a functional organization) will charge higher prices and locate products closer together than a decentralized structure (i.e. a divisional structure), given certain entry fee levels. The entry deterring effect of organizational choice was shown by choosing a divisional structure, although this might not be optimal from merely an internal organization point of view.

There are many extensions possible of the current analysis. We have limited ourselves to the delegation aspect of two well known organization structures. Other aspects of these structures are left out, like the relative advantage of a divisional structure regarding co-ordination and incentive problems, whereas a functional structure is relatively good at reaping the benefits of economies of scale. Other organization structures (e.g. a matrix structure, i.e. a hybrid of a divisional and functional structure) have not been considered. Issues like decisions regarding authority and responsibility relationships, the number of hierarchical levels, the size

Chapter 11 - Organizational Choice

and scope of the firm and remuneration schemes have not been treated, therefore we have not considered many aspects of the richness of internal organizations. Similar comments can be made regarding the industrial organization of firms. All these issues are interesting in themselves, but we have to limit ourselves in the scope of the analysis and don't imply some judgment about the importance of other issues. However, the main contribution of this chapter lies in providing a relationship between organizational choice and the industrial organization of firms.

Appendix

This appendix will derive the expressions of Table 1 for the case of one entrant on [b,1]. The other cases are obtained in a similar way.

Profits are equal to the price times the length of the segment of consumers being served. These segments will now be calculated. We have assumed that the whole market is served. A consumer located at x on the interval [0,b] is indifferent between buying at location a(=0) or b when

$C - x - p_a = C - (b-x) - p_b$

$\iff x = \dfrac{b+p_b-p_a}{2}$.

Similarly, a consumer located at y on the interval [b,c] is indifferent between buying at b or c when

$y = \dfrac{b+c+p_c-p_b}{2}$

and a consumer located at z on the interval [c,1] is indifferent between buying at c or a when

$z = \dfrac{1+c+p_a-p_c}{2}$

The profit functions are therefore

$\pi_a(p_a) = p_a (1-z+x)$
$\pi_b(p_b) = p_b (b-x+y-b)$
$\pi_c(p_c) = p_c (c-y+z-c)$.

The profits of a D-structure are determined by maximizing $\pi_i(p_i)$ with respect to p_i, where i = a, b or c. The solution to this system of three equations with three unknowns yields the profit maximizing prices and the associated profits. The profits of the F-structure are determined by maximizing $\pi_a(p_a) + \pi_b(p_b)$ with respect to p_a and p_b. The results are presented in table 1.

Notice that the assumption regarding the whole market being served insatisfied when $C \geq 3/4$.

References

Bonanno, G., and J. Vickers, 1988, Vertical Separation, The Journal of Industrial Economics, 36: 3, 257-265.

Brander, J.A., and J. Eaton, 1984, Product Line Rivalry, American Economic Review, 74: 3, 323-334.

Brander, J.A., and T.R. Lewis, 1986, Oligopoly and Financial Structure: the Limited Liability Effect, American Economic Review, 76: 5, 956-970.

Bull, C., and J.A. Ordover, 1987, Market Structure and Optimal Management Organizations, Rand Journal of Economics, 18: 4, 480-491.

Caves, R.E., 1980, Corporate Strategy and Structure, Journal of Economic Literature, 18: 1, 64-92.

Coughlan, A.T., and B. Wernerfelt, 1989, On Credible Delegation by Oligopolists: a Discussion of Distribution Channel Management, Management Science, 35: 2, 226-239.

Chandler, A.D., 1962, Strategy and Structure: Chapters in the History of the Industrial Enterprise, (Cambridge, Mass., The MIT Press).

Fershtman C., and K.L. Judd, 1987, Equilibrium Incentives in Oligopoly, American Economic Review, 77: 5, 927-940.

Hart, O., 1983, The Market Mechanism as an Incentive Scheme, Bell Journal of Economics, 74, 366-382.

Maksimovic, V., 1988, Capital Structure in Repeated Oligopolies, The Rand Journal of Economics, 19: 3, 389-407.

Nalebuff, B.J., and J.E. Stiglitz, 1983, Information, Competition and Markets, American Economic Review, 73, 278-283.

Schwartz, M., and E.A. Thompson, 1986, Divisionalization and Entry Deterrence, Quarterly Journal of Economics, 101, 307-321.

Smiley, R., 1988, Empirical Evidence on Strategic Entry Deterrence, International Journal of Industrial Organization, 6, 167-180.

Stiglitz, J.E., 1986, Towards a More General Theory of Monopolistic Competition, in Peston, M.H. and R.E. Quandt (Eds.), Prices Competition & Equilibrium, (New-York, Philip Allan / Barns & Noble Books).

Tirole, J., 1988, The Theory of Industrial Organization, (Cambridge, Mass., The MIT Press).

Vickers, J.,1985, Delegation and the Theory of the Firm, Conference Papers, Supplement to the Economic Journal, 95, 138-147.

Willig, R.D., 1986, Corporate Governance and Product Market Structure, in Razin A. and E. Sadka (Eds.), Economic Policy in Theory and Practice, (New York, Mac Millan).

# CHAPTER 12

TOP MANAGEMENT INCENTIVES FROM BONUSES AND FROM LABOUR MARKETS

H.G. BARKEMA
Tilburg University

Abstract

This chapter examines data about 137 top-managers of non-listed Dutch firms. I find that roughly half of these managers are insufficiently monitored, and that these managers are not positively motivated by their bonuses and by internal labour markets. In contrast, positive incentives from bonuses and from internal labour markets are measured for the other half of top-managers who are sufficiently monitored. The evidence provides some support for two important behavioral assumptions of agency theory: that managers are motivated by their bonuses and that they are motivated by internal labour markets. However it also indicates that in the absence of a market for corporate control, these assumptions break down in a non-trivial subset of firms.

1. Introduction

During the last two decades, principal-agent theory has become a major development in economics. Contributions to this theory appear regularly in almost all important economic journals, and the research flow shows no sign of diminishing. However, until today there is no unambiguous empirical support for two key implications of this theory: that agents are motivated by their bonuses and that they are motivated by the labour market. I will first discuss incentives from bonuses.

The 'standard' agency problem studied in formal papers in agency theory is the principal's problem of selecting a value maximizing contract with one agent for one period. This contract speficies the agent's pay as an increasing function of an unbiased estimate of his effort. Papers in this field characterize the pareto-optimal contract given various assumptions about preferences of principals and agents, the information that principals have about the effort of agents at the end of the period, etc. (Ross, 1973; Harris and Raviv, 1976, 1978; Holmstrom, 1979; Shavell, 1979). These standard agency models have been expanded to include multiple agents (Holmstrom, 1982), multiple time periods (Hart, 1983; Holmstrom, 1987), and multiple activities (Holmstrom and Milgrom, 1990)[1].

An important implication of this theory is that agents are positively motivated by expected bonuses. Consistent with this implication, a number of empirical studies have measured a positive relation between managerial pay and firm performance (Larcker, 1983; Murphy, 1985; Benston, 1985; Coughlan and Schmidt, 1985; Tehranian and Waegelein, 1985; Brickley, Bhagat and Lease, 1985). In itself, this evidence is consistent with the agency 'story' that bonuses motivate managers to enhance firm value. However it is well known that this evidence is ambiguous, since it can also be explained by other hypotheses, including tax and signalling hypotheses (Miller and Scholes, 1982; Hite and Long; 1982, Warner, 1985; Raviv, 1985, Bhagat, Brickley and Lease, 1985). In fact, recent evidence in Jensen and Murphy (1990) suggests that the relation between pay and firm performance is so weak that managers are unlikely to be significantly motivated by their pay.

An analogous story applies to the case of incentives from labour markets. That managers are motivated by internal and external labour markets is implied by Fama (1980), Lazear and Rosen (1981), and so on. Consistent with this implication, it is measured in a number of empirical studies that top managers in firms that perform poorly are more likely to leave the firm (Benston, 1985; Warner, Watts and Wruck, 1988; Weisbach, 1988; Jensen and Murphy, 1990). This evidence is consistent with the agency story that top managers are motivated by boards of directors that fire them in case they perform badly. However, as these studies point out, the evidence can also be explained by alternative hypotheses: such as that if firms perform badly, managers are more likely to leave the firm voluntarily, because sustained poor firm performance acts as a bad signal about their actions, which in turn reduces their future income.

The present chapter uses a new methodology to test whether managers are motivated by their bonuses and labour markets. This methodology is based on recent principal-agent theory in Holmstrom and Milgrom (1987, 1990). This theory assumes that managers are endowed with limited amounts of time and attention, which they allocate to various activities, such as work, family time, leisure, and so on, depending on the relative personal costs and gains associated with these activities. Hence expected gains from work, (from bonuses and from career moves on internal and external labour markets), are predicted to increase the time and attention that rational managers devote to work[2]. These predictions are tested in this paper on 1985 data about 137 top managers of non-listed firms in the Netherlands.

This chapter is structured as follows. Characteristics of the sample are discussed in section 2. Initial tests of the hypotheses are presented in section 3, and more elaborate testing is presented in section 4. The chapter ends with some conclusions and suggestions for further research.

2. Sample

The data set that is analyzed is obtained from the 1985 HAY data set. Managers in this data set are employed in a wide range of firms and industries. None of these firms is listed on the Amsterdam Stock exchange or any other stock exchange. In order to control potential omitted variables-problems associated with firm size and firm structure, I have only analyzed data about top managers of firms that have multiple executives on the board of executives and a formal chairman on the board. This leaves a data set of 137 top managers.

The time that a manager devotes to work is operationalized by what seems to be a natural indicator of this theoretical variable: the number of hours that the manager devotes to work per week[3]. The manager's bonus is operationalized as his total bonus which is dependent on last year's performance (of the firm, the division or individual performance)[4]. Whether the manager expects to be mobile or not is operationalized by a dummy variable, valued 1 if the manager expects to be mobile on the labour market in the future and 0 otherwise[5].

3. Some initial empirical results

The following model was estimated:

$$y = \beta_1 x_1 + \beta_2 x_2 + \varepsilon_1 \tag{1}$$

where:

y	= the number of hours that the manager works per week;
x_1	= the manager's bonus;
x_2	= a dummy variable valued 1 if the manager expects to be mobile, and 0 otherwise;
β_1, β_2	= coefficients;
ε_1	= an error term.

The variable y is available in the data set at the ordinal level. Therefore this model and other models in this paper are estimated on the basis of matrices of polyserial and pearson product moment correlations. The model is estimated by means of LISREL: a flexible framework for econometric analysis (Joreskog, 1973a, b, 1977; Joreskog and Sorbom, 1981; Joreskog and Wold, 1981). Maximum likelihood-estimates of model (1) are presented in table 1.

	β_1	β_2
estimate	0.11	-0.03
t-value	1.25	-0.32

Table 1.

LISREL Maximum likelihood-estimates of model (1).

The results in table 1 can be interpreted as follows. The coefficient associated with the bonus (β_1) has the expected sign, contrary to the coefficient associated with the labour market (β_2). Neither coefficient is significant at the 0.05 level (both t-values are ≤1.64, assuming a one sided test). So the hypotheses that managers are motivated by their bonuses and by labour markets are **not** corroborated. Furthermore, the explanatory value of the exogenous variables is very low: $r^2 = 0.01$.

The above results imply that either the test, or the theory is wrong, or both. In the rest of this chapter I explore the possibility that the theory is right but the test is wrong. In section 3.2, I examine potential problems associated with the test of the hypothesis that managers are motivated by their bonuses. In section 3.3 potential problems associated with the test of the hypothesis that managers are motivated by labour markets are examined.

3.1. Incentives from bonuses

One possible test error is that the model is underspecified and that other effects neutralize the positive incentive effect from bonuses. One such potential negative effect has recently been recognized in agency theory by Baker, Jensen and Murphy (1989). These authors cite psychologists and behaviorists who argue that bonuses demotivate managers because extrinsic rewards erode intrinsic interests. Now suppose that both effects -the motivation effect hypothesized by agency theory and the demotivation effect hypothesized by behaviorists and psychologists- exist simultaneously. Then the demotivation effect could very well neutralize the motivation effect, resulting in the overall insignificant incentive effect from bonuses measured earlier.

The prediction that both effects exist simultaneously -the motivation effect and the demotivation effect- is tested in the following way. In section 4 the data set will be partitioned into two subsets: one subset of managers who perceive their income as strongly related to their effort, and one subset of managers who perceive a weak relation between their income and effort or no no relation at all. If both effects exist simultaneously, then it is expected that 1) managers are negatively motivated by their bonuses in settings with a weak or non existant relation between income and effort,

Chapter 12 - Top Management Incentives

because the demotivation effect is likely to dominate; 2) managers are more positively motivated by their bonuses in a setting with a strong relation between income and effort than in a setting with a weak or non existant relation between income and effort, because the motivation effect is expected to be stronger in the former setting. Both predictions will be tested in the next section.

I end this subsection with the following comment. The existence of contracts that imply that managerial income is weakly or not at all related to effort is puzzling from the perspective of orthodox principal-agent theory. It is, however, less puzzling in view of the characteristics of my data set, that contains managers of non-listed firms. Since these firms are non-listed, the boards of directors of these firms are not disciplined by the market of corporate control, which may allow them to shirk with respect to their task of disciplining top managers.

Obviously, that boards of directors are not disciplined by the market of corporate control does not necessarily mean that they are not disciplined at all. Directors could be disciplined by other markets, such as product and factor markets, that threaten the firm's survival if directors do not sufficiently discipline top management. Directors could also be disciplined by inside stockholdings. These disciplinary effects on boards of directors are likely to vary across firms and industries (Demsetz and Lehn, 1985; Lambert and Larcker, 1987). Hence variations are expected in the degree to which directors discipline top management. Whether such variations indeed occur is also tested in section 4.

3.2. Incentives from labour markets

In theory, the insignificant incentive effect from managers that expect to be mobile on labour markets could be due to the fact that the positive incentive effect from expected mobility on internal labour markets is dominated by the negative incentive effect from expected mobility on external labour markets. Such negative incentive effects from expected mobility on external labour markets could arise because external mobility implies that managers escape settling up for past behaviour within their firm. This is easily illustrated by means of the analysis in Fama (1980).

Fama studies conditions under which managers face full ex post settling up via the labour market, such as an infinite number of periods, each preceeded by a recontracting. Fama assumes that the manager's contracted wage in any period t is the expected value of his marginal product, $\bar{z}_t$, where $\bar{z}_t$ follows a random walk with steps that are independent of the random noise, e_t, in the manager's measured marginal product z_t. Hence the manager's measured marginal product is:

$$z_t = \bar{z}_t + e_t \tag{2}$$

Muth (1960) has shown that the expected value of the marginal product evolves according to:

$$\bar{z}_t = \bar{z}_{t-1} + (1 - \emptyset)e_{t-1} \tag{3}$$

where $\emptyset$ is a parameter ($0 < \emptyset < 1$) that is closer to zero the smaller the variance of the noise term in the marginal product equation (1) relative to the variance of the steps in the random walk followed by the expected marginal product.

Now suppose, contrary to Fama, that managers face only a limited number of times of recontracting in the future. This seems realistic in case of the managers in my sample, who have often reached the last or next to last step in their career[6]. More specifically, suppose that managers face only one additional round of recontracting. Suppose also that, as a by-product of day-to-day operations, more recent information is available about the actions of managers on internal labour markets than on external labour markets. Then it is expected that $\emptyset_e > \emptyset_i$, where e and i denote the external and internal labour markets, respectively. Finally, suppose that managers can either keep their present job or be promoted internally or externally. This increases their productivity with fraction α[7]. Thus, the degree of ex post settling up in these three instances is, respectively:

$$(1 - \emptyset_i) \tag{4}$$

$$(1 - \emptyset_i)(1 + \alpha) \tag{5}$$

$$(1 - \emptyset_e)(1 + \alpha) \tag{6}$$

Because $\alpha > 0$, (5) dominates (4): a manager that expects to be mobile internally faces a higher degree of settling up than if he keeps his present job. Hence the prospect of an internal promotion induces the manager to select a higher level of effort than if he expects to keep his present job. Whether (6) dominates (4) depends on the specific values of the parameters α, $\emptyset_i$ and $\emptyset_e$. One possible outcome is that a manager faces less settling up if he is mobile externally than if he keeps his present job. This results in a lower level of effort in case of anticipated external mobility.

In sum: managers are expected to be positively motivated by anticipated mobility on the internal labour market. Whether they are positively or negatively motivated by anticipated mobility on external labour markets (relative to keeping their present job) is an empirical matter. In view of my earlier empirical results, I expect that anticipated external mobility induces negative incentives, since this would account for the overall insignificant motivation effect from labour markets that I measured earlier.

Chapter 12 - Top Management Incentives

Whether managers are indeed positively motivated by anticipated mobility on internal labour markets and negatively motivated by anticipated mobility on external labour markets is tested below.

4. More empirical tests of hypotheses

Before I test the more specific hypotheses about incentives from bonuses and from internal and external labour markets that were derived in the previous section, I will first test the hypothesis that boards of directors of non-listed firms (that are not subjected to the market of corporate control) are imperfectly disciplined to discipline top management.

4.1. Discipline from the market of corporate control

If the market of corporate control acts as a disciplining mechanism of last resort, directors are motivated to specify pay packages for managers that maximize shareholder wealth[8]. Consistent with formal models in agency theory, these packages are expected to specify objective procedures that define the manager's income as an increasing function of an unbiased estimate of his effort. In a multi-period setting, the objective measurement of effort and subsequent administration of punishments and rewards is expected to be carried out regularly.

If, on the other hand, the disciplining effect of the market of corporate control is absent, it is expected that the directors of at least a subset of firms will shirk with respect to the monitoring of managers, or even administer rewards on other grounds than the managers' contribution to shareholder wealth. In that case it is expected that managers are evaluated 'loosely' and subjectively, that criteria for evaluation are not well-defined, and that evaluations are carried out on an irregular basis.

The Hay data set allows for a test of these conjectures. The survey that generated the data contained questions about whether managers are evaluated informally (rather than formally), irregularly (instead of regularly), and on general grounds (instead of on specific, well-defined criteria). Answers to these questions were scored on a seven point scale. The scores of the 137 managers are summarized in table 2[9].

The empirical results of table 2 are consistent with the interpretation that in at least a subset of firms, directors are imperfectly disciplined to monitor managers. A substantial number of managers is evaluated informally rather than formally (35 managers score ≤ 3), irregularly rather than regularly (86 managers score ≥ 5), and on general grounds rather than on the basis of specific criteria (30 managers score ≤ 3).

score	1	2	3	4	5	6	7	
informally	17	9	9	28	17	25	24	formally
general grounds	7	13	10	25	20	20	29	specific criteria
regularly	8	4	16	12	18	23	45	irregularly

Table 2.

Empirical results about how directors evaluate managers.

4.2. The agency hypotheses subjected to test

In this section I test the predictions about whether managers are positively or negatively motivated by their bonuses and by the internal and the external labour market. The test is constructed as follows. Managers are separated into two groups: a group D of managers (of firms) with a deficient monitoring system, and a group ND of managers that are not subjected to deficient monitoring. Managers are partitioned over groups D and ND depending on their score on the question whether or not a relation exists between their pay and their performance. The scores of these managers range from 1 ('non-existent') to 7 ('clearly present'). Managers that score closer to 'clearly present' (that is, score ≥ 5) are distributed to ND. Managers that score closer to 'non-existent' (that is, score ≤ 3) are distributed to D. The estimation results for group ND (N = 56) and group D (N = 59) are presented in table 3. In this table, b_1 is the coefficient associated with incentives from bonuses, and b_3 and b_4 are the coefficients associated with incentives from the internal and external labour markets, respectively[10].

The results presented in table 3 for group ND corroborate the hypotheses. In firms where monitoring is in order, managers are positively motivated by their bonuses and by the internal labour market. Both effects are significant. The sign of the coefficient associated with the external labour market is indeed negative but insignificant. The estimation results for group D are also consistent with predictions. Bonuses in these firms have a negative effect on motivation, which is consistent with the hypothesized demotivation effect. The internal labour market induces a positive but insignificant motivation effect, which is not surprising in view of the fact that these managers work in firms where rewards (possibly promotions) are loosely tied to individual

Chapter 12 - Top Management Incentives

performance. The motivation effect from the external labour market is negative and significant. Finally, the r^2 for group ND and and for group D (0.12 and 0.22, respectively) is much larger than the r^2 obtained in the previous section (0.01). This suggests that the separate modelling of motivation and demotivation effects from bonuses and from internal and external labour markets produces much better explanations.

	group ND			group D		
	b_1	b_3	b_4	b_1	b_3	b_4
coeff.	0.32	0.42	-0.14	-0.34	0.14	-0.31
t-value	2.03	2.27	-0.82	-2.40	0.92	-2.14
	$r^2 = 0.12$			$r = 0.22$		

Table 3.

Estimation results about whether managers are motivated by their bonuses and by the internal and the external labour market, for 'deficient' firms (group D) and for 'non-deficient' firms (group ND).

5. Summary and conclusions

In this paper I examine 1985 data about 137 top managers of non-listed firms from a wide variety of industries in the Netherlands. Since these firms are non-listed, boards of directors of these firms are not disciplined by the market of corporate control to monitor top managers. Consistent with this view, I find that top managers of roughly half of the firms in my data set are evaluated irregularly, informally and on rather general criteria, and do not perceive a clear relation between their individual income and their performance.

For the latter subset of managers, I find no empirical support for two important implications of agency theory: that managers are positively motivated by their bonuses and by labour markets. In fact, a demotivating effect from bonuses is measured for these managers, which is consistent with the psychologists' and behaviorists' view that extrinsic rewards erode intrinsic interests. Opposite results are measured for the subset of firms where managers perceive a clear relation between their income and individual performance. Consistent with agency theory, I find that top-managers in these firms are positively and significantly motivated by their bonuses and by internal labour markets. Furthermore, my empirical results suggest that managers are demotivated by the prospect of external mobility.

These results are interesting both for theoretical and for practical reasons. From a theoretical point of view, they suggest that the agency implications that managers are positively motivated by their bonuses and internal labour markets are empirically valid, but only in a limited subset of firms. Secondly, they suggest that interactions exist between external and internal control systems. In the absence of external control from the market of corporate control, internal control systems (such as bonus schemes and internal labour markets) break down in a non-trivial subset of firms. More theoretical and empirical research is required to unravel the precise interaction between external and internal control systems. A first step in this direction has recently been made by Morck, Shleifer and Vishny (1989).

The above results are also interesting from a practical point of view. They suggest that internal control systems (bonus schemes, internal career systems) can either be benificial or detrimental to firms, depending on how they are used. Internal control systems can be benificial if they are implemented in such a way that managers perceive a clear relation between their individual rewards and performance. In that case managers are positively motivated by these systems. In contrast, internal control systems can be detrimental if they are implemented in a manner that managers do not perceive a clear relation between rewards and performance. In that case, no positive incentives are induced by internal career programs, and managers are demotivated by bonus systems. Furthermore, my results suggest that managers who anticipate leaving the firm should be encouraged to do so as soon as possible, since the prospect of external mobility induces them to work less hard than managers who expect to remain with their firm.

Notes

1 For an overview, see Hart and Holmstrom (1987) and their more than 130 references.

2 For a more complete description of this methodology, see Barkema (1991).

3 The data seem relatively reliable because after the survey (that is conducted every two years, in cooperation with the Dutch Center of Executives and Directors, the NCD), executives obtain feedback about how their scores relate to the average scores in their industry. Hence executives have an incentive to signal information.

4 The data set contains information about bonuses that are actually paid (ex post), while managers base their action on expected bonuses (ex ante). Therefore, I assume that the bonus paid in 1985 (the year of the survey) provides information about the bonus that managers anticipate for 1986. If this assumption is incorrect, the

Chapter 12 - Top Management Incentives

empirical test may yield insignificant motivation effects even if such motivation effects exist 'out there'.

5 The data set contains information about whether the manager <u>wants</u> to be mobile in the future, and not whether he <u>expects</u> to be mobile. In the Netherlands, managers are seldom fired, hence the manager's wish to be mobile is more or less a necessary condition for mobility. I assume that whether the manager's <u>wants</u> to be mobile (or not) provides information about whether he <u>expects</u> to be mobile (or not). If this assumption is incorrect, no motivation effect from the labour market may be measured, even if this effect exists in 'reality'.

6 Additional theory and evidence also suggests that managerial contracts are not renegotiated for an infinite number of times. In practice, long term contracts, specified either formally or informally, seem to be the rule rather than the exception. Furthermore, explanations for long term contracts abound in the economics literature. If workers are risk averse, firm value may be increased by long term contracts that insure the worker against unemployment (Baily, 1974; Azariadis, 1975; Holmström, 1983). Long term contracts also allow firm specific investments such as training costs (Williamson, 1985). In addition, incumbent managers may contract informally so as not to endanger each other's position (Faith et al., 1984). Finally, competition on the labour market as a means of disciplining managers has negative side effects because productive lower managers are not necessarily productive higher managers, due to differences in required skills (Baker et al., 1988).

7 Positive fractions of α and β ensure, within the context of our setting, corresponding increases in expected wages of managers. These higher wages may induce higher levels of utility in these other jobs, which is a necessary condition if the manager wishes to be mobile at all.

8 A number of studies have presented evidence consistent with the hypothesis that the market of corporate control enhances firm efficiency. Negative abnormal returns have been measured after the adoption of measures that restrict the functioning of the market of corporate control, such as poison pills and restrictions of voting rights (DeAngelo and Rice, 1983; Lease, Mc Connel and Mikkelson, 1983; Malatesta and Walkling, 1988; Ryngaert, 1988; Jarrell and Poulsen, 1988). Furthermore, Morck, Shleifer and Vishny (1988) document lower q-ratios for firms where boards of directors own more than 5 % of the shares of the firm (which reduces the probability of a hostile takeover).

9 Due to missing data, the number of scores in row 1 - 3 do not add up to exactly 137.

10 The questionnaire that generated the data also distinguished between whether managers expect to be mobile on the internal or on the external labour market.

11 Also a more homogenous set of managers could have been selected, e.g. that score ≥ 6 on the question whether pay is related to performance. The estimation results are in this case (N = 37): $b_1 = 0.44$ (t = 2.18), $b_2 = 0.54$ (t = 2.50) and $b_4 = -0.12$ (t = -0.61), $r^2 = 0.22$. As one would expect, the motivation effects from bonuses and the internal labour market are even more pronounced than in the less homogenous group ND of table 3.

References

Azariadis, C., 1975, Implicits Contract and Underemployment Equilibria, Journal of Political Economy, 83, 1183-1202.

Baily, M., 1974, Wages and Employment Under Uncertain Demand, Review of Economic Studies, 41, 37-50.

Baker, G.P., M.C. Jensen and K.J. Murphy, 1990, Compensation and Incentives: Practice vs. Theory, Journal of Finance, 43: 3, 593-616.

Barkema, H.G., 1991, Are Managers Indeed Motivated by Their Bonuses?, Research Memorandum FEW 481, Department of Economics, Tilburg University, The Netherlands.

Benston, G.J., 1985, The Self-Serving Management Hypothesis; Some Evidence, Journal of Accounting and Economics, 7, 67-84.

Bhagat, S., J.A. Brickley and R.C. Lease, 1985, Incentive Effects of Stock Purchase Plans, Journal of Financial Economics, 14, 195-215.

Brickley, J.A., S. Bhagat and R.C. Lease, 1985, The Impact of Long-Range Managerial Compensation Plans on Shareholder Wealth, Journal of Accounting and Economics, 7, 115-129.

Coughlan, A.T., and R.M. Schmidt, 1985, Executive Compensation, Management Turnover, and Firm Performance, Journal of Accounting and Economics, 7, 43-66.

DeAngelo, H., and E.M. Rice, 1983, Antitakeover Charter Amendments And Stockholder Wealth, Journal of Financial Economics, 11, 329-360.

Demsetz, H., and K. Lehn, 1985, The Structure of Corporate Ownership: Causes and Consequences, Journal of Political Economy, 93, 1155-1177.

Fama, E.F., 1980, Agency Problems and the Theory of the Firm, Journal of Political Economy, 88: 2, 288-307.

Faith, R.L., R.S. Higgins and R.D. Tollison, 1984, Managerial Rents and Outside Recruitment in the Coasian Firm, American Economic Review, 74: 4, 660-672.

Harris, M., and A. Raviv, 1976, Optimal Incentive Contracts with Imperfect Information, Grad. Sch. Ind. Adm., working paper 70-75-76, Carnegie Mellon University. Published in 1979 in the Journal of Economic Theory, 20: 2, 231-259.

Harris, M., and A. Raviv, 1978, Some Results on Incentive Contracts with Applications to Education and Employment, Health Insurance and Law Enforcement, American Economic Review, 68: 1, 20-30.

Hart, O.D., 1983, Optimal Labour Contracts Under Asymmetric Information: An Introduction, Review of Economic Studies, 3-35.

Hart, O.D., and B. Holmstrom, 1987, The Theory of Contracts, in Bewley (ed.), Advanced Economic Theory (Cambridge, University Press).

Holmstrom, B., 1979, Moral Hazard and Observability, Bell Journal of Economics, 10: 1, 74-91.

Holmstrom, B, 1982, Moral Hazard in Teams, Bell Journal of Economics,13, 324-340.

Holmstrom, B., 1983, Equilibrium Long-Term Contracts, Quarterly Journal of Economics, 98, 23-54.

Holmstrom, B., and P. Milgrom, 1987, Aggregation and Linearity in the Provision of Intertemporal Incentives, Econometrica, 55: 2, 303-328.

Holmstrom, B,. and P. Milgrom, 1990, Multi-Task Principal-Agent Analyses, Working paper 45, May 1990.

Jarrell, G.A., and A.B. Poulsen, 1988, Dual-Class Recapitalizations as Antitakeover Mechanisms: The Recent Rvidence, Journal of Financial Economics, 20: 1, 129-152.

Jensen, M.C., and K.J. Murphy, 1990, Performance Pay and Top Management Incentives, Journal of Political Economy, 98, 225-264.

Joreskog, K.G., 1973a, A General Method for Estimating a Linear Structural Equation System, in A.S. Goldberger and O.D. Duncan (eds), Structural Equation Models in the Social Sciences (New York, Seminar Press).

Joreskog, K.G., 1973b, Analysis of Covariance Structures, in P.R. Krishnaiah (ed), Multivariate Analysis III (New York, Academic Press).

Joreskog, K.G., 1977, Structural Equation Models in the Social Sciences: Specification, Estimation and Testing, in P.R. Krishnaiah (ed), Applications of Statistics, (Amsterdam, North Holland).

Joreskog, K.G., and D. Sorbom, 1981, Lisrel-VI, Analysis of Linear Structural Relationships by the Method of Maximum Likelihood, (Mooresville, Indiana, Scientific Software).

Joreskog, K.G., and H. Wold, 1981, Systems Under Indirect Observation: Causality, Structure, Prediction, Part I and II, (Amsterdam, North Holland).

Lambert, R.A., and D.F. Larcker, 1987, An Analysis of the Use of Accounting and Market Measures of Performance in Executive Compensation Contracts, Journal of Accounting Research, 25, Supplement 1987, 85-125.

Larcker, D.F., 1983, The Association Between Performance Plan Adoption and Corporate Capital Investment, Journal of Accounting and Economics, 5, 3-30.

Lazear, E.P., and S. Rosen, 1981, Rank-Order Tournaments as Optimum Labor Contracts, Journal of Political Economy, 89: 5, 841-864.

Lease, R.C., J.J. McConnell and W.H. Mickelson, 1983, The Market Value of Control in Publicly-Traded Corporations, Journal of Financial Economics, 11: 1, 439-471.

Malatesta, P.H., and R.A. Walkling, 1988, Poison Pill Securities: Stockholder Wealth, Profitability, and Ownership Structure, Journal of Financial Economics, 20: 1, 347-376.

Miller, M., and M. Scholes, 1982, Executive Compensation, Taxes, and Incentives, in W.F. Sharpe and C.M. Cootner (eds), Financial Economics: Essays in Honor of Paul Cootner (Englewood Cliffs, NJ, Prentice Hall) 179-201.

Morck, R., A. Shleifer and R.W. Vishny, 1988, Management Ownership and Market Valuation: An Empirical Analysis, Journal of Financial Economics, 20: 1, 293-315.

Morck, R. A., Shleifer and R.W. Vishny, 1989, Alternative Mechanisms for Corporate Control, American Economic Review, 79, 842-852.

Murphy, K.J., 1985, Corporate Performance and Managerial Renumeration; an Empirical Analysis, Journal of Accounting and Economics, 7, 11-42.

Raviv, A., 1985, Management Compensation and the Managerial Labor Market, Journal of Accounting and Economics, 7, 239-245.

Ross, S.A., 1973, The Economic Theory of Agency: The Principal's Problem, American Economic Review, 63: 2, 134-139.

Ryngaert, M., 1988, The Effect of Poison Pill Securities on Shareholder Wealth, Journal of Financial Economics, 20: 1, 377-417.

Shavell, S., 1979, Risk Sharing and Incentives in the Principal and Agent Relationship, Bell Journal of Economics,10: 1, 55-73.

Tehranian, H., and J.F. Waegelein, 1985, Market Reaction to Short-Term Executive Compensation Plan Adoption, Journal of Accounting and Economics, 7, 131-144.

Warner, J.B., 1985, Stock Market Reaction to Management Incentive Plan Adoption: An overview, Journal of Accounting and Economics, 7, 145-149.

Warner, J.B., R. L. Watts and K. Wruck, 1988, Stock Prices and Top Management Changes, Journal of Financial Economics, 20, 461-492.

Weisbach, M., 1988, Outside Directors and CEO Turnover, Journal of Financial Economics, 20, 431- 460.

Williamson, O.E., 1985, The Economic Institutions of Capitalism, (New York, The Free Press).